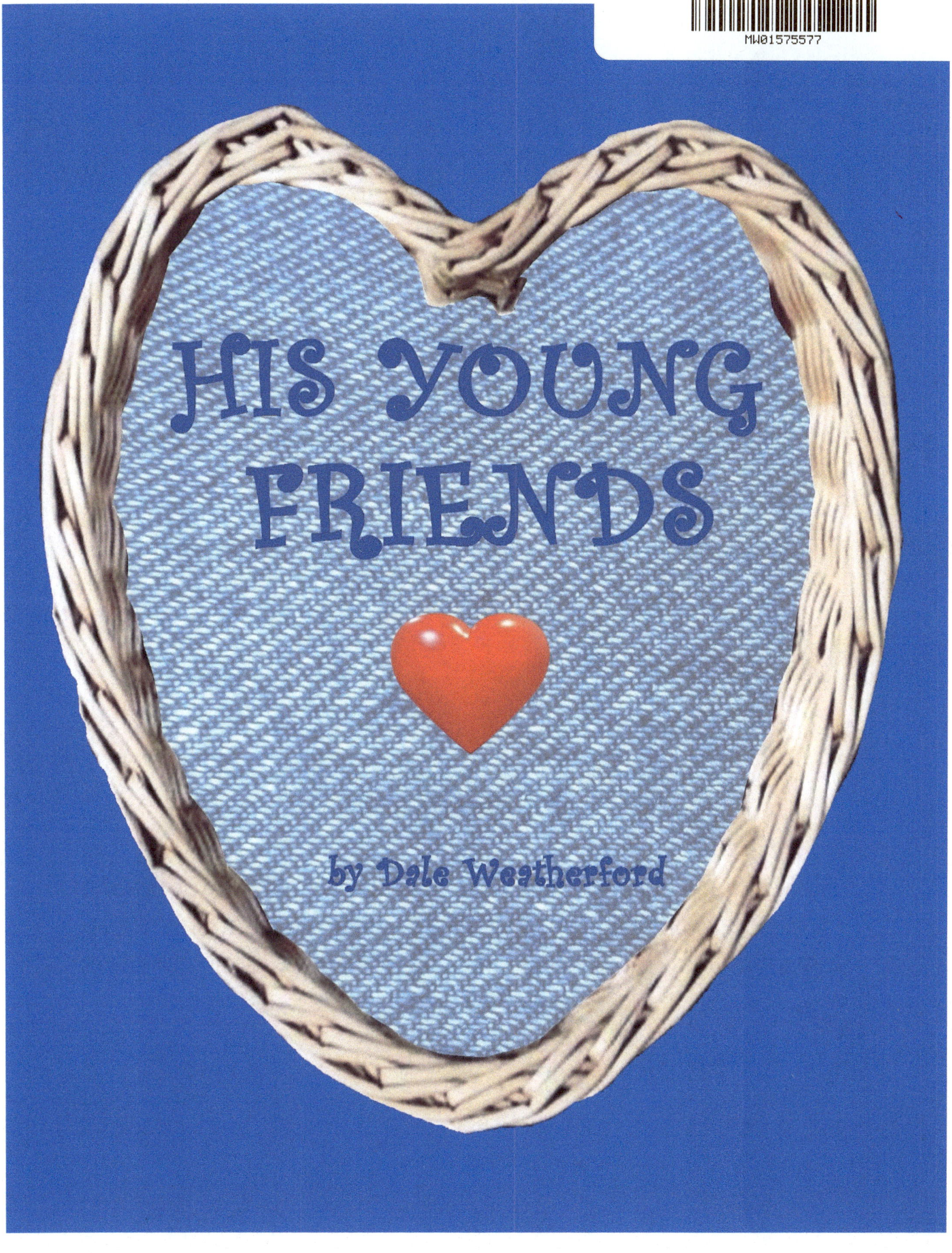

HIS YOUNG FRIENDS

by Dale Weatherford

Copyright © 2021 by Dale Weatherford
All rights reserved

All Scripture is taken from The Holy Bible, New International Version. Copyright © 1973, 1978, 1984 International Bible Society. Used by permission of Zondervan Bible Publishers.

ISBN 978-1-7363315-0-7

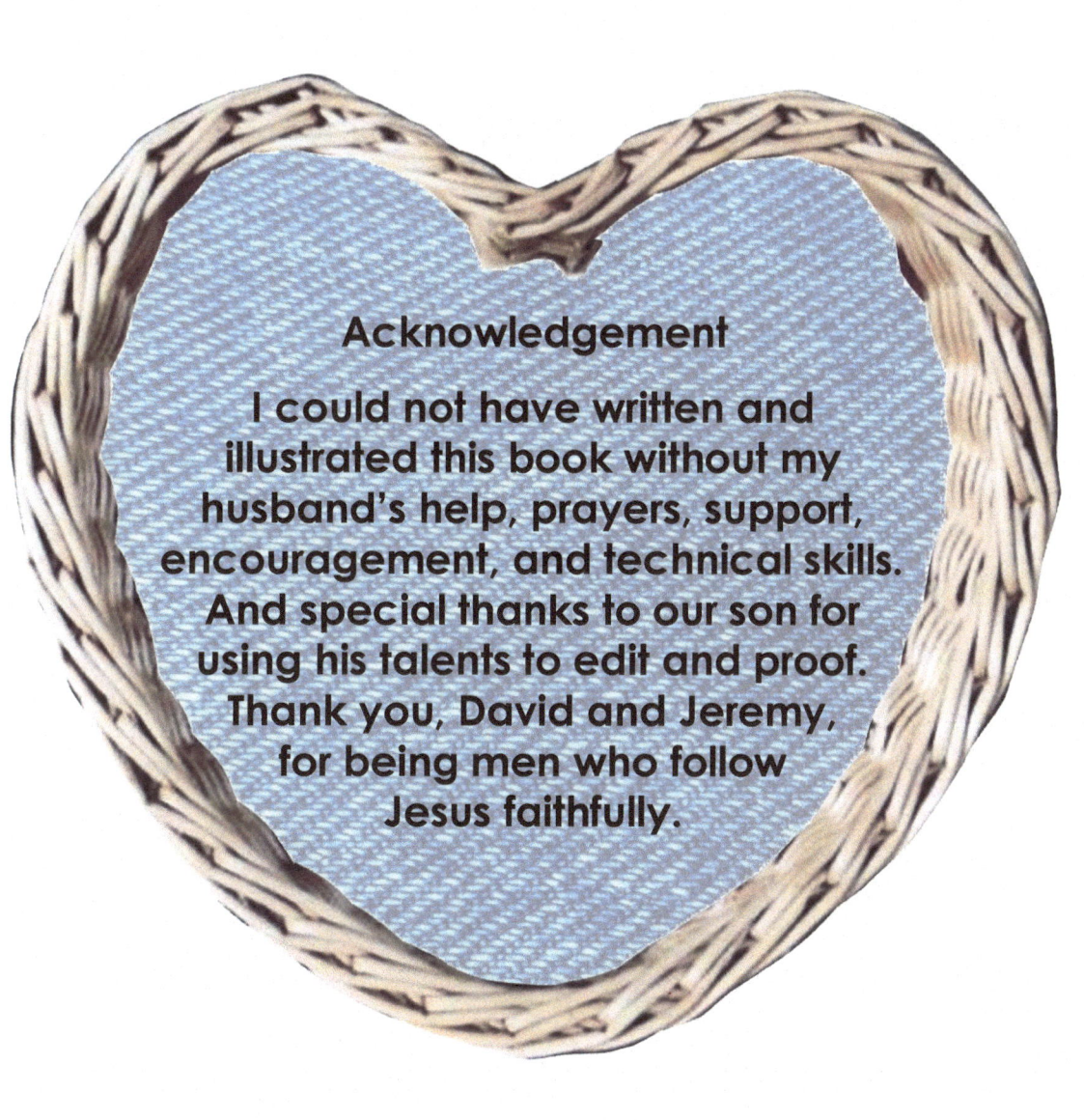

Acknowledgement

I could not have written and illustrated this book without my husband's help, prayers, support, encouragement, and technical skills. And special thanks to our son for using his talents to edit and proof. Thank you, David and Jeremy, for being men who follow Jesus faithfully.

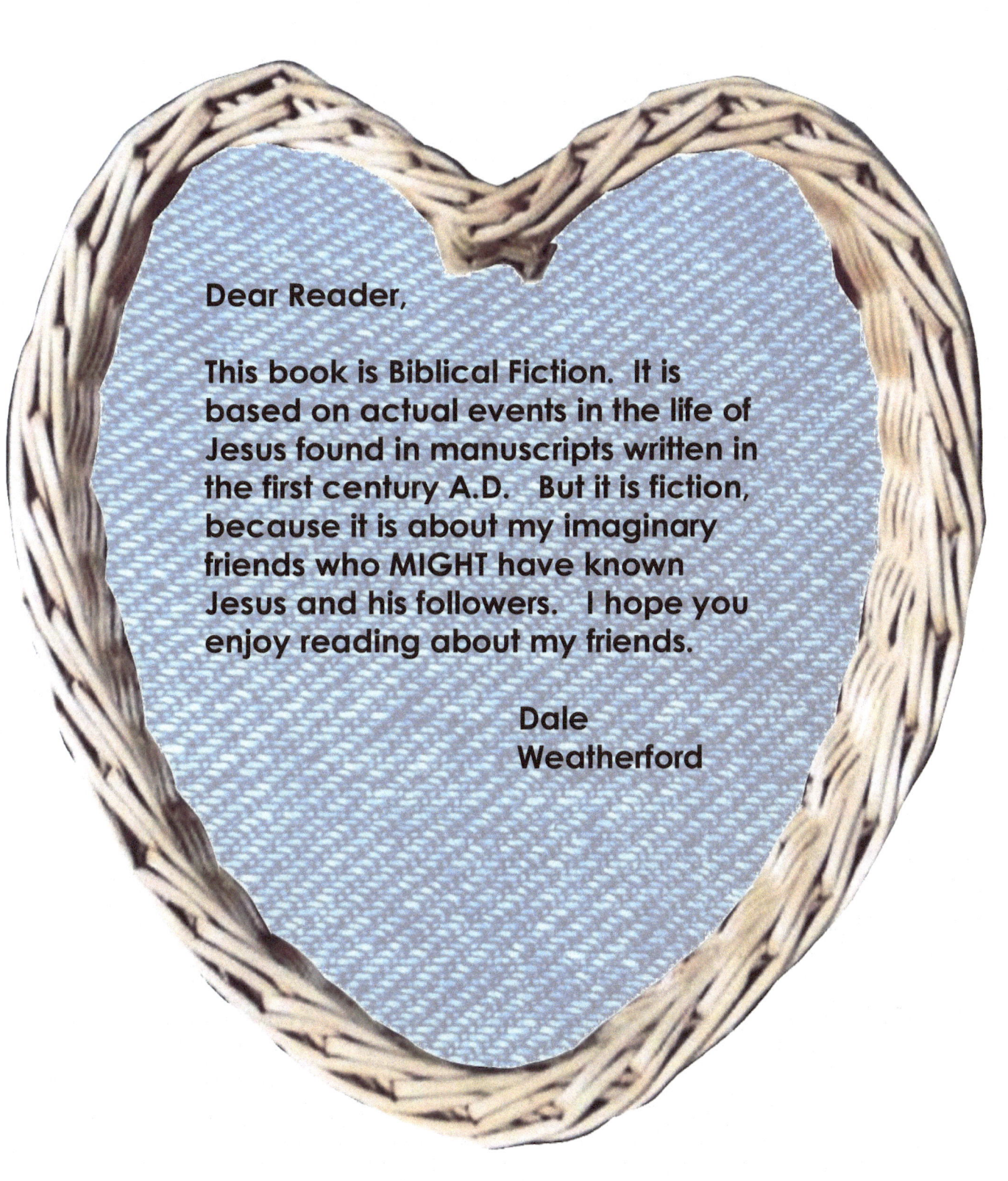

Dear Reader,

This book is Biblical Fiction. It is based on actual events in the life of Jesus found in manuscripts written in the first century A.D. But it is fiction, because it is about my imaginary friends who MIGHT have known Jesus and his followers. I hope you enjoy reading about my friends.

Dale Weatherford

The Stories Of

1. DAVID 1
2. RACHEL 31
3. JOSIE 67
4. NOAH 91
5. ORLY 117
6. LUCRETIA 125
7. CALEB 165
8. BENJI 183
9. SAMSON & SOLOMON 213
10. JUDITH 231
11. JOEL 245

12 LAILA 267

13 REUBEN 283

14 DINAH 307

15 AARON, DANIEL & GIDEON 331

16 ARIAL, HAVA & MIRIAM 369

17 KOBE 385

18 GERSHAM & MARIO 425

19 MICHAEL 439

20 GABRIELA 451

21 MATTISON 473

22 JONATHAN & JENAY 491

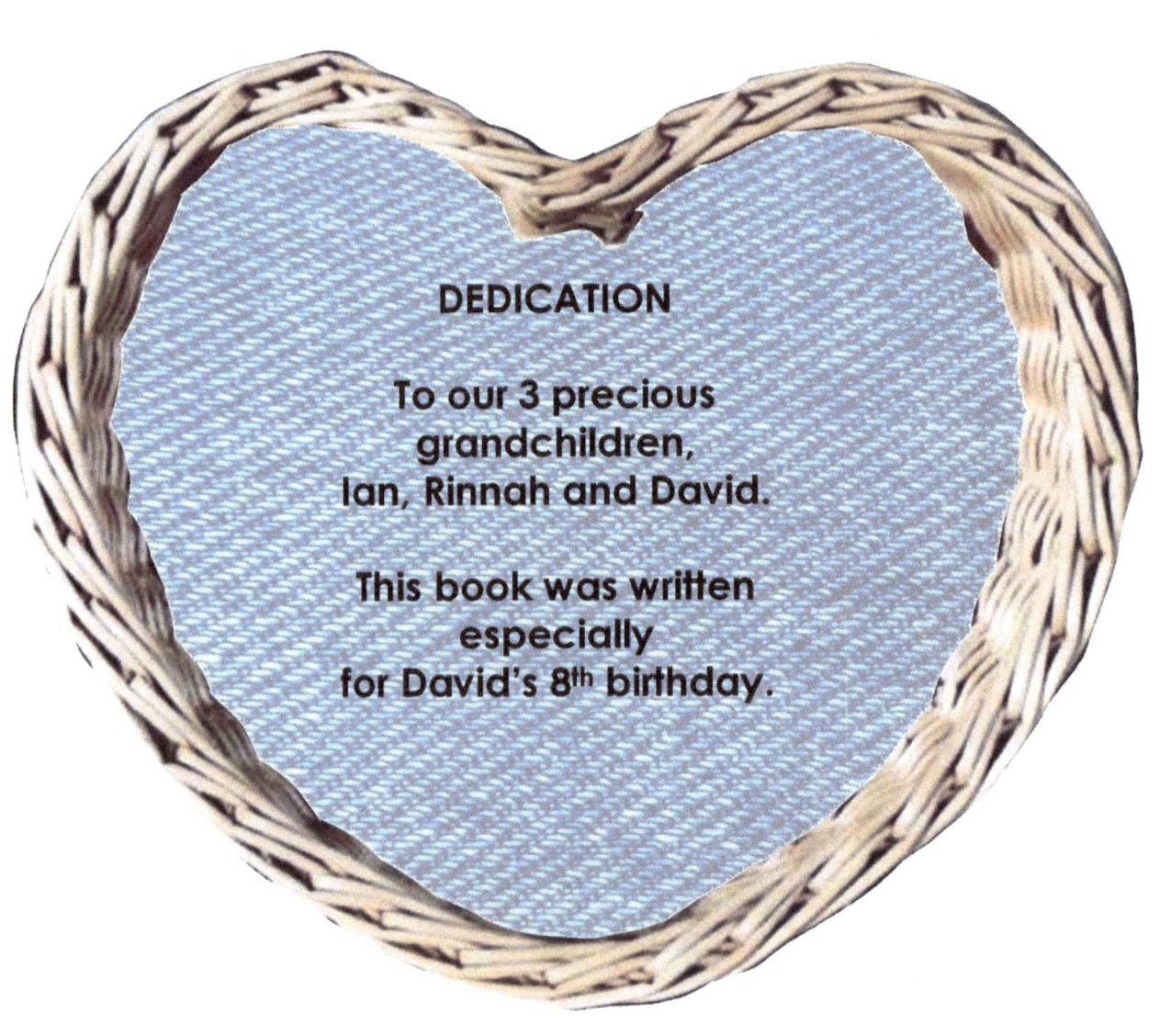

DEDICATION

To our 3 precious grandchildren,
Ian, Rinnah and David.

This book was written especially
for David's 8th birthday.

Chapter 1
THE STORY OF DAVID

"Good morning, David, I'm so glad your mother let you come early to help. I was just heading out to the market. Bring me the baskets. We must hurry to find a good chicken. Uncle Zechariah should be arriving this afternoon and I want to make a special dinner for him."

David loved going to the market with Aunt Elizabeth. There were so many interesting things to taste and see and he knew if he was a good helper, she would buy him some honey as a treat. Quickly, he gathered up the baskets and together they began the walk to the market.

There were lots of tents set up and so many things to see. But when Aunt Elizabeth said she wanted a chicken — she meant a real live chicken; one with feathers and a beak and sharp claws. David hoped that she didn't think he was strong enough to carry it, because he wasn't really sure he wanted to touch it. He was relieved when Aunt Elizabeth motioned for Elrod, her servant, to take the chicken home and begin preparing it.

David helped Aunt Elizabeth carry the baskets that she filled with fruits and vegetables and then they hurried home. It would be a busy day to prepare the special meal.

Everyone was in a festive mood because they knew that soon Uncle Zechariah would return, and he would bring them news of all the wonderful things that he had seen and done while he was in Jerusalem. David's parents were coming for dinner, too, so they could all hear Uncle Zechariah's news.

Jerusalem was the capital city of Israel. The temple was up on a high hill overlooking the entire city and you could see it for miles around. David's whole family went there three times a year for special holy feast days unless someone was sick or there was a new baby to care for. But this was Uncle Zechariah's time to go alone to work at the temple. He did this every year and returned with news from all over Israel and the surrounding areas. Uncle Zechariah was a priest, and he served his village in the Judean hillside most of the time. But every year, he spent two weeks working at the temple. And now he was on his way home. David could hardly wait.

David helped Aunt Elizabeth in the kitchen when he could, but most of the time he just watched all the servants rushing around preparing dishes and getting the table ready for the meal. "Would you like to help me with the bread?" asked Aunt Elizabeth.

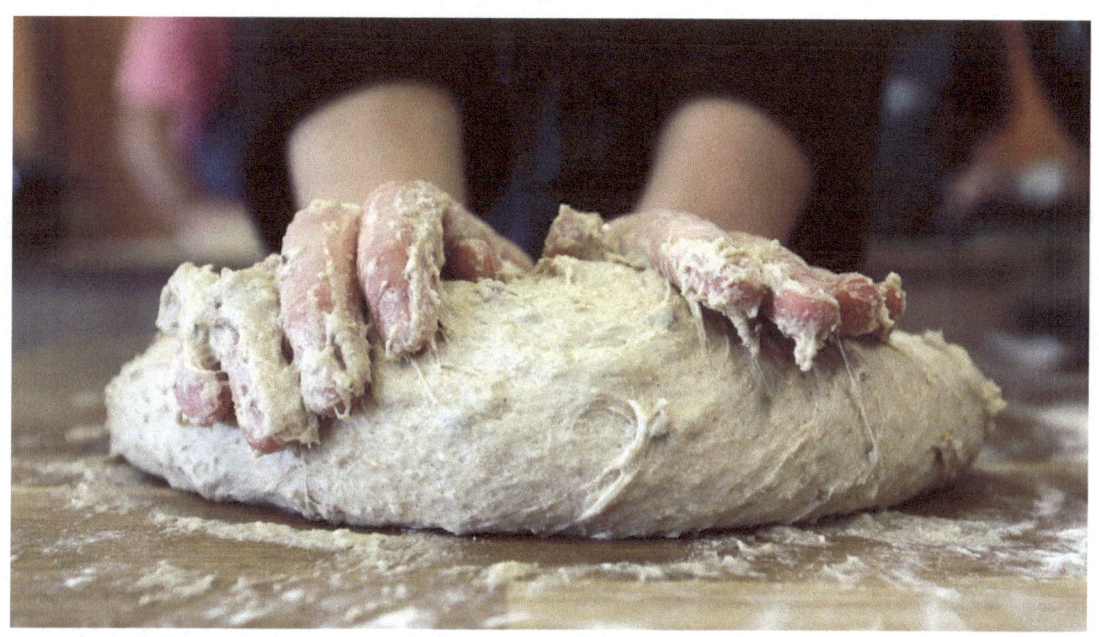

"Of course!" said David. Kneading the bread was his favorite part. He loved the way the sticky dough became firmer and firmer as he mashed it with his fists. He felt proud that he was old enough and finally strong enough to handle the dough. But his favorite part was when the dough was safely tucked into a pan to rise, and Aunt Elizabeth would hand him a handful of raisins to push deep in the dough. She would slip him a few extra ones and would always say, "And here's the chef's tip!" He would bow grandly and accept the raisins as his special reward. Yummmmm! He loved raisins.

Aunt Elizabeth wanted to rest for a while during the afternoon heat, so David wandered outside and played with the goats while the adults rested.

He daydreamed about what it would be like to work in the temple. He would like to light the candles and burn the incense, but he wouldn't want to kill the lambs and other animals used in sacrifice. He didn't like that part at all. He wondered what Uncle Zechariah did while he was at the temple this time.

Sometimes he worked in the kitchen and cooked. Other times he worked to repair the curtains and cushions. Sometimes he polished all the beautiful gold and silver decorations and one time he even got to climb to the top of the temple ceiling and dust the beautiful carvings there. That would have been fun.

Uncle Zechariah was a great storyteller, and everyone looked forward to hearing about all the people he had met. He had a loud, storytelling voice that kept everyone listening and his stories were always filled with laughter and fun.

As David thought about Uncle Zechariah, he realized that even though Uncle Zechariah was a joyful and fun man to be around — he was also very serious about his love for God. He wanted to obey God's rules and he really cared about his family obeying, too. David continued to wonder what it would be like when he was old enough to become a priest and work at the temple.

"David," called Aunt Elizabeth.

"Coming, Aunt Elizabeth!" David quickly darted into the house to see what Aunt Elizabeth wanted.

"Hand me the scroll of the prophet Isaiah. As I was resting, I kept thinking about it and I want you to read it with me."

David had to stand on top of a chair to reach the rack of scrolls but finally found the one that his aunt wanted. He handed it to her, and she skillfully unrolled it to find the words she was looking for.

David was proud that Aunt Elizabeth could read and understand the Holy Scriptures. Her dad, who was also a priest, had taught her as a child and unlike most of the women in the community, she could read well.

She read:

> "…. The virgin will conceive and give birth to a son, and will call him Immanuel. [1]

"Have you learned this verse in Hebrew school?"

"Yes, Aunt Elizabeth."

"Do you understand it?"

David felt a little troubled by the question because he thought he did, but he wasn't exactly sure. But he wanted Aunt Elizabeth to be proud of him, so he gave it his best shot.

"*The virgin* means a young woman who is not married."

Aunt Elizabeth nodded for him to continue.

"And it says she will have a baby and will name him Immanuel."

"Very good! You have learned your lessons well. But have you ever thought about what the name *Immanuel* means?"

Uh-oh, that's not the question I was expecting. He thought she would ask if he knew that this verse was a prophecy about the coming of the Messiah. "No, Aunt Elizabeth, I guess I don't know. I'm sorry."

"David, do not ever be sorry for not knowing the answer. Only be sorry if you do not want to learn the answer!"

"Yes, Ma'am. I do want to know what *Immanuel* means because it will tell me something about the Messiah."

"What a smart little boy you are! I am proud of my nephew! *Immanuel* is the word I was thinking about as I rested. *Immanuel*, in Hebrew, means *God with us*. Now, if this baby, the Messiah, is going to be named 'God with us', I think that there's going to be something very, very special about him. I think he will be God." Aunt Elizabeth seemed to forget that David was even in the room and David wasn't sure if she was praying or just deep in thought.

Just then he heard the servants rushing around and one announced that they could see Uncle Zechariah coming down the road and he had two guests with him. David didn't even wait for Aunt Elizabeth but rushed out the front door and down the steps to meet him.

But something was wrong. All the buzz and hustle of the servants stopped as everyone realized that something was different.

It was not unusual for Uncle Zechariah to bring home fellow travelers to spend the night or eat a meal with them.   But there was something definitely wrong. Uncle Zechariah's strong hearty greeting did not ring out. Usually you could hear him as he shouted, "Home, sweet home!"

But instead, the three men walked quietly up the steps to greet Elizabeth. While everyone stood around anxiously wondering what was going on, the two men, who were priests from surrounding villages, told Aunt Elizabeth the news about her husband.

The priests told Elizabeth that Zechariah had gone into the Holy Place of the temple and:

> **When he came out, he could not speak to them. They realized he had seen a vision in the temple, for he kept making signs to them but remained unable to speak.[2]**

And they reported that ever since that day, Zechariah had been unable to speak.

Quickly Aunt Elizabeth took charge. She ordered the servants to return to their jobs and asked that dinner be served as usual. She invited the priests to stay for dinner, but they were eager to get to their own homes. She sent Uncle Zechariah to rest and cool off after his hard journey and she sent David to get some cloths and a pan of water to cool Uncle Zechariah's face.

David was glad there was something he could do to help. Nothing like this had ever happened before. *What will happen if Uncle Zechariah is sick?* David hurried to get the water and tried not to think about anything else. Uncle Zechariah stretched out on the cushions in the living room and the servants fanned him with palm branches to make him as comfortable as possible.

As David laid the cool cloths on his uncle's forehead, he thought to himself that he had never seen Uncle Zechariah look healthier. He didn't <u>look</u> sick. And there was that same twinkle in his eyes that showed he was filled with joy and almost bursting with news.

Uncle Zechariah took David's hand and placed it on his heart. David knew that Uncle Zechariah was telling him that he loved him. David took one of Uncle Zechariah's hands and brought it to his heart. That made Uncle Zechariah smile even bigger — but he shook his head meaning "no." Now, David was really confused.

Uncle Zechariah grinned and pointed to his ears and gave David the "thumbs up".

Just because Uncle Zechariah couldn't speak, didn't mean he couldn't hear! David laughed and that made Uncle Zechariah laugh too, even though no sound came out. Then David declared loudly, "I love you, Uncle Zechariah and I'm so glad you are home!"

Soon David's parents and more friends arrived. Everyone was seated around the table. But Uncle Zechariah couldn't lead in the evening prayers, so David's Abba prayed and thanked God for the meal and for Uncle Zechariah's return. (Abba is what Jewish children call their daddy).

While the meal was excellently prepared, everything felt strange. Everyone was trying to make signs so that Uncle Zechariah could understand them. David had to keep reminding them that Uncle Zechariah's ears worked just fine. They all wanted to ask questions but the only thing they could understand was just what the other priests had told them.

The meal ended earlier than usual to allow Uncle Zechariah to get some rest and David went home with his parents. As David walked beside his Abba, he asked him what was wrong with Uncle Zechariah. His Abba said that he didn't know the answers, but that he was certain that God would reveal whatever it was soon.

"But I don't like not knowing and I don't like to wait!"

"I know, son. I don't think anyone enjoys those things, but sometimes God has plans that are too big for us to handle all at once, so he shows us just little bits at a time. Remember the Scripture we studied a few weeks ago:

'For my thoughts are not your thoughts, neither are your ways my ways,' declares the Lord.[3]

"Someday we'll understand it. And for now, we must trust that God knows what is best. And I assure you, David, God will let us know when we need to know it."

"I love you, Abba."

"And I love you, little David."

The next few months were very busy ones for David and for his Abba. Hebrew school had started again and because Uncle Zechariah was unable to teach, David's Abba, who was a priest-in-training, was teaching all the classes. That meant that David needed to help even more at home.

David worked hard on his schoolwork each evening. After school there was always work that needed to be done in the garden and other things that Mother needed help with. After dinner he would work on his studies by lamplight until bedtime. It seemed that he had more homework than ever. He wanted to make his Abba and his Uncle Zechariah proud of him and knew that they expected him to do his very best.

One of David's chores was gathering produce from the garden before going to school. He would pick the fruits and vegetables so Mother could use them or give them away to people who needed them that day.

Sometimes while he was in the garden, he would think about his time with Uncle Zechariah and Aunt Elizabeth. He wished he had more time to spend with them. It had been several months since that night Uncle Zechariah came home and was unable to talk.

Once when David had taken them some fresh melons, he found them sitting at the table with scrolls laid out all around them. Even though they seemed very glad to see him, he could tell that they were busy with some serious studies, and he didn't want to bother them.

He gave them both hugs and told them he loved them. Uncle Zechariah took David's hand and placed it over his heart. That made David feel especially loved. He missed learning from Uncle Zechariah, but he didn't think it would be polite to say so — so he didn't.

Sometimes at school some of the older boys talked about Uncle Zechariah and said things that made David feel sad. Sometimes they said that God was punishing Uncle Zechariah for something evil that he must have done. David wanted to punch them in the face, but he knew that his Abba and Uncle Zechariah would not like that at all. So, he would just turn away and find other friends to talk with. But that didn't stop the sick feeling in his stomach.

When David finally talked with his Abba about it, his Abba gave him some suggestions that helped him be bolder. "But I'm very proud of you for not fighting. Fighting never solves the problem."

"Yes, Abba, and thank you!"

The next time the boys began to say that Uncle Zechariah was being punished, David's heart began to beat really fast. His hands got all sweaty and he felt sick to his stomach, but he spoke up, even though he was afraid of what the older boys would do. David boldly said, "Don't forget that Job's friends were wrong when they judged him. Remember that the Scripture says:

> **… judge your neighbor fairly.[4]"**

Then David walked away. Instead of feeling sick, he felt proud that he had stood up for Uncle Zechariah. He knew he couldn't change the boys' minds, but he knew that inside he felt taller and stronger because he had done what was right.

A few months later, David's Abba announced that they were going to eat their Sabbath meal with Uncle Zechariah and Aunt Elizabeth and a very special guest. (*Sabbath* means *rest*. The Jewish Sabbath was from Friday sundown to Saturday sundown.)

After school, David and his Abba washed and put on clean clothes for the occasion. Then David walked with his parents to Uncle Zechariah's and Aunt Elizabeth's home. He hoped the special guest would be someone his age. Maybe they could go out in the yard and play ball together after dinner. Or maybe it was someone who could explain what had happened to Uncle Zechariah. David's mind was racing all over the place with excitement.

But when they arrived, the only unexpected person there was David's cousin, Mary. She was a few years older than David and David would have much preferred to entertain her younger brother who was his age. They lived in Galilee and couldn't visit often. He was really, really disappointed. Not only was it just his cousin Mary, but she was looking and acting very grown up and didn't want to play in the yard with him.

 David knew that Uncle Zechariah wouldn't mind if he looked at his scrolls and soon David totally forgot the grownups as he read through the story about the prophet Daniel being thrown into a lion's den.

He joined the adults for dessert, and then everyone said their "good-nights." Mary would be leaving in the morning and David politely wished her a safe journey and tried to say all the right things.

As David walked home with his parents he grumbled about the "special" guest only being cousin Mary. His parents looked shocked and maybe saddened, but he wasn't sure what their exchanged glances meant. There were a lot of things about grownups that he just didn't understand yet. And right now, he just wanted to get home and out of his dress-up clothes.

It was only a few weeks later when an exciting guest did arrive. David's family was just finishing dinner when there was a loud knock at the front door. Elrod, Uncle Zechariah's servant, looking very excited, yelled, "It's time! It's time!" and left with no other explanation.

"David, bring me the bag that is sitting by my bed." Mother and Abba were talking quietly but urgently. They seemed to be making plans for an escape. But then Mother kissed David and was out the door before he could even ask what was happening.

"Abba?"

"Yes, David."

"What's going on? And where is Mother going?"

"It's time for the baby to come. We must pray for God's safety."

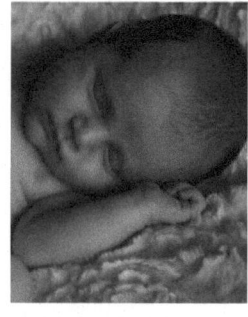

"Baby! What baby? We're going to have a baby?" David's head was exploding, and he had so many questions he couldn't form the words — they kept tripping over his tongue. It sounded more like "bay-bay-bay-bay".

David's Abba looked at him closely and realized that David was feeling very confused.

"Come, Son, sit down and let's talk." They sat together on the cushions in the living room and David's Abba brought him some juice to drink.

"Now, Son, what is it that you don't understand?"

"Abba, I don't understand anything!" wailed David.

"Okay. So, let's start with Elrod's announcement that Aunt Elizabeth's time has come."

"Aunt Elizabeth? Has she died? I thought this was about a baby?" David placed his hands over his face and rocked back and forth. Now, he was not only confused but very scared.

"Son, didn't you know that Aunt Elizabeth was going to have a baby?"

"A baby? Aunt Elizabeth? She's old enough to be my grandmother. She can't have a baby!"

Now Abba laughed and threw his arms around David. "I'm so sorry that I assumed you knew all about it. But you have been very busy this term at school and not paying attention to things around you."

"So, why did Mother leave so quickly?"

"Well, your mother will need to be there to help Aunt Elizabeth with the birth and probably to keep Uncle Zechariah calm! Your mother will stay with Aunt Elizabeth until she is strong enough to take care of the baby. It may be a couple of weeks because, as you know, Aunt Elizabeth is old and not as strong as she used to be."

David felt much better after talking with his Abba. Both David and his Abba had studies to complete before bedtime, but it seemed strange to be in the house without Mother. The house seemed empty somehow.

David and his Abba were glad to be busy at Hebrew school all the next day. David worked in the garden for a while after school. Just before Abba got home, Elrod came with the announcement that a healthy baby boy had arrived, and that Aunt Elizabeth <u>and</u> Uncle Zechariah, and the baby were all doing fine.

David was proud to get to announce the news to his Abba and his Abba was relieved that all was well. They ate a simple meal prepared by their servant Mira, but they both missed Mother.

"Abba?" asked David.

"Yes, Son."

"Abba, why wasn't I told that Aunt Elizabeth was going to have a baby?"

His Abba thought a few minutes and said, "I guess we assumed that you knew. I promise you; we weren't hiding it from you."

"Abba?"

"Yes, Son."

"How will Uncle Zechariah teach the baby all the things he needs to know when he can't talk?"

"I guess you and I will have to help teach him to be a man of God. That's a big responsibility. Do you remember the Shema, God's command to parents?"

"Yes, Abba, the Shema says,

> **Hear, O Israel: The LORD our God, the LORD is one. Love the Lord your God with all your heart and with all your soul and with all your strength. These commandments that I give you today are to be on your hearts. Impress them on your children. Talk about them when you sit at home and when you walk along the road, when you lie down and when you get up.[5]**"

"I'm sure your little cousin will look up to you and follow your example. You will need to be careful that you do not lead him into bad things."

"Abba, I forgot to collect the fruits and vegetables this morning and some of the apricots were ruined. I had to throw them away. I'm sorry."

"I'm sorry, too, Son. We don't want to waste food that others could use. Times are hard and your chores are important. Don't forget again."

"I won't, Abba. And I will try to be a good example for my new cousin. Does he have a name yet?"

"No, not yet. New boy babies get their names when they are eight days old. There will be a large party to celebrate."

One week later, David and his Abba hurried to Uncle Zechariah's home to join in the celebration. All the neighbors had gathered and brought gifts to share with the happy couple.

David found several of his friends from Hebrew school and they played ball on the far side of the yard so they wouldn't disturb the adults. But the boys quickly joined the party when they noticed that the dessert table was available. Many neighbors had helped to fill the dessert table with goodies to add to the celebration.

When it was time for the Naming Ceremony, David recognized the priest who was leading it as one of the men who had brought Uncle Zechariah home from Jerusalem and told Aunt Elizabeth what had happened. He knew that he was a good friend of Uncle Zechariah's.

Once again, David's thoughts turned to how this little boy would learn all he needed to know when his Abba would be unable to teach him. But David's attention was caught by some commotion around Aunt Elizabeth. It seems there was some argument about the name of the baby.

The neighbors had told the priest that the baby's name would be Zechariah, Jr. and Aunt Elizabeth was saying, "No! His name will be John." The neighbors continued to argue with her saying that that wasn't the right name, and it looked like Aunt Elizabeth might start crying.

Uncle Zechariah was motioning for David to come. He ran quickly to his uncle's side. He motioned for David to find his writing tablet in the house. David ran inside and looked around. He spotted it on the kitchen table and quickly sprinted to Uncle Zechariah.

> **... he wrote, "His name is John." Immediately his mouth was opened and his tongue set free, and he began to speak, praising God.[6]**

David was not the only one surprised when Uncle Zechariah's voice began to boom out. Everyone in the yard turned their full attention to him and listened.

"Praise God for sending his Messiah! He promised that he would come, and we've waited and waited. He promised that he would rescue us from our enemies."

What does this mean? All the people were asking the same question as David, and everyone was talking at once. *Is this little baby the Messiah?*

Uncle Zechariah raised his arm to quiet them and continued. This time he turned and touched baby John on the head.

Uncle Zechariah said:

> **"And you, my child, will be called a prophet of the Most High; for you will go on before the Lord to prepare the way for him."[7]**

It was very late that night before the party broke up. Everyone wanted to hear again what had happened to Uncle Zechariah in the Holy Place at the temple. He told the story over and over about seeing an angel who told him that baby John would be a prophet to prepare the people of Israel for the Messiah.

Mother was going to stay one more night to help Aunt Elizabeth, so David and his Abba walked home alone. They walked in silence since both of them were filled with thoughts and questions. They had much to think about.

When they arrived at home, David knew just what his Abba would do. He took down several scrolls and rolled them out on the table. Together they read some of the prophecies concerning Messiah. But it had been a long day and David soon headed to bed.

"Abba?"

"Yes, Son"

"Is this <u>really</u> happening? Or am I just dreaming?"

"David, it <u>is</u> really happening, and I believe that Messiah is very, very near."

"I hope so, Abba."

"I hope so, too, Son. Good night. I love you."

1. Isaiah 7:14
2. Luke 1:22
3. Isaiah 55:8
4. Leviticus 19:15
5. Deuteronomy 6:4-7
6. Luke 1:63-64
7. Luke 1:76

Zechariah & Elizabeth
Luke 1:5-7

Zechariah Hears Great News
Luke 1:8-22

Mary Visits Zechariah & Elizabeth
Luke 1:39-56

Daniel in the Lion's Den
Daniel 6:13-23

Birth of John the Prophet
Luke 1:57-58

Naming of John the Prophet
Luke 1:59-66

Zechariah's Prophecy
Luke 1:76-79

Chapter 2
THE STORY OF RACHEL

Mary was bored from being stuck inside the dark barn. She was feeling stronger and Joseph had gone out to look for work. He said he would be back to check on her at noon, but until then it was just her and the baby. She was tired of resting and the baby was sleeping, so she gently opened the front door of the barn.

"Who's there?" demanded a stern but childish voice.

"It's me, Mary. And who are you and <u>where</u> are you?" Mary didn't feel threatened by the voice — just curious as to where it was coming from.

A mass of dark curly hair popped out from between some bales of straw that were stacked just outside the door. "Hi! You scared me. I didn't know you were here. Usually I hear everything."

When Mary looked closely, she realized that the girl in front of her was blind. "What are you doing?"

"Oh, I was just pretending that this was my house and well … you know. But what are <u>you</u> doing here? This is Uncle Omar's barn!" the girl demanded.

"Well, your Uncle Omar said that we could stay here for a few days until we could find a place — as long as we didn't mind sharing with a few goats and a donkey."

Rachel liked Mary's voice. She didn't seem to be afraid of Rachel's blindness and she sounded gentle. Rachel was a pretty good judge of voices.

"His name is Pete."

"Whose name is Pete?"

"My donkey. And the goats are Rosa and Beta."

"Well, that's very good to know! And who might you be?"

About that time, baby Jesus announced himself with a loud wail. Mary turned and ran quickly into the barn with Rachel on her heels.

"A baby!"

Mary quickly picked up Jesus and tended to his wet blankets, then she settled him on her breast.

"Why don't we go to your make-believe house and get acquainted?" Mary suggested. The child quickly moved the hay bales so that they could sit on them and talk.

"I'm Mary and this is Jesus. He's four days old and seems to be very hungry these days. My husband and I came here from Nazareth in Galilee and now we need to stay until I can get strong enough to travel. Now, it's your turn."

Rachel was delighted that Mary seemed interested in her. "I'm Rachel and I have two little brothers. My Uncle Omar owns this barn and I come here to hide, I mean," she quickly changed her story, but Mary noticed it. "I come here to check on Pete.

"May I touch baby Jesus? I won't hurt him. I know how to be gentle."

Mary agreed and Rachel moved to her side. She very gently touched his toes. Mary realized that because Rachel couldn't "see", she was using her touch to get a picture of him. She counted each toe and then found one of his hands.

Rachel giggled when baby Jesus clasped hold of her finger and wouldn't let go. Rachel was so gentle with him, and Mary realized that she was an experienced big sister and could be trusted to keep Jesus safe.

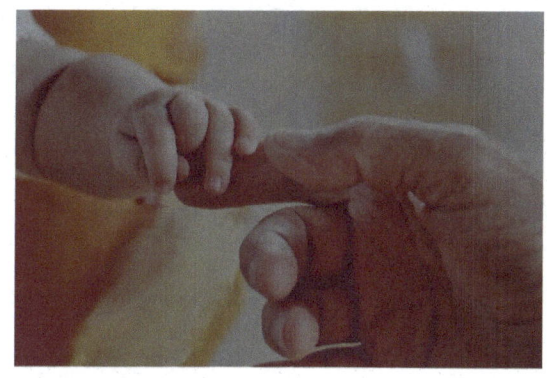

Rachel was filled with questions and before Mary noticed, the morning had passed. She saw Joseph headed toward the barn. Rachel heard the footsteps and quickly scampered off without even saying goodbye.

Joseph kissed baby Jesus before telling Mary the big news. Because Bethlehem was so filled with people, lots of workers were needed — especially carpenters who could repair yokes and wagons. He had found a position already, and soon they would have something besides goat's milk, and some stale bread to eat.

Joseph drank a cup of goat's milk, but then needed to rush back to work. He promised to bring her something wonderful for dinner and reminded her to get her rest. He kissed them goodbye and started off at a run to get back to the shop on time.

Mary knew she needed to rest, so just as soon as she got Jesus fed again and settled into the little makeshift crib (a cow's old feeding trough), Mary stretched out on the hay and was quickly asleep. Feeding a newborn every few hours was a lot of work and her body needed to heal.

It was late afternoon before Jesus woke her this time and she cleaned out his bed and washed him in a pan of water. He seemed to enjoy the bath. "Your Abba is bringing home a good supper and you need to be clean and smell good for him. He's worked hard all day to take good care of us. He'll be home soon."

"Hello. Mary? It's me, Rachel. May I come in?"

"Certainly Rachel, I was just finishing up giving Jesus a bath. Do you think you could hold him while I repack my bag of supplies? I don't want the mice to get into them."

Rachel sat on the hay and held baby Jesus on her lap just like her mother had taught her to hold her brothers. Pete kept sticking his head over his pen and kissing Rachel's ears and neck. Rachel would giggle and shoo him away.

Rachel chatted happily and Mary found out that Rachel was eight years old, and that she had been blind since birth. Her two little brothers were a handful for her mother and there was another baby on the way. Rachel was supposed to be sitting by the street leading to the synagogue to beg for coins. But apparently, she often sneaked away and hid at her uncle's barn and played with Pete instead.

Mary realized how much she missed her younger brothers and sisters. Having Rachel around helped pass the time even though she was only half listening.

"So, do you?" Rachel asked.

"I'm sorry, Rachel, I was thinking about how hungry I am and hoping Joseph will be home soon. What was your question?"

"I was just wondering if you believed the shepherds?" repeated Rachel.

"Oh, Rachel, I must have missed something because I'm not sure what we are talking about."

Rachel's face fell and Mary thought she saw a look of distrust. Mary took both of Rachel's hands in hers and assured her that she wanted to listen, and she wanted to answer her question. She apologized for not listening carefully. "Please start all over at the beginning and I'll try my best to answer you."

Rachel seemed pleased with that and began her story all over again. It seemed that four nights ago there had been some commotion out in the street with people running and shouting. She had gotten out of bed, but her parents would not let her go outside to check out what was happening.

They told her it was probably the Roman soldiers celebrating something, and it would be no place for a girl. Rachel had obeyed, but she heard enough from the shouting to figure out that these were not Roman soldiers — they were shepherds who had seen something that had excited them and they were intent on waking up the whole town to tell them the news.

The next morning, Rachel had gone to beg outside the synagogue as usual, but all the beggars could talk about was what the shepherds had said the night before.

The shepherds said that an angel had appeared in the sky and said:

> ... "Do not be afraid. I bring you good news that will cause great joy for all the people. Today in the town of David a Savior has been born to you; he is the Messiah, the Lord. This will be a sign to you: You will find a baby wrapped in cloths and lying in a manger."[1]

"Mary, did you hear the noise that night?"

"Yes." Mary was not sure what to tell the child, but she knew that she would not lie to her.

Excitedly Rachel asked, "Did they come here, Mary? Did they come here?"

"Yes, Rachel, they came here."

"Mary, does baby Jesus sleep in a manger?"

"Yes, Rachel, he does."

Now Rachel could hardly sit still.

"Mary, is baby Jesus the Messiah? Is he the One we've been waiting for? Oh, Mary, I got to touch him! I got to hold him. Oh, Mary, is baby Jesus the Messiah?"

"Well, Rachel, I believe he is."

Rachel sat perfectly still as if she were just listening to the air around her.

She kept saying, "Oh! Oh my!"

But Jesus had other plans and let out a pitiful wail that made them both laugh.

He was a four-day-old man demanding his dinner. Mary quickly cleaned his makeshift crib, and he began to nurse greedily. His smacking noises made Rachel giggle.

"Gotta go!" and Rachel quickly disappeared.

This time Mary realized that Joseph was approaching. What an exciting evening they shared! Joseph had been paid well and he had purchased a feast for the two of them. He had bought two pomegranates, two cucumbers, an onion, and two fresh rounds of bread. With the goats' milk, they felt that it was a feast fit for royalty.

The carpenter had told Joseph he could continue to work if he wanted the job. Joseph planned to get caught up on their food supplies, and then start saving a little to be able to move out of the barn. But in the meantime, they were content.

Joseph held Jesus while Mary cleaned up their dinner and packed it all securely away. While she worked, she told Joseph about her visitor that day. He was glad that she had made a new friend.

Together they watched Jesus and agreed that he was much, much bigger than the day before. They discussed what else she could have said to Rachel. They didn't want to lie, but they also didn't want to draw attention to him. They knew that God was depending on them to protect Jesus as much as they could, but they weren't always sure of what they were supposed to do.

Mary was still talking about Rachel when she realized that both Joseph and Jesus were fast asleep in the hay.

Mary picked Jesus up and put him in the manger to keep him safe and then lay down to think over her busy day.

Early each morning, Joseph had to feed Pete the donkey and then milk Omar's two goats and carry the milk to the nearby inn. That was their payment for the use of the barn, but Omar had told them they could keep as much milk as they needed for their own use. Then Joseph had to take the water jar to the well and fill it, because Mary was supposed to be resting and not lifting heavy things. She would need fresh water to keep Jesus clean, wash his clothing, and of course for drinking water.

Joseph had barely left for work when Rachel knocked at the barn door. Mary invited her in and decided to put her to good use. "Rachel, do you think you could hold Jesus while I wash my hair? I feel much stronger after eating such a good meal and Joseph brought me some extra water. It would feel so good to have my hair clean." Rachel happily agreed and settled onto the hay so that baby Jesus would be safe in her arms. Mary quickly washed her hair and began combing it out when she heard Rachel singing to baby Jesus. Rachel was such a little girl, but her voice was big and strong and pure and beautiful. Baby Jesus was fascinated by her voice and was soon fast asleep. Mary felt tears in her eyes because of the amazing beauty of the child's voice. "Rachel, who taught you to sing like that?"

"My Grandmother taught me all the Psalms. I love to sing."

The eighth day for a Jewish boy baby is very special. Usually the entire family and sometimes the whole community gathered for the Naming Ceremony and birthday party. But here in Bethlehem, Mary and Joseph didn't know anyone and couldn't afford to feed them if they did.

Joseph had asked the priest to come for a private ceremony in the afternoon and Joseph's boss had generously given him the entire afternoon off. They had planned for a quiet time for just the three of them. Joseph had not had much time with Jesus, and this would be the perfect time. But they didn't know that Rachel had other plans!

After noon, there was a knock on the door that they assumed would be the priest, but instead Rachel had brought quite a crowd. There was Rachel's mother and dad and her two little brothers. Thankfully, her mother was carrying a large raisin cake and her dad was carrying a loaf of honey bread.

Uncle Omar and his wife were bringing some jugs of fruit juice. Behind them were a couple of Rachel's friends who begged with her every morning at the synagogue.

Mary and Joseph were thrilled to meet Rachel's family and friends. When the priest arrived for the Naming Ceremony, Jesus was given his name, and everyone proclaimed the party a success.

Long after the women had taken the children home, Joseph stayed up late in the night to talk with Rachel's dad, Obadiah; her Uncle Omar; and the two beggars. They sat in front of the barn on the hay bales and talked about Israel's future. They, too, wanted to know what all the excitement with the shepherds was about. Joseph answered their questions as best he could. These were fellow Jews who were looking for the Messiah as eagerly as he was. But he decided to not volunteer any information — just answer questions.

They all agreed that Jesus must be going to be very special, and that God had great plans for him as they shook hands and parted ways. They also agreed to be on the lookout for a house for Joseph and Mary to rent.

About a week later, a small one room house had been found that Joseph felt they could afford to rent. When Mary told Rachel about the upcoming move, she was sad until they discovered that the house was actually closer to her house and they would live on the same street just a few doors down.

Since Mary had carried all she owned on her back, moving day was not a big operation. With Rachel's help, Mary had just about everything moved before Joseph got home. He had assured her that he would stop by the barn after work and pick up his heavier pack and check to make sure they hadn't forgotten anything.

The days passed a little quicker now that Mary was feeling stronger. She could prepare a meal over a fire in the backyard and keep the house tidy without mice and spiders in every crevice. It felt more like camping-out than being at home because they had no furniture, but at least it was cleaner.

Mr. Omar offered Joseph the job of continuing to feed the donkey and milk the two goats in exchange for all the milk they could use, and Mary began to dream of having butter and cheese on a regular basis. Rachel visited often and Rachel's mother also stopped by occasionally for a quick visit.

When Jesus was 40 days old, Mary and Joseph woke early as usual. Today would be a special day. Mary got up and tended to Jesus while Joseph left to go feed Pete and milk the goats. By the time he returned, Mary had fed and dressed Jesus and prepared a quick breakfast. Joseph helped Mary strap baby Jesus to her so that her hands would be free to carry a few small bags of baby supplies. Joseph carried the bedding and some extra food just in case the trip took longer than expected.

They shut the door to their little house and prayed for God's protection as they traveled. It was only six miles to Jerusalem, but this was their first time to make the trip together as a family with a baby.

Joseph wanted to make sure they had everything they needed. They began their walk just as the sun peeked over the hills. Mary thought she might could see the sparkle of the temple even from there.

As they walked further and further, they were joined by fellow travelers, all headed to Jerusalem. Mary and Joseph enjoyed the time to be together, but they also joined some of the other travelers in singing the Psalms as they approached the temple.

Jesus stirred and Mary reminded Joseph that they needed to find a place to change him and feed him before going into the temple. Joseph suggested they go into the olive garden just outside the gates. There, they could rest from their walk and make sure Jesus was at his best before taking him into the priest for the ceremony.

It was good to sit in the cool of the garden. Mary hadn't walked that far in a while and needed to catch her breath. Joseph produced a couple of apricots from his sack and they just relaxed for a few minutes.

Joseph left Mary and the baby in the cool of the garden while he sprinted across the ravine and into the temple grounds to purchase a lamb to sacrifice. He was shocked at the increase in prices and discovered that they could only afford two turtledoves.

He carried the birds carefully in one hand, while helping Mary with the sacks and other supplies for Jesus. They entered the courtyard of the temple and began to walk up the steps to the court of women. There, two things happened that Mary and Joseph would never forget.

They got home late that night and Mary was so tired she hardly remembered shutting her eyes. Thankfully, the fresh air helped Jesus sleep through the night, but it was still early when he woke and demanded attention. The sacrifice at the temple had been to thank God for their firstborn son, and the priest declared Mary fully recovered from giving birth.

She wanted the day to be special. Maybe she would go to the market later, or maybe to the synagogue. She hadn't realized how tired she was of being cooped up in the house.

When Rachel knocked on the door, Mary was eager to see her young friend and make plans for the day. Of course, Rachel wanted to hear every detail about the trip. Mary tried to describe the magnificent temple and all the people that she had met.

"But Rachel," Mary said, "two incredible things happened when we walked into the temple, and I can't wait to tell you!"

"You know I want to know everything! What happened?"

"Rachel, do you remember asking me about the shepherds and the angels?"

Suddenly, Rachel was quiet and still, "Oh, Mary, I think about that all the time. Did you see an angel? Do you know if Jesus really is the Messiah? Oh, Mary. Please tell me everything!"

"Well, Joseph and I walked into the temple courts. We had just walked up the steps into the court of women when this old man — they said his name was Simeon — came and held out his arms as if he wanted to hold baby Jesus. I wasn't sure whether it was safe, but Joseph nodded — so I placed baby Jesus in his arms and let him hold him.

He began to pray very loudly, and he told God that he would be happy to die now because he had seen the Messiah."

"Oh, Mary," Rachel gasped. "That's the second time someone has said that Jesus is the Messiah. What else did he say?"

"I didn't understand all of it, but he said something about Jesus being a light to the Gentiles and the glory of Israel. Oh, and he also said that the Holy Spirit had told him to come to the temple courts yesterday morning to meet us. Isn't that amazing?"

Rachel was very quiet and still. Then very quietly she whispered, "You said there were two things that happened? What was the other one?"

"Well, while that man was just standing there holding Jesus and praising God, a very old lady came up. She looked like she was over 100 years old. I've never seen anyone so old.

"Her face was radiantly beautiful, and she began to tell everyone around us that Jesus was the redemption of Israel. Some people told us that she was Anna, a prophetess. Everyone was crowding around wanting to see Jesus. I guess I felt a little afraid for him, but he seemed to be having a great time and was just looking around like royalty.

"Well, after we gave our sacrifice, we went back to the olive garden to rest a while before starting home. Joseph didn't want me walking in the heat. We ate an early dinner and rested until closer to sundown before we started home. And today is my first day of being free!"

"Mary, it seems like a lot of people think that Jesus is the Messiah."

"Yes, it does."

"I wonder why suddenly everyone is talking about the Messiah. We've waited forever. I wonder why now?"

"God keeps his promises, Rachel, no matter how long it takes."

The next few days were exciting ones for Mary, and she was determined to get to know her new community.

The first thing that changed was Mary getting to go to the water well instead of Joseph. It was a little awkward to figure out how to hold Jesus and still manage to carry the water jar on her head, but she soon figured it out.

She made friends with the ladies who all met at the well each morning. Her head was spinning with recipes and advice on raising Jesus and which vendors had the best prices at the market — all the things that women throughout the centuries have discussed together. She soon knew everyone's name and the names of their children. They all welcomed her to the community.

Many mornings, if Jesus was being cooperative, Mary would walk to the synagogue to pray. Rachel was usually sitting with her friends begging — but would come running when she heard Mary's footsteps. They would hug and let Rachel play with Jesus for a few minutes before Mary would take him into the synagogue with her. But as Mary began to pray day after day for her family back home and her new friends here, she prayed often for little Rachel.   She had become a really good friend, and Mary was praying that God would show her how to help Rachel.

One afternoon as Rachel visited and tried to play with baby Jesus, he was being fussy. Mary asked Rachel to sing a Psalm for him.   Rachel very naturally began to sing to baby Jesus these words:

It is good to praise the Lord
and make music to your name,
O Most High,
proclaiming your love in the morning and
your faithfulness at night,
to the music of the ten-stringed lyre and the
melody of the harp.
For you make me glad....[2]

Jesus calmed down immediately and fell asleep.   Suddenly, Mary had an idea.

"Rachel, I want to ask you to do something very special for me."

"I will try, Mary, you know I will. What can I do for you?"

"Rachel, tomorrow morning when you go to beg by the side of the road, will you sing this Psalm for me?"

"Oh, Mary, I can't sing for people. I would be so scared. Besides, I would disturb the people and they would tell me to go away."

"Rachel, will you sing for Jesus? You know he loves your songs. I will bring him and let you sing to him. That's my request. Will you do it?"

Rachel tossed and turned all night. She had never sung in front of other people. In fact, Mary and Jesus were probably the only ones who had heard her sing since her grandmother had died. Oh, she was scared. But she had promised, and a promise was a promise.

The next morning, sure enough, Mary and Jesus came to Rachel's spot. Mary knelt on the ground beside Rachel and held baby Jesus in her lap. She whispered to Rachel to just sing to Jesus and pretend there was no one else around.

Rachel took hold of baby Jesus' hand, and he clung tightly to his friend. She began very, very quietly. As she relaxed, Mary could tell that she was enjoying just lifting her voice in worship.

By the time she finished, a small crowd had gathered. They clapped appreciatively and asked for another song. With Mary's encouragement, Rachel began to sing one Psalm after another. Baby Jesus kept trying to put Rachel's fingers in his mouth, and that kept Rachel from paying attention to the crowd that was gathering. When Jesus began to get fussy and hungry, Mary had to leave. By then Rachel was enjoying singing, and the crowds were encouraging her to keep on. Mary thanked God for showing her how to help Rachel use her talent.

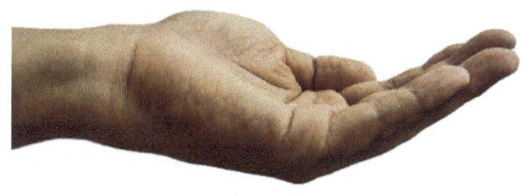 Rachel began staying longer and longer at her spot by the synagogue because she loved helping the people prepare their hearts for worship.

She became known as the little girl with the big voice. Rachel was able to help her parents with expenses. No longer did Rachel feel like she was begging. Now she considered herself a singer who was paid for her ministry to the people.

And often, she could contribute to her friend's buckets. That made her feel really good inside. Her two crippled friends had protected her when she was just a scared little girl, and now she could help them.

"Rachel, what are you doing up? You are usually asleep by now."

"Yes, Abba. I'm sorry to disturb you, but don't you hear it?"

"Rachel, you know that I can't hear the things you hear. Just tell me — hold it — there is something going on." He went to the door and looked out. Rachel was right behind him.

"What is it, Abba?"

"I'm not sure…."

"Abba, I can't see but my ears tell me that there are camels and lots and lots of people. They are going east toward the synagogue, but Abba, what do they look like?"

"Rachel, I'm not sure, but it looks to me like they are royalty from somewhere. They are not Roman or Israeli or Egyptian. I don't know where they are from, but their robes are beautiful and so colorful with lots of jewels."

"Abba, they have stopped! Why are they stopping?"

"I can't tell, Rachel."

"Abba let's go see! I think they have stopped at Mary and Joseph's house!"

"No, I think we should stay here and not get involved. We don't know who these people are or what they might do."

"Abba, I must know. I don't want to disobey you, but I think it has something to do with baby Jesus being the Messiah. Please, please go with me."

"All right, Rachel, but stay with me and don't go running off. Hold my hand tightly."

The road was completely blocked by the large, ornately dressed crowd. But Rachel and her dad were able to squeeze around the crowd and get close enough to tell that indeed, everyone was focused on Mary and Joseph's house. Rachel's Abba, Obadiah, later said it seemed to glow like a spotlight was shining on it.

Rachel's Abba saw that Joseph was in the front yard talking with a group of men who were dressed like kings. Rachel and her Abba couldn't hear what was being said but everything felt friendly and safe.

The men talked a few minutes and then Joseph went back into the house. Shortly he returned with Mary. She was carrying Jesus in her arms.

A bright star seemed to shine down on all that was happening. Rachel's Abba, Obadiah, watched as the men who looked like kings and all their attendants fell on their faces and worshiped Jesus. Abba fell to his knees to worship and Rachel joined him. He watched as Mary and Joseph held Jesus up high so that all could see him. Even the camels and horses knelt, and there was absolute silence.

Rachel wanted to ask what was happening but knew that her whisper would be heard. So, she waited. Mary would tell her in the morning.

Then the men talked with Joseph some more, gave him some packages, remounted their camels, and the entire group left as quietly as they had come.

Rachel and Abba walked slowly back to their home. Her Abba tried to explain to her what he had seen, but he couldn't explain what he felt inside his heart. Somehow, he <u>knew</u> that this was the Messiah and that these foreign kings were in some way pledging their allegiance to him.

He wasn't sure what it all meant, but he knew that God had plans for Jesus that were most unusual. He was grateful that Rachel went straight to bed without a fight. He sat up for a while and debated walking down to talk with Joseph, but finally decided he'd better try to get some sleep.

He had just managed to doze off when he heard a tap at the window.

"Obadiah. Wake up! Can you help me?" Obadiah recognized Joseph's voice and he quickly ran to the front door.

"Joseph! What's wrong? How can I help?"

"You have been a good friend and I need a friend tonight. An angel has told me that King Herod will try to kill Jesus and that I must be gone by morning."

"Gone! Where will you go?"

"I don't want to tell you because it would put your family in danger. God will protect us. But we must leave. Now!"

"How can I help you, my friend?"

"I have a long list, so listen carefully."

"I'm listening."

"Here is my rent money for this week. Please give it to my landlord with my apology. And please tell my boss that I had a family emergency and had to leave."

"Okay. No problem. What else?"

"Please tell Omar I can't take care of the goats and donkey and thank him for all he's done for us.

"And Obadiah, please tell Rachel how much we love her and thank her for being Mary's friend."

Suddenly a blur launched itself into Joseph's arms. "Oh, Joseph, I can't bear for you and Mary and Jesus to leave. I heard what you said, and you must hurry. And Joseph, you must take Pete. You will need to take your tools and baby supplies and food. It will be a long journey, and Jesus is getting too heavy to carry. Take Pete."

Joseph tried to protest, but Rachel insisted. Joseph tried to pay for the donkey, but Obadiah insisted that it would save them from having to buy food for him.

So, it was decided. Obadiah went to Omar's barn to get Pete and the sacks that they would need to pack a load on his back. Joseph and Rachel ran to the house to help Mary pack. Rachel held baby Jesus and told him over and over to not forget her.

Long before daylight, they had everything they owned packed on Pete and were headed south into the hill country after tearful goodbyes.

"Abba, if Jesus is the Messiah, we'll see him again, won't we?"

"Yes, Rachel, I'm sure we'll see him again."

"Abba, I <u>know</u> he's the Messiah. I just know it, deep down inside of me."

"Rachel, I'm proud of you for giving them Pete. Are you sure that's what you wanted to do?"

"Oh, yes, Abba! Jesus loves Pete as much as I do, and Joseph will take good care of him. And, Abba, it feels so good to be able to help. They have helped me so much."

"I love you, Rachel. Try to get some rest. It's almost morning."

"I love you, too, Abba.   I hope you can rest, too."

_____

[1] Luke 2:10-12
[2] Psalm 92:1-4

The Birth of Jesus
Luke 2:1-7

The Shepherds' Visit
Luke 2:8-20

Jesus was Named
Luke 2:21

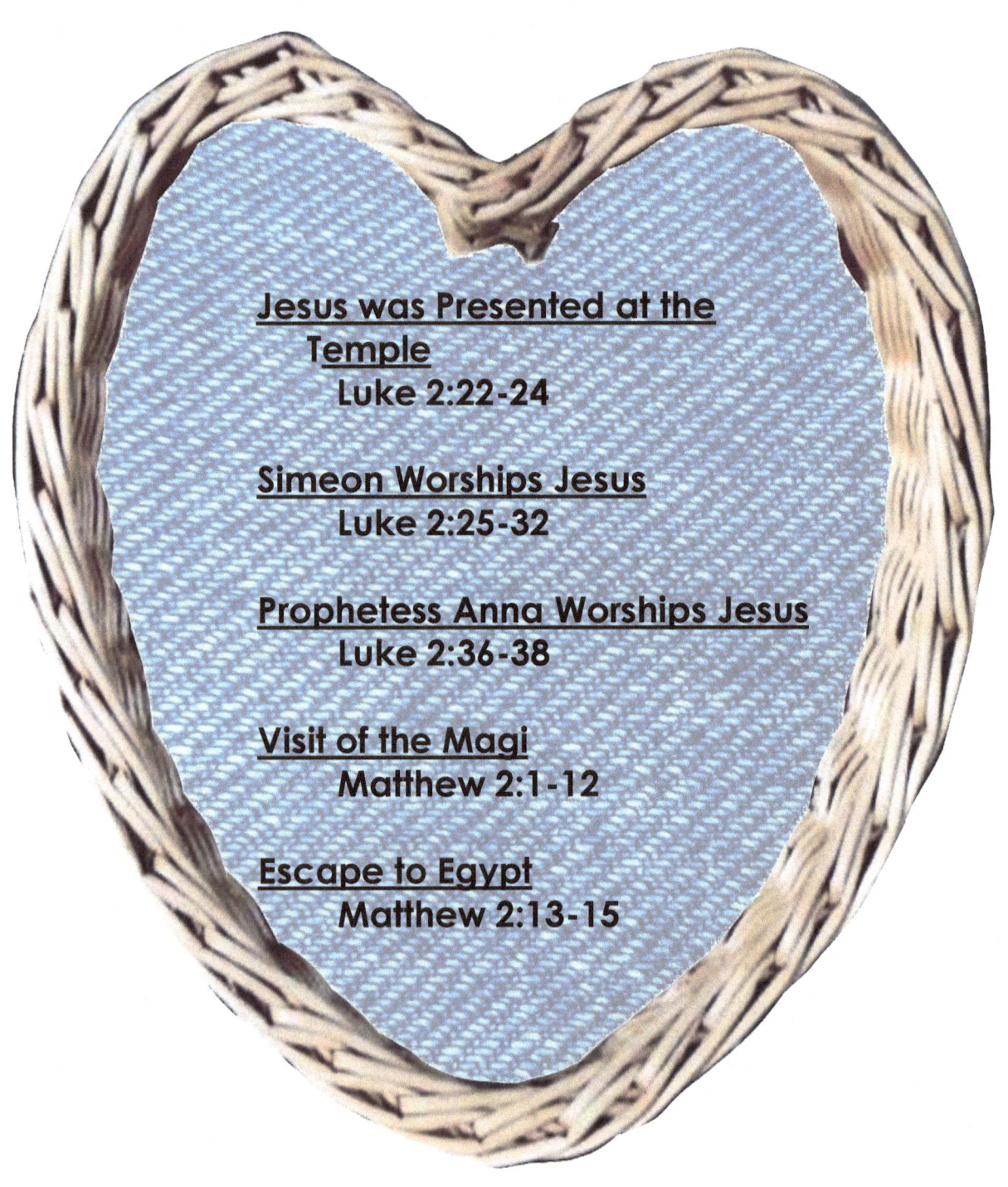

Jesus was Presented at the Temple
Luke 2:22-24

Simeon Worships Jesus
Luke 2:25-32

Prophetess Anna Worships Jesus
Luke 2:36-38

Visit of the Magi
Matthew 2:1-12

Escape to Egypt
Matthew 2:13-15

Chapter 3
THE STORY OF JOSIE

"Josie!"

"Coming, Mama."

"Josie, I need you to watch Rebecca and Ruth while I go to the well. I thought I had enough water, but I'm going to need another jug full. They should stay asleep. But if they wake up, you need to be here so they won't be afraid or get into mischief."

The twins were only three years old and were taking a late morning nap because they loved to wake everyone up at dawn!

"Okay, Mama. I'll stay right here until you get back."

"I know you will, Josie. Thank you."

Josie was only seven years old, but he knew that his mama depended on him — and that made him feel good inside. He knew that Jesus had gone fishing with his buddies, but he wondered where his other two brothers were. He looked out the window and, as usual, James was sitting in the garden daydreaming. He was two years older than Josie but spent most of his time thinking and planning instead of working. Jude was busy picking cucumbers.

The whole family was working today to get everything ready for their big trip. Each year they went to visit their Abba's brother in Jerusalem for Passover.

Josie knew that many of their neighbors and relatives from Nazareth would also be traveling, and they would see them along the way. It would be like a camping trip with lots and lots of friends.

Jewish men were required to attend three holy days in Jerusalem each year. Josie's Abba went alone for the other two festivals, but for Passover, Abba's entire family got together at Uncle Obed's and Aunt Rachel's home.

Josie was so excited — not only for the journey, but for the three days of playing with his cousins. He was trying to count how many cousins would be all together, when his mama returned.

"Josie, thank you for watching the girls. Now go down to the barn and see if you can find the sacks that we use to pack supplies on Pete. Bring them to me. We need to make sure they don't have holes in them if we are going to pack all this food I'm cooking."

Josie raced off toward the barn. He loved to help, and he thought he knew just where to find the sacks that Mama needed. Sure enough, the sacks were stacked right where he expected, but when he picked up the ropes, he found that mice had chewed them to pieces. He carried the sacks and the pieces of rope back to the house to show Mama.

"Josie, you know the way to Uncle Zeke's, don't you?"

"Of course, Mama."

He knew the way, but it was a long walk. They lived on the opposite end of Nazareth — but there was no way to get lost since there was just one long street.

"Do you think you and Jude could take Hulda and Hilda over there? They will need to be milked twice a day and I don't want Uncle Zeke to do that much walking." Josie assured her that he and Jude could handle the goats just fine.

"Jude, go with your brother and listen to Josie. You boys stay on the road. The goats will follow you as long as you stay on the road. On your way back, stop at Abba's shop and ask him to bring home some fresh rope for Pete's bundles. Can you remember all that? Stay on the road, ask Abba to bring rope, and come straight home. We've got lots to do before sundown."

"Yes, Mama," they said together.

Josie and Jude headed to the barn. Jude was only five years old but could handle the goats almost as well as Josie. "Let's take a small bag of grain, just in case we need to bribe them," said Jude.

"Good idea."

Josie opened the pen and the goats seemed happy to see the boys. They followed them without any problems. The boys talked to them and scratched their ears, and all went well — until it didn't.

They were about halfway to Uncle Zeke's when suddenly the boys saw a group of Roman soldiers riding on horses coming down the road. They were coming fast, and Josie and Jude just barely had time to jump out of the way. They were safe, but the goats discovered the pasture and began to graze.

Josie offered them a handful of the grain they had brought, but the goats just ignored the boys. They much preferred the tender green plants and they just kept right on munching. Josie and Jude pushed and pulled and begged and pleaded, but nothing that they tried could get the goats to budge.

Finally, Josie and Jude sat down on the side of the road. Jude began to cry, and Josie was about to decide that they should go tell their Abba.

About that time, a neighbor walked by and asked the boys what was wrong and if he could help. Josie pointed to the goats and told him their story. The kind neighbor chuckled, "Jude, stop your crying and come see what I've got." He led the way to his back yard and into his garden. There he picked two large cucumbers. "Do you know what goats love better than grass?"

Both boys were smiling now because they knew how hard it was to keep the goats out of the garden. The boys thanked their neighbor, then ran quickly into the field to bribe the goats. Sure enough, once Hilda and Hulda realized that the boys had cucumbers, they tried to get a second bite. But Josie and Jude ran fast, and the goats chased them all the way to Uncle Zeke's. After the goats were safely in the pen, they gave them the last of the cucumbers. That's a trick they would have to remember!

Now they needed to stop by Abba's shop to ask him for rope, then their job would be done. They wondered if there would be any time to play today since there was so much work to be done.

Abba said that he would bring the rope with him and reminded them to go straight home as Mama would need lots of help.

When they got home, Jesus was busy packing skins filled with olives and olive oil. Everyone enjoyed eating bread dipped into the olives and oil for their breakfast. It was perfect for an on-the-go breakfast while they were traveling.

James was busy packing vegetables into the sacks. Rounds of bread were cooling on every surface and Josie thought it looked like a feast day. Mama quickly put the younger boys to work packing almonds and raisins. She was packing a skin with pickled fish for dinner on the road.

The little girls were playing contentedly in the middle of the chaos, and Josie noticed Mama was giving them raisins to keep them happy.

The walk to Jerusalem would take six or seven days depending on the weather and everyone's health. Then they would stay with Uncle Obed and Aunt Rachel for three days to celebrate the Passover. Because it was mostly downhill on the way home, it would only take about five days to return.

It was a great sacrifice for the Jewish families to close their businesses and leave their farms and gardens for so long, but that's what they did each year because that's what the Jewish Law required.

About an hour before sunset on Friday, Mama began to wrap the bread with cloths. She and James began to set all the supplies into piles so that they could use the table for the Sabbath meal. Jesus started the fire in the backyard and began to fry the fish he and his friends had caught that morning.

When Abba arrived home, he praised each boy for their help with preparations. He brought a supply of rope for the sacks, and he brought a sturdy walking stick that he had carved for Mama. He kissed her tenderly and she assured him it would help tremendously for the hike. They had a lively meal, but soon everyone was yawning after such a hard day's work.

As a family, on Saturday morning, they went to the synagogue for worship. Abba worshiped with the men, but Jesus helped Mama with the twins and his younger brothers. He admitted to Mama that it was hard to worship with a wiggly three-year-old in his lap.

The afternoon passed slowly as everyone was thinking about the upcoming trip. The boys played quietly in the backyard and entertained their sisters.

Just before sundown, Abba called the family together. He gave each boy a chore to complete. He told them they would only have a few minutes of dusk after the Sabbath ended.

He encouraged them to work quickly just as soon as the sun went down, but before it became too dark to work.

When everyone had finished their chore, they would eat a late supper and go to bed soon, because they would need to be up very early for the trip.

Jesus was assigned to pick all the apricots that were ripe because he was the tallest. James and Jude were to pick any vegetables that were ready in the garden. And Josie was assigned to help Mama set out the bread and cheese for their late supper.

When they all had finished their tasks and Joseph had lit the candles, they enjoyed their last supper at home for a while. Abba assigned each boy a chore for the morning and then everyone headed to bed.

It was still dark when Mama called the boys to get up. They discovered that Pete was already packed with all the food and bedding, and Abba had strapped some baskets on Pete's back for the girls to ride in. The boys added their blankets to Pete's sacks and joined the family for a quick breakfast. Mama worked on getting the twins dressed and fed while Abba made sure Pete's load was secure. When they shut the door to their little house, Abba led them in prayer that God would protect them on their journey.

The road was pretty deserted when they first started out, but soon Josie began to recognize several other families from Nazareth. Some families walked faster and some slower, but they were all headed to Jerusalem for the same reason. They had a long way to walk each day, but it felt relaxed. They were busy walking, but it was different because there was time to talk and sing and play games.

Sometimes Josie walked with his friends from school, sometimes with one of his brothers, and sometimes with one or both of his parents. He spent some of his time walking with his cousins, and some time entertaining his sisters.

James and Josie gave the twins piggy-back rides to help them keep up when they were tired of riding in the baskets. And Jesus often let Jude ride on his shoulders when he got tired of walking. Josie felt so happy inside because usually everyone was so busy. But this trip seemed like one of the most special times of his life — and they weren't even to Jerusalem yet!

At sunset, they would set up camp where they could find water nearby and join whatever group was already there. Just about everyone along the way was traveling to Jerusalem for Passover even though they were from many different villages all over Galilee.

They made a lot of new friends, and there were always other kids around to play with. After dinner each night, the group would sit and talk and sometimes sing songs before falling asleep under the stars.

On Thursday night, the group they camped with was feeling confident that they would reach Jerusalem before the Sabbath began at sundown on Friday. But Friday ended up being a harder day than Abba expected.

The girls were getting tired of riding in the baskets. Abba put Jude on Pete and he and Mama carried the girls most of the way. The road was becoming much steeper and Pete seemed to go slower than ever. He couldn't be persuaded to walk faster even though his burden was getting lighter every day after each meal.

Gone was the leisurely walking and sweet fellowship. Josie felt like he was being shoved along by the crowd and occasionally, Abba would have to grab him to keep him from being pushed out of sight. Everyone felt pressed by the crowds. They stopped often to rest, and were surrounded by vendors selling water, wine, fruits, and vegetables to the weary crowds.

By early afternoon, Abba spotted a good camping site and declared that it was time to stop for the night. Josie was relieved to be off the road, but also sad that they would not get to spend the Sabbath with their family in Jerusalem.

The boys helped Abba unpack Pete and they all began to relax. The girls were able to run around and stretch their legs without fear of being crushed and Jesus discovered a small stream not far away.

Jesus and James got permission to go fishing and Josie and the younger kids started collecting firewood. Everyone agreed it was the best tasting fish they had ever eaten.

While they were eating, other families began setting up camps around them and soon a large group had formed to celebrate the Sabbath together. All day on Saturday, the children played quietly, and the grownups visited and rested.

As expected, Sunday morning found the roads completely clogged with people. It was almost sundown before Josie and his family arrived at Uncle Obed's home in Jerusalem. Abba's younger brother and sister and their families had arrived a few hours earlier. There was noisy chaos as everyone was laughing and hugging and getting reacquainted. They were so glad to have the trip behind them and to be able to stay in one place for a few days.

Passover that year began on Monday night at sundown. The entire family prepared all day on Monday for the Seder feast that night. The men and older boys were going to a nearby farm to pick out some lambs for the feast.

Abba had already told Jesus and James that they would go with him, but he gave Josie his choice. He told him that they would pick out a lamb and then kill it. Josie decided he wasn't quite ready to see that and his Abba assured him that that was okay.

He stayed and played with his other cousins and helped keep Jude and the girls entertained. The women were all busy cooking and preparing for the special meal that would happen soon after sundown.

That night, Uncle Obed led the Passover Seder meal, just like it was happening in all the other Jewish homes. Because Jude was the youngest attending the Seder, he got to ask the beginning question, "Why is tonight different from all other nights?" Then Uncle Obed told the story about the first Passover that happened over 1500 years earlier.

"Israel was held in slavery by the Egyptians. God sent Moses to tell the Pharaoh, Egypt's king, to let the people go free. When Pharaoh said, 'No way,' God sent nine bad punishments on the Egyptians. But Pharaoh still said, 'No way!' So, God told Moses to tell the Israelites to kill a lamb and put the blood of the lamb on their doorway. God protected the Israelites because they obeyed him but punished all the Egyptians very severely. The Egyptians decided it was time to let the people go. And that's when Israel moved out of Egypt and became a great nation. So, every year Jews celebrate the Passover to remember when God's punishment passed over them because of the blood of the lamb on their door."

It was a very special night and more special because Josie's family could be all together.

The next morning the men were going to the temple to offer a sacrifice. Jesus wanted to go but was reminded that he wasn't allowed in the men's area of the temple until he turned 13. He would have to wait one more year. So, he watched as his Abba and uncles and older cousins went to the temple.

Jesus asked his mother if she would take him to the temple. She said that she planned to go that afternoon with the women, but she would need him to watch the girls. Josie could tell he was disappointed.

Josie wondered how different next year would be when Jesus would be 13 and could make his own decisions. He wondered if Jesus would camp with the family or even come for the Passover. It would be his choice because he would legally be a man. Josie didn't want to be all grown up — at least not yet — and he wasn't sure how he felt about Jesus being grown up either.

It was good to be with his cousins, but secretly Josie was looking forward to the journey back home. The trip here had been very special with everyone together and so relaxed. He was getting tired of all the noise and chaos of having 20 cousins and eight adults cooped up in one house.

The three families from Nazareth had decided to stay one extra day to try to avoid the crowds. Even though Passover lasted for a whole week, many would only stay for the Seder meal and leave on Tuesday or Wednesday.

So early Thursday morning, Pete and the other donkeys were packed. The three families thanked their hosts and with lots of tearful goodbyes began the slow journey out of Jerusalem and back on the road to Nazareth. Leaving Jerusalem was crowded, but not nearly as bad as the uphill journey coming in had been.

It was a pleasant day, and everyone seemed to be happy to be back on the road. Since it was downhill, Pete was more cooperative, and the families spread out. They had agreed to camp together the first night and had already chosen a particular spot in a pleasant valley, so there was no need to make sure they stayed together.

The older boys asked if they could run ahead. Once again, it felt like vacation. Josie was pleased that James seemed to spend more time with him than usual. He was glad Jesus was having fun with his older cousins, but he missed him. Josie and James tried to make the trip easier for Jude whose short legs tired out quickly even going downhill. And the twins seemed content to ride in their baskets if someone would stay close and talk with them.

 One by one the families arrived at the planned campsite for the night and began to prepare dinner. It had been a much easier journey down the mountain, and everyone wanted to talk about the things they had seen and heard while in Jerusalem.

But Mama and Abba were becoming concerned that Jesus had not joined them, and dinner was almost ready. Josie could see the worry on Mama's face. His Abba was beginning to ask around if anyone had seen Jesus. When every family replied "no", the grownups began to gather and try to determine where they had last seen him. No one could remember seeing Jesus since the night before in the backyard at Uncle Obed's house.

After several minutes of intense discussion, it was decided that Abba and Mama would return to Jerusalem together and that the children would go home with their cousins. The group would deliberately travel slowly so that maybe Jesus and his parents would join them by tomorrow night. But if not, of course, Josie's aunts and uncles would care for them.

Josie's uncle gave them a lantern and a skin of oil. Abba and Mama quickly threw together two small packs for bedding and food, kissed the children goodbye, and started back up the mountain they had just climbed down. It would normally be too dangerous to travel at night, but the roadside was so filled with campers that it seemed safe.

Josie lay awake for a long time looking at the stars. Nothing bad like this had ever happened to his family. He couldn't cry earlier, but now that Jude and the girls were asleep, he couldn't stop his sobs. James moved over closer to him and held his hand. Josie was pretty sure that James was crying, too, but they must take care of their family now. What if Mama and Abba never came back?

But the next thing Josie knew, the sun was peeking over the mountain, and it was time to get breakfast and back on the road. The uncles helped James and Josie get Pete's sacks strapped on securely. Then they continued their journey down the mountain, every step taking them farther from Jerusalem. Josie felt that his heart was being torn in two.

He wanted to go back to be with Mama and Abba and Jesus, but he knew he had to be obedient. Occasionally a tear escaped as he worried about his parents and brother. James and Josie took turns leading Pete and let Jude ride him as much as he wanted.

The aunts took care of the girls. And since they had decided to delay as much as possible, it was an easy day and would have been fun except for the situation.

They stopped early that night to prepare for the Sabbath. The grownups were trying to keep the brothers from worrying, but everyone was concerned about a 12-year-old boy alone in Jerusalem. Outwardly they kept assuring the boys and themselves that the absent trio would probably join them sometime tomorrow.

It was harder to go to sleep on Saturday night because no one was tired after the Sabbath. They had rested all day and played quiet games with the cousins. They had even waded in a stream and caught some tadpoles.

Rebecca and Ruth were too young to be worried and were delighted with all the attention of their cousins. Josie was glad that they weren't crying for their mama — because he knew that if they started crying, he might just join in!

Sunday morning was a mixed blessing — it was good to be on the road again instead of sitting still, but it also meant another day further from Jerusalem. It was a long day. And one long day turned into another. Now there were very few people on the roads, and they could make good time.

Josie overheard the grownups discussing who would keep them when they reached Nazareth. It was decided that the three boys would go to their uncle's house, while the two girls would go with their aunt. Josie felt like his world was falling apart.

On Wednesday night they made camp for the last time. Everyone was tired and Josie was in no mood to play. He ate his supper quietly and intended to just crawl into his blanket and cry — when shouts began to ring out. Jesus came running into the camp and scooped up his three little brothers all in one big hug. Mama and Abba followed. Everyone made room and found food and water for them. Questions would have to wait for the travelers to catch their breaths.

Abba motioned for Jesus to join him and they stood before the curious group. Abba said, "Jesus stopped to help a group of people and he lost track of time. We are proud of him and hope you will accept his apology." Jesus then looked around at each person in the group and offered his apology for worrying them.

Josie knew that there were things that he didn't understand. He knew he was proud of his big brother, but he always wondered what really happened.

Do you think that maybe 30 years later he read what Mr. Luke wrote about that event and said, "Oh, now I understand!"

Mr. Luke wrote in his manuscript:

> **After three days they found him in the temple courts, sitting among the teachers, listening to them and asking them questions. Everyone who heard him was amazed at his understanding and his answers.**[1]

[1] **Luke 2:46-47**

The Passover
   Exodus 12:1-11

Names of Jesus' Siblings
   Matthew 13:55-56

Jesus' Visit to the Temple
   Luke 2:41-52

Chapter 4
THE STORY OF NOAH

Noah was going to his Abba's store to sweep the floor and help with restocking the shelves. When Hebrew school was out for a break next week, he could spend all day with his Abba. On school days, he could only work for a couple of hours and then help him lock up. When he arrived, things were strangely quiet. There was not a single customer inside, and his Abba was just sitting behind some bins looking unhappy. "Abba, where are your customers?"

"I don't know Noah, I don't know. For two days now, I have had only one customer. That is not good."

"No, that's not good, Abba. I heard today at school that there is a new teacher in town and the rabbi (a Jewish teacher) said he was teaching bad things. Do you think all the people are listening to him and don't have time to shop?"

"Hmm, I have not heard that. Noah, watch the store for me, I am going to ask Rabbi Joshua what is going on."

"I think I can handle these crowds!" Noah said sarcastically as he continued sweeping.

When Abba returned, he reported to Noah that there was indeed a new teacher in town who was claiming to be a prophet and had a message from God. The Rabbi felt that once the people realized he was a fake, life would return to normal and there was nothing to worry about.

"That's good to know," agreed Noah.

But each day the store remained empty except for one day when Mrs. Mahala, an old lady, came in and said she needed candles and then decided she didn't, and left.

On Friday night Noah and his Abba locked up the store and walked slowly home. Abba reported a total of one paying customer the entire week. But Mother had the Sabbath meal ready when they arrived home, so they washed up and agreed not to fret about it.

After the little ones were tucked in bed, Noah was whittling on a toy boat for his little brother when he overheard his parents discussing the new teacher.

Mother reported hearing interesting things at the well from some who had gone to listen to the new teacher. Most of them believed he really was a prophet. They said his name was the prophet John and he was telling people that they needed to be baptized.

"Baptized!" Abba exploded. "But that's ridiculous. This must be some new religion. You be careful what you listen to at the well!"

"You know I'm careful who I listen to! But Joab, you need to know that just about every family in the village has gone to listen and the only one who says anything bad about him is Rabbi Joshua. What if he really is a prophet from God?"

Abba spent the Sabbath fretting about his lack of customers and wondering what he should do. He knew his wife was not a gossip, and she knew which women to listen to and which ones to ignore. She was a wise woman. Maybe he should check this out.

As the family ate dinner together on Saturday night, Abba surprised everyone.

"Noah," he said, "since you are out of school this week, I want you to open the store by yourself tomorrow morning." Noah was only 11, but he had been helping in the store since he was seven and knew where everything was. And since the store was obviously not going to be crowded, he assured Abba that he could handle it.

Abba then stated that he was going to go and check out this teacher and see why everyone was listening to him. He wanted to determine for himself whether he was a fake or a prophet.

Noah hardly slept Saturday night. He was so excited to be allowed to run the store all by himself. That was a big responsibility. *What will I do if the store becomes crowded and I can't handle all the orders?* Then he would assure himself that wasn't going to happen and would turn over and try to get some more sleep.

On Sunday morning, he ate a quick breakfast and darted out the door with a quick goodbye to his mother. She said that she and the little ones would bring him a snack later just to make sure he was doing okay. "I'll be fine, Mother. Don't worry!" Noah said. But secretly he was relieved that she would be checking on him — just in case.

As he put the key in the door, Noah felt so proud of opening the shop. He carefully put the key away and began sweeping the front entrance. Opening the shop would have been a lot more fun if there was someone to see it! But there was not a single person on the street. The town was totally empty.

Noah usually was busy putting out new merchandise, but since no one was buying anything, there was no room for new things. He rearranged some shelves to make them more attractive, but really and truly — there was nothing to do.

He dusted all the shelves twice. He walked round and round and played hopscotch with himself. He counted to 1000 and recited all his Hebrew letters. He carved two more boats for his little brothers and was just about to try to stand on his head, when his mother and three little brothers arrived.

Mother sat and talked with him for a little while, but she needed to get the little ones down for a nap, so soon it was back to silence and four walls.

But Mother had brought a sack filled with grapes. Perfect! He decided that for every Hebrew Scripture he could remember from school, he would reward himself with a grape.

When he couldn't remember any more Scriptures, he started singing songs. <u>Finally</u>, the sun began to set, and Noah made sure everything was put away properly. The CLOSED sign was hung, the door was locked, and then he ran as fast as his legs would carry him all the way home. He was so glad to be home. He hugged his mother and then played with his brothers while she finished dinner. He was so glad to not be stuck in a perfectly quiet store.

They had already started feeding the little ones when Abba arrived. He was strangely quiet and refused to answer any questions until the little ones were in bed.

"Noah, come to the living room and talk with your mother and me."

"Yes, Abba."

"How did it go at the store today?"

"There were no customers again. It was boring, but I thank you for trusting me to be in charge."

"You are a good boy. Did you lock the door and put up the CLOSED sign?"

"Yes, Abba." Noah felt sad that his Abba would ask. He knew the routine.

"Good. Because I want you and Mother to go with me tomorrow to hear the prophet John. I believe that he is sent from God and I want you both to hear him, too."

"But Joab, what about the little ones? I can't keep them quiet to listen to a teacher," his mother said.

"No, no. It's not like that. Whole families are going to listen to him and there are kids everywhere. No one is telling the children to be quiet. It's not like the synagogue. It's, it's — well, you'll just have to see for yourself. I would like both of you to join me tomorrow to listen."

"But Abba, what about the store?" Noah asked.

Abba laughed, "Did you make any money today?" When Noah shook his head, Abba said, "Tomorrow we will learn things that are more important than any money we could make."

Noah felt confused. All he'd ever heard his Abba talk about was making money so that they could buy nice things. He wondered what this prophet was teaching.

Early the next morning, Mother prepared a nice breakfast and packed some snacks for the day. They ate quickly and started out. Noah carried his baby brother. His parents had their hands full with the toddlers.

Soon they were surrounded by others headed to the Jordan River where the prophet was teaching. Families were spread out all over the riverbank. Noah couldn't remember ever seeing this many people in his life. He recognized a lot of the townspeople, but most of them were strangers from further away. He waved at school friends.

A strange-looking man appeared near the river and began talking to the crowd. His voice was loud enough for all to hear — even though the children were playing all around. He wore animal skins for clothes and his hair was uncombed. But Noah soon forgot about his looks. He was listening to what he was saying.

Noah understood some of what he heard that day, but he also had a lot of questions that he wanted to ask Abba on the way home. One thing he understood was that this prophet was saying that he had been sent by God to prepare the way for the Messiah. Now that was big news! Noah knew that it had been 400 years since God had spoken to his people, the Jews, through the prophet Micah. Noah wondered if it was even possible for God to still speak to people.

While Noah thought about those kinds of questions, he also heard the prophet John saying that being God's special chosen people wasn't just about being a Jew, but about how you treated other people. He talked about being kind and sharing and taking care of each other and not bullying. Noah had never heard anyone speak like this.

Noah heard John the prophet say:

> ..."Anyone who has two shirts should share with the one who has none, and anyone who has food should do the same.[1]"

Noah had been taught to look out for himself and to always grab the best before anyone else beat him to it. His dad had told him that he was better than everyone else and he deserved the best in life. Even Rabbi Joshua taught his students to put down people who were different from themselves. That's just the way it was. Food was scarce and everyone looked out for themselves.

Something inside Noah's heart felt excited and afraid all at the same time. *Wouldn't it be great if everyone started being good to each other? The world would be a much better place. But that would be impossible!*

On the way home, his dad announced that he wanted to come back tomorrow and asked Mother and Noah if they wanted to come, too. They both agreed that they would like to hear more.

So, Monday morning, the store remained closed again. Noah and his parents and little brothers all went back to the Jordan River to listen to the prophet John. The crowds seemed to have doubled. They couldn't find a place very close, but the prophet's voice was strong enough that they could hear clearly.

About an hour later, a group of Jewish religious leaders arrived. They solemnly made their way through the crowds right up to the front.

You could tell that they were important people because they were dressed in expensive robes with long tassels and their faces were very serious and sad.

Noah's heart stopped. He could tell that angry words were being spoken. *Why would the Jewish leaders be unhappy with the prophet sent by God?*

The people were getting restless because they couldn't hear what was happening, when suddenly the prophet's voice rang out loud and clear.

> ... **"You brood of vipers! Who warned you to flee from the coming wrath? Produce fruit in keeping with repentance.[2]"**

"Abba, what does that mean?"

"Noah, just listen and I'll explain it on the way home. Stay here and help your mother, I've got some business to take care of."

And with that, Abba whispered something to Mother and started toward the front of the crowd. Noah watched wide-eyed wondering what was going to happen. There seemed to be a long line of men waiting to talk with the prophet.

After each man would talk with him, the prophet would take them out into the Jordan River and dunk them under the water. Noah realized that was what the prophet called *baptizing*.

Noah kept watching until his own dad reached the front of the line. He, too, talked with the prophet, and then they went out into the water together and the prophet baptized his Abba.

Now Noah's head was exploding with questions. *What does it all mean? What is going on?*

Noah watched as his Abba came dripping back to his family. He was wearing a huge smile and gave Mother a long hug. They decided it was time to leave since it was getting late in the day and the boys were getting hungry.

But of course, the toddlers took up all of Abba's attention on the way home. Abba announced at dinner that he wanted to hear the prophet's teaching one more day, then they had to open the store. Mother decided she would stay home with the younger boys and catch up on housework and cooking.

Noah and his Abba agreed to leave earlier than usual on Tuesday morning so they would be able to beat the crowds and see and hear the prophet better.

Noah lay awake for quite a while trying to figure out what all had happened. He knew it was big — but his eyes just wouldn't stay awake to figure out the answers. Before the sun was up, Abba was shaking him. They ate quickly and then began to walk toward the Jordan River as the first hints of sunrise began.

"Noah, I know you have many questions. I want you to know that I don't have all the answers, but I'll do my best to tell you what I know. Why don't you ask the questions and I'll see if I can answer them for you, or maybe we can figure them out together."

Noah was surprised to hear his Abba speak so humbly. His Abba had always had all the answers and didn't need help with anything. Noah was so surprised he forgot what he wanted to ask. Finally, he simply asked, "What was the baptism about?"

Abba smiled and nodded approvingly at his question. "That's a good question, but I'm not really sure of the answer." He thought a few minutes and then said, "I think it would be easier to explain if we backed up a little bit. Do you know what repentance means?"

"I think it means being sorry for your mistakes and mess-ups."

Abba nodded again but said, "That's what most people think, but really repentance means turning around and going the other way. It's like you are headed to the Jordan and you decide to turn around and go home instead.

"I was headed in a direction that didn't make God happy. I decided to repent or turn around and head in a direction that does make God happy."

Noah's eyes got big. "How do you know what makes God happy?"

"Well, Son, the prophet has been teaching that it makes God happy when we follow his Laws and love other people instead of just thinking about what we need and what we want."

"So, you repented and told the prophet you were going to change?"

"Yes. But I did it in front of a lot of people. I was baptized to make a promise to change. Does that make sense?"

"I think so. But how will you change?"

Noah's Abba laughed deeply. "I have no idea! All I know is that I want to be more like God wants me to be. He'll have to teach me. Maybe we can teach each other. You are studying the Hebrew Law at school, maybe you can teach me what I need to do."

"Abba, I remembered my other question."

"What is it, Son?"

"Why did the prophet call the Jewish leaders a brood of vipers? That's not very nice."

"No, it wasn't very nice. But now that you are growing up, I guess it's time for me to be honest with you about why I don't go to synagogue very often and I haven't been to the temple in Jerusalem in years."

"You said you were too busy at the store."

"Yes, but there is something more. You see, I agree with the prophet. I don't like that the Jewish leaders tell us to keep the Laws, but they don't keep them themselves. Now, I don't want to be critical, because I'm not doing a very good job, either — but sometimes it seems that they are just cruel and mean to the poor, or the widows, or the crippled people. I don't think that's right.

"And I think the prophet John said it exactly right. If they want to be leaders of our people, then they should be good examples — not bad ones. I believe he was asking them to repent, too."

"And that's what made them mad?" asked Noah.

"I think so. You see, sometimes if I catch you doing something wrong — you quickly say you are sorry. But sometimes, when I catch you doing something wrong, you just try to hide it or blame it on your brothers — and I know that you aren't going to quit or change. You don't want to repent."

"I think I understand. Thanks, Abba, for talking with me. I'll try to listen better today. We've got a great place to be able to see and hear everything and it's getting really crowded. I think the prophet will begin teaching soon."

"Look over there, there's even more of the Jewish leaders over to the right. I hope they aren't going to try to stop the prophet from teaching."

Soon the prophet John began teaching. He again said that he was preparing the way for the Messiah and that people needed to repent and get their lives right with God. Again that afternoon, a line of men formed who wanted to be baptized. Even though Noah and his dad couldn't hear what was being said privately, Noah understood now that each man was telling the prophet that he wanted to repent and be baptized to show that he was serious about changing his life.

But then Noah noticed something strange. A man approached and talked with the prophet and the prophet fell on his knees and it looked like he was worshiping the man.   There was a loud murmur coming from the Jewish leaders and everyone was watching to see what would happen next. The man helped the prophet to his feet and together they went into the Jordan River.

Noah didn't know what to think, but he knew that his heart was doing flips. The man's face was so kind and gentle — almost holy. Noah couldn't find words to describe it. But as he watched, the prophet baptized the man.

> **As soon as Jesus was baptized, he went up out of the water. At that moment heaven was opened, and he saw the Spirit of God descending like a dove and alighting on him. And a voice from heaven said, "This is my Son, whom I love; with him I am well pleased."[3]**

The crowd was perfectly silent. Even the Jewish leaders were silent.

John dismissed the crowd, and everyone headed home. Everyone was asking, "Did you hear that?" and, "Was that God's voice?" or "Is this man the Messiah?"

"Abba, I want to come back tomorrow!"

"I know, Son. I was planning to open the store tomorrow, but I think I want to be back tomorrow, too. I just don't want to miss seeing the Messiah. Maybe he will speak tomorrow."

"Who knows what will happen tomorrow!" exclaimed Noah.

They excitedly told Mother what she had missed as they sat down to a wonderful meal. They agreed that they would go back together to the Jordan again tomorrow, and they would wait to open the store on Thursday.

On Wednesday morning they were so far away it was hard to hear or see what was going on. Some estimated that there were four or five thousand people along the riverbank.

It was near the middle of the morning when the crowd was rewarded by the arrival of Jesus. Everyone had been looking for him. When he appeared, it seemed that everyone's head turned to him instead of to the prophet John.

The prophet announced loudly:

> ... **"Look, the Lamb of God, who takes away the sin of the world! .... I have seen and I testify that this is God's Chosen One.[4]"**

Noah's Abba motioned to Mother and Noah that it was time to head home. The crowd was going crazy shouting that the Messiah had come, and he was afraid the little ones would be trampled.

"What will happen now, Abba?"

"I don't know, Noah. We'll just have to wait and see. I must admit that I don't know enough of the Jewish prophecy to know what comes next. I have looked for the Messiah all my life, but I have no idea what it all means."

Noah took his brothers into the back yard to let them play for a while.

"Noah, I'm going to go to the store and check on things and make sure all is ready for opening tomorrow. Come with me. Mother will watch the boys."

"Coming, Abba." Noah raced to catch up with his Abba who was already ahead of him. Abba seemed to have something on his mind and Noah had to hurry to keep up with him.

The store was the same as when Noah left it on Sunday except for the accumulated dust. They got busy dusting and were preparing to lock up when his Abba stopped.

"Noah, go get two packages of those candles that Mrs. Mahala was looking at the other day."

"But Abba, she changed her mind and said she didn't want them."

"Noah, be obedient."

"Yes, Abba, I'm sorry."

Abba went to the back of the store and picked up a large skin of lamp oil. It was the expensive kind that didn't give off as much smoke as the regular oil. Now Noah was really curious.

Abba locked the door, but instead of starting home, they headed into a poorer section of town. Abba knocked on the door of a small house and Mrs. Mahala answered. She was very surprised to see them. Abba asked her where he could put the lamp oil for her so it would be easy for her to reach.

When Abba explained that the oil and candles were free, Mrs. Mahala was shocked. Abba explained that he just wanted to reward a faithful customer. He apologized for not giving her the candles when she came in earlier last week.

Mrs. Mahala was crying now. She said, "I have known you since you were a little boy and I've never known you to give anything away for free. You have always been a good businessman."

Abba replied, "I may have been a good businessman, but I wasn't a good man. I want to do what God's Law says, and it says that we should take care of the poor and the widows. I have not done my part to take care of you since your husband died last year. You both were my faithful customers, and today I am simply saying thank you.

"Come Noah, Mother will wonder why we are late for dinner."

_____

[1] **Luke 3:11**
[2] **Matthew 3:7-8**
[3] **Matthew 3:16-17**
[4] **John 1:29, 34**

John the Prophet Preaches
Luke 3:2-16

Jesus' Baptism
Mark 1:9-11

John Announces the Messiah
John 1:29-34

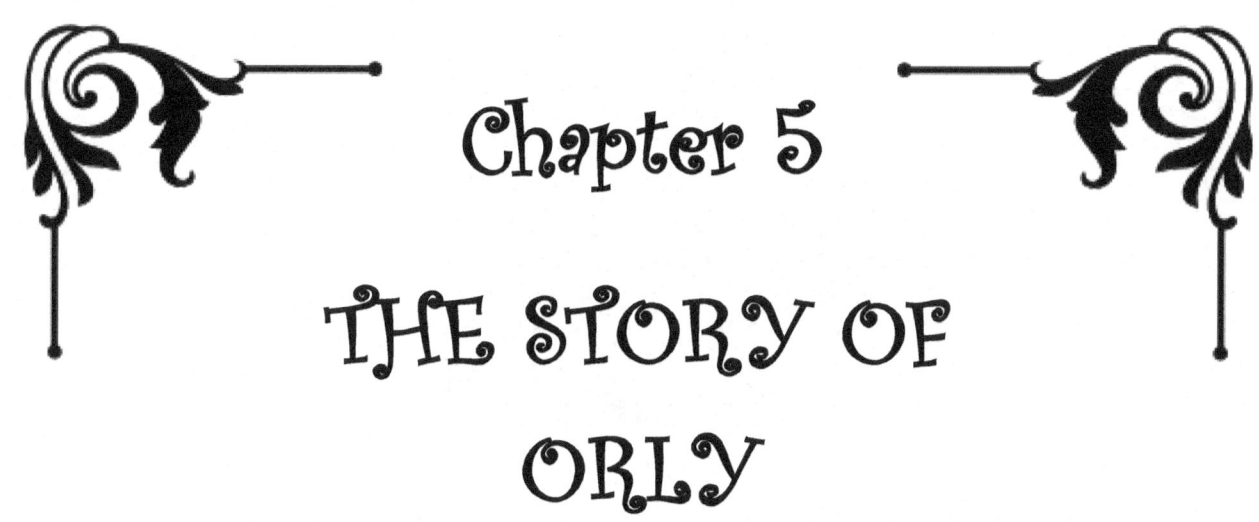

Chapter 5
THE STORY OF ORLY

Orly still couldn't believe what his eyes had seen that day. He lay in the dark on his blanket and just couldn't quit thinking about it. Finally, he slipped out of the room and went outside to the front courtyard to look at it again. There was a full moon, and he could easily walk around without needing a lamp. He didn't want to wake anyone else up. He needed time to think.

His mind started all over at the beginning. For the past several weeks he and all the other servants had been really busy getting ready for the wedding of Master Kenan's son. Orly's mother was in charge of the kitchen and she had been working night and day to prepare for the big day and that meant that he had not had a break in weeks. Work, work, work.

But that's what you expect when you are a slave. He and his mother had been slaves since he was five years old. He was nine now and they still had two more years to work before they would be free. He used to spend a lot of time crying about being a slave and dreaming about being free, but he and his mother were well cared for and he was happy here. But he didn't get up to think about that.

He wanted to try to figure out exactly what happened....

Let's see. Oh, yeah, I was busy pulling onions because Mother had heard that more relatives from Nazareth were coming and she was afraid they wouldn't have enough food prepared. She was going to make more of her wonderful fish sauce.

The lambs were roasting over the fires and the servants were turning them carefully so that they would be perfect for the meal.

Yesterday, a lady named Mrs. Mary had arrived from Nazareth. She was a sister to Master Kenan and had come to help with the preparations. She was very kind to me and even slipped me a cookie for helping her carry the trays out to the courtyard.

Then mid-afternoon, Master Kenan's son, the groom, went to collect his bride and it seemed that the whole town decided to come to the wedding celebration. Mother was giving me directions. Mrs. Mary was giving me directions. Master Kenan was giving me directions. And Mrs. Kenan was giving me directions — all at the same time! Maybe that's why I can't remember exactly what happened. It was quite a busy day!

I remember that Mrs. Mary's son, Mr. Jesus, arrived with a large group from Nazareth. Apparently, these were some cousins and maybe some friends of Mr. Jesus.

The lambs had been put on platters and the vegetables brought from the kitchen to the courtyard, and the men were lined up at the ceremonial washing jars. It had taken me all week to get those water jars completely full, but Master Kenan had insisted they have plenty of water for washing before the meal. The men were required by Jewish tradition to ceremonially wash their hands before eating.

I remember thinking that soon the guests would all be busy eating and maybe there would be food for the servants in the kitchen. My legs were dead tired, and my head ached. But I learned a long time ago not to complain. A good slave was always cheerful and eager to help.

As the meal began, I noticed that the ceremonial water jars were almost empty, but that was okay, because everyone was done with the washing for now. I figured I should probably make some trips to the well so that there would be water in case of latecomers. But there was plenty of time to take care of that later.   I needed a break!

Some servants were assigned to wave palm branches over the food to keep away the flies and gnats. Some were busy refilling bowls and returning the empty bowls to the kitchen to get refills. But since I wasn't assigned to those tasks, I knew that I could slip into the kitchen and rest for a few minutes and grab a bite to eat.

Mother had set aside some plain bread and cheese for the servants and there were probably 10 of the male servants already ahead of me with the same idea. Sitting down felt wonderful and the food was just what I needed. But I had just gotten a bite when Mrs. Mary came running in calling for help.

Or course everyone stood up immediately. She said that they were almost out of wine and that her son would tell us what to do. I assumed she wanted us to go and purchase some wine. We all walked outside and reported to her son, Mr. Jesus.

Mr. Jesus asked us to fill up the ceremonial water jars with water.

To give you an idea of how much work I'm talking about, here's what the Bible says:

> **Nearby stood six stone water jars, the kind used by the Jews for ceremonial washing, each holding from twenty to thirty gallons.**[1]

Now, a slave doesn't ask questions, he just obeys — but let me tell you — I wasn't a happy camper. That's a <u>lot</u> of work.

At least this time I had help. It only took us about 30 minutes to get them filled to the brim. And all the while, I was thinking *this is stupid! Who cares about the water jars? What we need is wine for the guests.*

Then Mr. Jesus turned to Hosea, the oldest of the slaves who had helped fill the jars. He told him to dip some of the water into a cup and take it to the Ruler who was leading the wedding ceremony. I could see Hosea shaking because he knew he was going to get a beating for giving the Ruler water to drink instead of wine. He was shaking so hard that the water was spilling out all over the place. But like I said, we had learned to be obedient.

Here's the part I don't understand. Hosea had water all over him when he returned to us — but the Ruler said it was the best wine he had ever tasted! He complimented Master Kenan for serving the best wine last instead of first.

What happened between Hosea handing the water to the Ruler — and the Ruler drinking it? I can't figure that out. But for the rest of the night, we dipped water out of those jars and served it to the guests. But when the people drank it, it was wine. I just don't understand.

I know it wasn't just a mind trick, because when a lady spilled her cup, it stained red. Water doesn't do that. And there was the smell of wine everywhere.

I knew that I couldn't sleep until I checked it out myself. So, here I am, standing out in the courtyard just a few hours before dawn. There's such a mess. I know it will be a busy, busy day for me when the sun comes up. But I must know.

 I dipped a cup into one of the jars. It was just water! I checked each of the six jars and they were all the same — just plain well water.

The only people who saw what happened were us 11 servants and Mr. Jesus's two friends. His two friends seemed pretty surprised, too.

Hmm. Who is this man named Jesus and what kind of supernatural powers does he have? I want to find out more about him.

---

[1] **John 2:6**

Chapter 6
THE STORY OF LUCRETIA

Lucretia stretched her back. She had been sitting at the loom all morning and was ready for a change. She was designing a pillow and weaving it carefully. Her mother could make a pillow in a couple of hours. Lucretia had been working on this one for almost a week.

Her parents assured her that her hands would get stronger as she grew. After all, she was only 10.

Lucretia had been helping with her parents' business all her life, but she had only started on the loom a couple of weeks ago. Before that, her job was dying the wool before it was made into yarn. Her brother's new wife wanted that job, so Lucretia was learning to weave.

It had been her secret desire for many years to learn to weave, but she had to wait until her parents felt she was old enough. Her first pillow had some loose threads, so she was working extra hard to get this one perfect. But right now, she needed a break. She stood up and asked her mother if she could walk down to Deborah's booth. She promised she wouldn't stay long.

Deborah's family had a pottery booth just four doors down and the girls had practically grown up together. "Good morning, Mrs. Hannah, what a beautiful pot you are making."

"Good morning, Lucretia, and thank you. You just missed Deborah. I sent her for a delivery. She should be back soon — or you could go to meet her if you wish. She went to Mrs. Tumal's house."

"I know where that is. I think I'll walk to meet her. Then I've got to get back to work."

"Yes, Deborah has work to do, too. Don't be slowpokes!" But even as she spoke, Lucretia could tell that she was smiling, and not upset that Lucretia was Deborah's friend.

In the town of Antipatris (an-TIP-uh-tris), most of the people were Roman citizens. There were very few Jews. Sometimes the Romans were mean to the Jewish families, and sometimes the Jewish families were mean to the Romans. But Lucretia and Deborah were best friends forever and nothing would ever change that!

Lucretia and her family were Romans and they believed in many gods, but really worshiped none of them. They just worked hard and hoped that the gods were pleased with them. Deborah and her family were Jewish and worshiped the God of Israel. Deborah had told Lucretia many, many stories about her God and that he was the only true God — at least the only one with any true power. Lucretia listened and wondered. Sometimes, she would be invited over for Sabbath dinner and she would hear Deborah's family recite verses from the Jewish Scripture. Lucretia thought that it was beautiful poetry and felt a longing to know more about this God that Deborah worshiped. But she knew that her parents would never agree for her to become a Jew.

"Shalom," was a Jewish greeting that Deborah had taught Lucretia and they greeted each other when they met. It meant "peace on you and yours."

"I've got to hurry back to my loom, but I wanted to say hi. I've been really busy for the past several days and just haven't found the time to visit."

"I'll walk you back to your booth. How is your pillow turning out? Do you think you will finish it today?" asked Deborah.

"Oh, no. I had to rip out a section yesterday because I had missed a stitch and had dropped another thread, so I can't decide whether I'm moving forward or backward."

"Oh, I'm sure you'll figure it out. It seems pretty complicated to me. I'm sure I could never weave a pillow. Maybe Mother will let me try the wheel soon."

"That would be exciting — I know you'll be great at it. Gotta go. Shalom!"

"Shalom!"

Lucretia nodded to her parents as she came into the booth. Her papa was making cushions and her mother was weaving on the huge blanket loom. She returned to her pillow loom and felt a burst of energy to tackle it once more.

As the sun began to set, Lucretia helped her parents put away the supplies and lock up the little booth. They walked home together but it seemed to Lucretia that there was a sadness between them tonight. She wondered what had been said while she was away from the booth.

She didn't have to wonder long.

Not a single customer had bought a cushion or blanket or pillow today or, for that matter, all week. Papa felt that maybe everyone in town had already bought all they wanted. They needed a new market, or a new product.

Lucretia was glad that they were including her — but it seemed like a terrible dinner discussion to her. *Why so gloomy?*

Cushions, blankets, and pillows were all they had ever made, and this town was all she had ever known. She got busy with her chores and went to bed early. She planned to get up early and finish her pillow tomorrow.

The next morning, she busied herself with her pillow design and was working intently when a surprise visitor came into the booth. "Uncle Livius!" Everyone left their work and the three of them peppered him with questions.

Uncle Livius and Aunt Longina had lived in Antipatris until two years ago. They were also weavers of cloth, but they focused on making togas and heavy robes out of the colorfully dyed wool. They had moved to Jerusalem to see if the market there was better. Now, Uncle Livius was reporting that their business was booming, and he had come back to ask his little brother to join him.

"Lucretia, stay here at the store until closing. We'll take Uncle Livius home and let him rest a while. Lock up carefully and come straight home for dinner."

"Yes, Papa."

After the adults left, Lucretia continued to work on her pillow.

"Shalom!" Deborah said as she entered the tent.

"Shalom! I was so busy with my pillow, you totally surprised me."

"Where are your folks?"

"My Uncle Livius — you remember him — came for a visit. They went home and left me in charge. But as you can see, that's not a really busy assignment."

"The pillow is coming along beautifully. I love the deep orange color you are using. It is beautiful — a work of art!"

"Thanks."

"Lucretia, what's wrong? You seem troubled."

"Well, it's just that the business is not going well, and my parents are actually talking about moving."

"No!"

"That's exactly what I said. But then today, in walks Uncle Livius and he's bragging about how well his business is doing and right now he's trying to talk Mother and Papa into moving there and joining his business."

"Oh, Lucretia, that's terrible, but I've got to run. I stopped by to invite you to join us for Sabbath meal tonight — but I guess, if you've got company, that won't happen. Could you come over tomorrow to visit? I'll be free all day and we could catch up then. You don't have to let me know now, but if you could come — please do. I want to hear what's going on."

"I'll come if I can. I'm almost finished with the pillow, so they should let me. But I don't know what Uncle Livius' plans are. Shalom!"

"Shalom!"

Deborah walked slowly back to her parent's booth. She knew that they needed her to be working, but her thoughts were on her friend. *What will I do if Lucretia moves?* Lucretia was her closest friend, and she would miss her terribly.

News had traveled quickly and all of Lucretia's six older brothers and sisters and their kids had arrived to visit with Uncle Livius. As the meal ended and the adults were still debating the proposed move, Lucretia had two choices: she could offer to clean up the kitchen and all those dishes, or she could take all her nieces and nephews into the back yard and give their parents a break. She decided she needed the distraction and herded the kids into the backyard where she found balls and bats for the older kids and some bean bags to toss for the little ones. She showed baby Julius how to dig with a spoon in the dirt and he was delighted. She wondered what was being decided about her future.

One by one the families collected their youngsters and left. They thanked Auntie Lucretia and gave her sweet hugs and kisses. When the last family had gone, Lucretia knew that she should go into the house and visit with Uncle Livius, but she could tell that he and her parents were still talking about markets and inventory and supply chains and she just didn't want to hear it.

She climbed to her favorite perch in the olive tree. She realized she hadn't climbed up here in a long time. It was her hidey-hole, her thinking place. And tonight, she needed to think.

Or maybe she didn't want to think.   She looked through the branches at the starry skies and remembered a saying that Deborah had taught her from the Jewish Scripture:

> **Be strong and courageous. Do not be afraid ..., for the Lord your God goes with you; he will never leave you nor forsake you.**[1]

Lucretia wished she knew a God like that.   She wished she knew Deborah's God.   A tear slipped down her cheek. She felt certain that her parents were deciding to leave Antipatris, and she knew she would have no choice.

Maybe tomorrow she could slip away for a while and visit with Deborah. Often, Lucretia's parents would let her go to Deborah's home on the Sabbath unless she was needed at the booth.

She climbed down from the tree and successfully slipped past her parents and into her bed.

The next morning, Lucretia quickly ate her breakfast and hurried to the booth. Her mother and papa were already there. She apologized for sleeping late, and they teased her that watching 14 nephews and nieces under the age of eight might have had something to do with her fatigue.

Lucretia noticed that instead of her parents setting out merchandise for sale, they were stacking and wrapping and labeling. Something was definitely up.

"Where's Uncle Livius?"

"He's gone to take care of some business. Lucretia, we need to talk with you."

"Okay." She sat down on one of the cushions nearby — feeling like her legs would collapse if she didn't sit down fast.

"Your mother and I have agreed that we need to relocate our business. Your brothers and sisters will stay here and run the farm and continue to provide all the wools and dyes that we will need. They may, in time, reopen this booth, but for now, we are just going to close it down and move to Jerusalem. We will live with Uncle Livius and Aunt Longina until we can find a house. They have already purchased the booth next to theirs when it became available last week."

"I don't want to leave Antipatris," said Lucretia quietly.

"We know. We understand. But we cannot continue to stay here and meet our needs. Our family is growing, and we have many mouths to feed. Your brothers and sisters depend on our selling products. If we can't sell, then we all go hungry."

Lucretia threw herself into her mother's arms and couldn't hold back the sobs. When she had calmed herself, she sat up and asked, "When? When will we be moving?"

"Uncle Livius has gone to purchase some oxen and a wagon from a friend out in the country. He should be back by late afternoon, then we will load the wagon tomorrow and leave on Monday.

We need to have the new booth opened in Jerusalem in time for their Passover Festival. It's the busiest time of the year there."

"Mother, Papa, may I go to Deborah's house today? She invited me to dinner last night, but I told her about Uncle Livius' visit. She said I could come anytime today, if possible. You know it is their Sabbath, so they will welcome me, and I want to spend time with Deborah."

"I think that would be a good idea. We will be very busy packing the wagon tomorrow and there won't be any free time. I will expect you home for dinner tonight, but you may stay all day if you feel welcome."

"Thank you. I know you need my help today, but I really want to see Deborah."

"We understand."

"Mother, may I give my pillow to Deborah?"

"Have you finished it?"

"Yes, I finished it after you left yesterday. I would like for you to check it. But I want to give it to Deborah, please."

Mother looked at Papa and they both agreed that that would be okay. They both knew how special Deborah's friendship was to Lucretia.

"And Lucretia —"

"Yes, Papa?"

"We will need to return to Antipatris twice a year to pick up the dyed wools for our business, so I think you can tell Deborah that you will see her again in the fall."

"Oh, Papa, thank you!" She gave her papa a huge hug and handed her pillow to Mother. Mother looked it over and handed it to Papa. They both were very pleased with her progress. They both agreed that she was learning very quickly and would soon be earning money for the family business.

Lucretia took the pillow, her heart filled with pride from her parents' praise, but every step took her closer to having to tell Deborah the news.

As expected, Deborah's parents welcomed Lucretia warmly. Deborah was in the back yard with her younger sisters. When she saw Lucretia's sad face, she asked her parents if they could walk down to the river. But first Lucretia gave Deborah the pillow. She and her parents exclaimed over its beauty, and Lucretia was proud that she had worked so carefully on it.

As the girls began to walk away from the house, Lucretia began to cry.

"You are leaving, aren't you?" Deborah asked.

"Yes. On Monday."

"On Monday! Oh, Lucretia!" Now both girls were crying. They continued to walk arm in arm toward the riverbank. There they found a grassy spot and sat down to face each other.

They had come here so many times and shared so many secrets and dreams together. They had imagined many things, but they had never imagined being separated.

"So, tell me everything," demanded Deborah.

"There's not much to tell. My parents and I will move to Jerusalem and live with my aunt and uncle and open a new booth there."

"Whoa! Stop right there. Did you say Jerusalem?"

"Yes, that's where Uncle Livius and Aunt Longina live."

"Lucretia, Jerusalem is so special. I've always wanted to go to Jerusalem!"

"Then you go! I don't want to!" Lucretia felt confused and angry.

Deborah continued, "I didn't mean it like that. I just mean, if you must move somewhere — then Jerusalem is the most wonderful place in the world to be."

"I don't understand."

"Don't you remember? Jerusalem is where the temple of our God is. He lives there. You could go to the temple and worship him! The whole city is holy. I've never gotten to go there, but someday, I will."

"But I'm not Jewish. I wouldn't be welcome there!"

"Yes, you would. My dad has told me all about the temple. The main temple is divided into two parts — one for men and one for women and children. Then outside that building is a huge courtyard that's for people from all over the world to worship. It's called the Courtyard of the Gentiles. That's you. You could go there to pray, and God would hear your prayers because he lives there. Oh, Lucretia, you will be living in the city of the true God. I am so happy for you. I will be sad — but I'm happy, too. How can I explain this?"

"So, you really think your God would hear my prayers if I went to this courtyard?" asked Lucretia.

"Oh, I <u>know</u> he would, Lucretia!"

"I have always wanted to know your God better. You know that. Maybe this move will not be so bad after all. And I forgot to tell you the good news. Papa says that he will be coming back in the fall to pick up supplies and I can come with him. So, I will get to see you every six months."

"And maybe I can convince my family to come to Jerusalem to visit you. We will always be friends," Deborah assured her. "Do you have to rush back to work?"

"No, the booth is already closed, and Papa says I can stay all afternoon if it's all right with your parents."

"Oh, goody. Let's wade in the river and cool off our feet."

All afternoon the girls visited and cried, laughed, and remembered the good times. They made promises to never forget each other and Deborah promised to pray that her God would bless her friend, Lucretia.

Lucretia wanted to say goodbye to Deborah's parents and little sisters, so she walked back to Deborah's house and said her goodbyes. Then she slowly walked home knowing that this would be the last time she would walk this road in a long time. How quickly things change!

Uncle Livius had found a wagon and two sturdy oxen to pull it.

Papa, Mother, Uncle Livius, and Lucretia sat down to a simple meal and then continued sorting and packing the household goods. Because Lucretia's oldest brother would be moving into the house, there was no need to take everything.

Lucretia had some keepsakes that she placed in her trunk. She had some sculptures that Deborah had made for her, and she packed them carefully in wool scraps so they wouldn't get broken on the trip.

She laid her clothes in the trunk and saved room for her bedding on top. Most of the wagon would be filled with inventory for the new booth.

Sunday was spent emptying the booth and locking it tightly. Her brothers might one day decide to re-open it. Or maybe in a few years she would return to Antipatris and open it as her own booth. The future was wide open. Anything could happen.

Papa and her older brothers spent most of the morning taking apart the blanket loom so that it would fit in the wagon. Her pillow loom was much smaller and wasn't a problem, and then they packed the two spinning wheels that turned the wool into yarn and threads.

Papa and Mother had already wrapped most of the inventory so that it was ready to be loaded. The yarn and other supplies were already packed and by noon they were ready to go to the barn and start loading the rest of the already dyed wool. They would leave the dye pots and the unprocessed wool for her brothers and sisters to prepare. Papa and Uncle Livius added sideboards to the sides of the wagon so that they could pack more wool.

They spent one last night in the only house Lucretia had ever known. Sleep came quickly because she was so tired. At sunrise, the family gathered to say a last goodbye. Her brothers and sisters and their wives and husbands and all her nieces and nephews came to wave goodbye.

Uncle Livius drove the wagon and Papa and Mother and Lucretia walked behind. Lucretia walked backward, waving for as long as she could see her nieces and nephews.

Then the adventure began. There were two seats on the wagon and four people. One of the men would drive the oxen while the other man walked. Lucretia let Mother ride as much as she wanted — she preferred to walk. It was a lot less boring than sitting on a hard wagon seat. She collected wildflowers and took in all the beautiful sights and sounds of the land around her. She thought about pillow patterns and kept her mind busy thinking about everything except home. One thought kept returning: her desire to go to the temple of the God of Israel and pray to him was getting stronger and stronger. She wasn't sure when to approach Papa, but she felt certain that he would be the right one to talk to about her wish.

Because the wagon was so full and had to travel slowly, they would not be able to make the trip all in one day. They spent the night at a friend's house about halfway.

The second and final day was a harder climb for both the oxen and the people. They had to stop and adjust the wagon load a couple of times as the cargo wasn't adequately tied to keep it from sliding out the back on the steep roads. They had to purchase more rope to anchor the load better.

As the incline became steeper, Lucretia could not keep her eyes off the golden glow at the top of the mountain. Uncle Livius told her it was the Jewish temple. He also reminded her family that it would be best if they would learn and practice the Sabbath rules. He explained how they were not to work or carry anything on the Sabbath. Lucretia was delighted to think that now she would only work six days a week instead of seven. But she wondered how she would spend the long day without Deborah.

About noon on Tuesday, the perfect opportunity to talk to Papa came. Uncle Livius and Mother had walked ahead and were out of hearing distance. Lucretia crawled up on the wagon seat beside her papa.

"Papa?"

"Yes, Daughter."

"Papa, you know that I have been friends with Deborah for my whole life."

"Yes, I know that you and Deborah are very close. I'm sorry you have had to leave your friend. And I am proud of the way you have handled it."

"Thank you, Papa. I have a request."

"I've already told you that you may come back with me in the fall and visit with her while I pick up supplies."

"Yes, Papa, and I thank you. That makes it a lot easier."

"Is there something else on your mind?"

"Yes, Papa. Deborah says that the temple of the God of Israel has a special place for foreigners to come and pray to him. Papa, I would like to go and pray to Deborah's God. I would like to ask him to bless our new business. Will you take me to the temple of the God of Israel? Please, Papa."

Papa seemed very surprised by Lucretia's request. He believed in many gods, but as he thought it over, it made sense to him to be on the good side of the God of Israel if they were going to do business there.   So he said, "Sure. I will take you to the temple if you are sure that foreigners are welcome."

Lucretia told him about the building for the Jewish men and women and children, and she told him how Deborah had said that the entire surrounding courtyard was available for all Gentiles who wanted to come and pray to the God of Israel.

Papa agreed that it sounded nice and said he would take her there once they got things unloaded and settled in.

"But Papa, I would like to go there soon. I feel it is important that we start out right."

"Okay, Daughter, but I must get the booth set up before this big feast that is coming."

"Yes, Papa. I understand and thank you."

Lucretia knew her papa would keep his promise. She hoped it would be sooner rather than later, but he <u>would</u> keep his promise. Now, her heart was filled with anticipation of what the visit to the beautiful temple would be like.

The last few miles into Jerusalem were incredibly crowded. Lucretia couldn't remember ever seeing so many people. She let Mother ride with Uncle Livius on the wagon seat, and she and Papa walked behind the wagon to make sure nothing fell off.

The next few days were a blur of activity as they settled into sharing a home with Uncle Livius and Aunt Longina. They also began arranging their new booth and the men had to re-assemble the largest loom.

Lucretia found the perfect spot for her loom so that she could work near the front and still watch the crowds. There was so much happening all around her and the new smells and sounds were exciting. Each night, she fell into bed exhausted.

They found a farmer just outside of town who would keep the oxen and the wagon for them. And Uncle Livius and Papa had found a house for them to rent that was only a few blocks away. They enjoyed their first Sabbath by resting and visiting all day and decided that the Jews had a great idea!

On Sunday, they moved into their new home and began preparing the new booth to open on Tuesday. The looms and spinning wheels were set up and were working fine. Papa and Uncle Livius only had to make some minor adjustments after the bumpy ride. They would spend Monday setting out inventory and then open on Tuesday. Passover would begin on Wednesday and they would be ready for the crowds. But one thing still bothered Lucretia: she wanted to go to the temple.

Sunday night as they sat down to a simple supper in their new home for the first time, Lucretia felt that the time was right to bring it up.

"Papa, have you got everything at the booth working and ready to start on Tuesday?"

"All we lack is putting out the inventory and settling back into the routine. But I do think we are ready. Is your loom working properly?"

"Yes, Papa, thank you. I've already started a new pillow and it is behaving now that you tightened that loose board. Thank you.

"Papa, do you think we could go to the temple tomorrow? I don't think it would take long and the crowds are getting bigger and bigger. I'm afraid the temple will be packed if we don't go soon. Would you take me to the temple tomorrow?"

"What's this? Why do you want to go to the temple of the God of Israel?" Mother asked.

"Deborah told me that there is a place there where foreigners can go and pray to the God of Israel. I just wanted to go and ask him to bless our new business," answered Lucretia.

Papa added, "I didn't see any harm in it, and I told her I would take her once we got settled in. So, I guess I need to keep my promise."

Mother seemed concerned and insisted that she would need both of them at the booth all day.

Lucretia looked pleadingly at her Papa.

"Are you willing to go at sunrise tomorrow morning?"

"Oh, yes, Papa. And thank you!"

Lucretia woke before the sun and quickly dressed. She heard Papa stirring and they ate a quick breakfast together.

They were surprised to see so many people headed to the temple this early. Some sang songs of worship and others were busy visiting with friends. No one seemed to notice Papa and Lucretia — that is until they entered the gates of the temple.

All at once, it seemed that all eyes were on them, and the friendly, worshipful atmosphere disappeared. Some shook their fists at them and muttered ugly words toward them. Lucretia sensed that Papa was about to turn and leave, but she pulled him to the left of the crowd. Once they were out of the main pathway, all Lucretia could see were cows. And oh, how bad it all smelled!

That obviously wasn't the way to the Court of the Gentiles. So, she pulled her papa back across the main entrance where once again they encountered rude words and threats. Lucretia wanted to see what was to the right of the temple entrance. Once across the main pathway, the people were not as packed together.

But there they saw people buying and selling sheep and lambs. Here the smells reminded her of home even though they were overpowering. There were also rows and rows of tables with boxes of doves.

Behind all that there seemed to be a small empty place that might be available for them to say a quick prayer. And Lucretia was determined that since she had made it this far, she was going to at least speak to Deborah's God.

Right up beside the back wall, there were piles of trash everywhere, but Lucretia picked a spot and knelt down to pray. Papa didn't know what to do, so he knelt beside her. Lucretia had seen Deborah and her family pray and so she simply said, "God of Israel, I want to know more about you — but I don't know how. I came to ask that you would bless our new business and…"

At this point she noticed an angry group of men headed toward them. They were yelling for her and Papa to leave and some were even throwing rocks. Lucretia finished her prayer quickly by saying, "and please protect us."

Papa and Lucretia didn't know whether to stay kneeling to protect themselves or to stand and try to run. Would the crowd leave them alone if they left — or would they kill them? They were terrified.

Then from the direction of the temple a strong young man came running toward them. His face was not angry. His eyes were kind and sad. "Don't be afraid," he said.

Then he turned toward the angry crowd and here's what the Bible says happened next:

> **...he made a whip out of cords, and drove all from the temple courts, both sheep and cattle; he scattered the coins of the money changers and overturned their tables. To those who sold doves he said, "Get these out of here! Stop turning my Father's house into a market!"[2]**

When the courtyard was cleared of all the animals, Papa and Lucretia ran as fast as they could to the nearest gate. They wanted to thank their rescuer, but didn't want to risk getting trapped inside again.

Papa and Lucretia decided to go home and change clothes before going to the booth. They didn't want to alarm Mother and needed some time to catch their breath before going to work.

Papa and Lucretia both had some cuts and bruises from the rocks that had been thrown at them. But after they sat and drank some tea they felt better.

"Papa?"

"Yes, Lucretia."

"Papa, the God of Israel heard my prayer and sent a rescuer for us."

"I hadn't thought of that. But you are right. I don't know what would have happened if the rescuer had not come at just that time."

"Papa, the God of Israel heard my prayer. Deborah said he would. That makes me happy."

"Daughter, I'm glad that makes you happy — but I don't ever want to go back to that temple. The Jews have made us feel so welcome in the community and the market. But we are certainly not welcome in their temple! Promise me that you will not ever go back there."

"Papa, I will not go there without telling you first. But I want to know more about the God of Israel. If he can hear and answer prayer like that — I want to know more. Deborah says he is the only One who has any power.

"Our Roman gods have never helped us. I don't want to make you unhappy, but I know that I want to know more."

"Daughter, you must follow your heart. I want you to be happy. Don't go to the temple without telling me — and I will probably go with you. But right now, Mother needs help at the booth. We are running terribly late and we must be ready to open the doors tomorrow."

Lucretia finished her tea and joined her Papa as they walked quickly to the booth. Mother wanted to hear all about their adventures and agreed with Papa that the temple was no place for Lucretia to go alone, and she wasn't so sure that she wanted Papa to go either!

Passover began on Wednesday night, and all day long families strolled the market looking for special decorations and food for their celebration. Papa and Mother sold more cushions, blankets, and pillows in one day than they had sold in a month in Antipatris.

 After dinner, Lucretia slipped outside into the back yard and knelt under the stars. She thanked the God of Israel for his protection and for his blessing of the new booth. Then she quickly got ready for bed and the start of another long day.

All week long, the booth continued to be very popular, and kept all three of them very busy.

How glad they were for the Sabbath Day of rest that was the law in Jerusalem. Lucretia spent the day relaxing and caught herself designing new pillows. But it also made her miss Deborah even more. Maybe soon she would meet other girls, but for now, she was content to visit with her parents and aunt and uncle and not be working at her loom.

How quickly the six months had passed. In only two more weeks, Lucretia and her Papa were headed back to Antipatris to pick up supplies. She would get to see Deborah. She was sad that Mother couldn't go, too, because there should be a new niece or nephew by now. It would only be a short visit, but her parents had promised that maybe next summer, they could all go for a real visit.

All the products in the booth were selling very well, but Lucretia's pillows were an especially popular item. It seemed she couldn't make them fast enough. This latest pillow reminded her of the Mediterranean Sea where she had visited her grandparents.

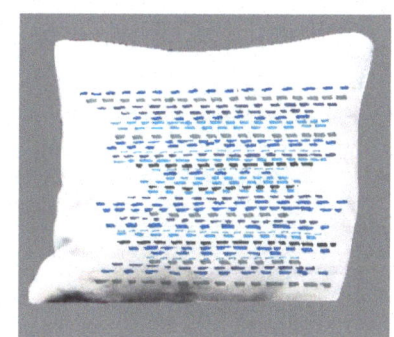

The pillow was beautiful, and she was proud of it. The lady who had seen it this afternoon had begged her to finish it for her in time for a dinner party tomorrow night and she had promised to pay double for it.

Papa and Mother had made it clear that she could not stay and work late unless one of the men stayed to protect her. After dark, the market area was not well lit, and they didn't want to take any chances with her safety. She knew her parents were ready to go home, so she asked Uncle Livius if he could stay late. He agreed because he, too, had promised to finish a toga that needed to be delivered tomorrow. So, it was decided.

When Mother and Papa left, they rolled down the sides of the booth so that from the outside, no one could tell that someone was inside working. Uncle Livius' booth was connected to theirs so he, too, closed down the outer sides and no one knew that the two of them were hard at work inside the booth. Uncle Livius was working in the back of his booth and Lucretia's loom was up close to the front of her booth.

Lucretia was daydreaming of working alone in her very own booth — when suddenly she heard men's voices just outside the tent. She froze for fear that they would hear her working inside. *What if they are robbers? Should I tiptoe back and get Uncle Livius?*

But suddenly ... she recognized that voice. That was the voice of the man who had rescued her and Papa at the temple. She would know that voice anywhere.

She remembered that he had looked straight at her and said, "Don't be afraid."

Now she sat perfectly still and listened to what he was saying to the other man.

Apparently, the other man was a Jewish rabbi, and her rescuer was trying to teach him something. They were talking about everyone needing a spiritual birth just like a physical birth. But she didn't understand much of that.

Then her rescuer said,

> "I have spoken to you of earthly things and you do not believe; how then will you believe if I speak of heavenly things? No one has ever gone into heaven except the one who came from heaven — the Son of Man. ... Everyone who believes may have eternal life in him."[3]

As the men walked off into the night, Lucretia replayed in her mind that day at the temple. She remembered that her rescuer had said:

> ...."Stop turning my Father's house into a market!"[4]

Who was her rescuer? Was he the God of Israel's son? Lots of Roman gods had sons and daughters, but Deborah had never told her about the God of Israel having a son. *What did he mean, "Everyone who believes may have eternal life?" What am I supposed to believe? Who is this man? And why did he stop right outside my booth to say these things?*

She was glad that it was only two weeks until she would see Deborah. She had much to ask Deborah and her family. There was much she wanted to know.

She finished her pillow and called to Uncle Livius. They carefully locked up the booth and carried their lamps home. Lucretia thanked Uncle Livius for staying late with her and told him good night. She had much to think about.

---

[1] **Deuteronomy 31:6**
[2] **John 2:15-16**
[3] **John 3:12-15**
[4] **John 2:16**

Jesus Clears the Temple Courtyards
John 2:13-16

Jesus Meets with Nicodemus
John 3:1-15

Chapter 7
THE STORY OF CALEB

"Good morning, Mith Mary," Caleb called through the back fence.

"Good morning, Caleb. You are up early, and I do believe you forgot to put your front teeth in — they seem to be missing!"

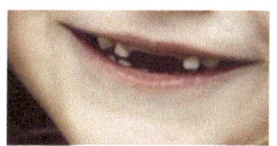

Caleb giggled at Mrs. Mary's silliness.

"Ask your mother if you can come over and see what I found in the garden this morning." She knew he would be right over.

In just a few seconds they were exploring a tiny nest of baby birds hidden in some bushes near the garden wall.

The mother bird was not happy with their exploring, so Mrs. Mary invited Caleb to come and sit closer to the house so Mother Bird could feed her little ones.

"Caleb, how are you going to eat if you keep losing your teeth? And how are you going to grow if you can't eat?" Caleb loved Mrs. Mary and proudly showed her the fresh new hole left by his latest loss.

"My goodness, I remember when my boys were losing their teeth. You know it means you are going to start growing very fast now!"

"Mith Mary, where are your boys?"

"Oh, they are all grown up. They started losing their teeth and the next thing you know — whoosh — they just grew up!"

Caleb's eyes got wide as he imagined growing up overnight.

"How many boys did you have?"

"I have five very special boys. Jesus, James, Joseph — who we call Josie, and Jude. Then I had Simon. He was my baby. And I have two little twin girls who are all grown up and are mommies now.   They all live around here except for Jesus. I'm sure you've met some of them. In fact, my grandson Jacob is the same age as you and you probably know him at school. I wonder if he's lost any teeth yet?"

"Where does Jesus live?"

"He lives in Capernaum, up in Galilee. But he comes and visits me sometimes.

"Oh, my, you startled me!"   Mrs. Mary stood and hugged a young man.

"Caleb and I were just talking about you and I was hoping that you would visit soon. Caleb, this is my oldest boy, Mr. Jesus."

"Good morning, Mr. Jesus. We were just looking at a bird's nest by the garden wall."

"Jesus, this is my neighbor, Caleb."

Jesus knelt down to get on eye-level with Caleb. "How many babies did you see?"

"Three!" exclaimed Caleb

"I'm glad you are a good neighbor to my mother. She gets lonely sometimes, so I'm glad you are visiting her and being a good friend," continued Jesus.

"Caleb," Mother called, "Come eat your breakfast or you'll be late for school."

Caleb tried to remember all the polite things to say as he hurried to obey his mother.

He was bursting with pride when he sat down and told his mother all about the baby birds and about meeting Mrs. Mary's oldest son, Mr. Jesus. "I think he's the nicest man I've ever met!"

"Well, that's quite a statement! But I tend to agree with you. Jesus has always been a very good man and very, very kind. I'm glad you got to meet him."

"Have you met him, Mother?"

"Oh, yes. He was just a little older than me and I've known him all my life. I mostly played with his younger sisters, but our families were friends and so I knew them all. My older brother, your Uncle Ben, worked with Jesus in his dad's carpenter shop.

"You'd better get busy or you'll be late for Hebrew school."

With a quick kiss, Caleb was out the door and running down the street toward the synagogue. He was glad today was Friday because there was always a spelling test on Fridays, and he loved spelling!

On Saturday morning, Caleb walked slowly between his parents toward the synagogue. His Abba would worship with the other men downstairs. Caleb and his mother and little sister would sit in the balcony with the other women and children.

Caleb wasn't tall enough to see over the railing but could peek through the slats to see what was happening down below. His mother was chatting with neighbors and friends, and the children played quietly at their mother's feet. There were several older boys leaning over the railing watching the men below. When the Ruler entered the room downstairs, everyone became quiet.

Shhhhhhhhhh!!!!

The Ruler selected a scroll and started to unroll it, but then paused and smiled when he saw someone he recognized in the crowd. Caleb tried to see who it was, but he couldn't see his face. The Ruler spoke to the man and invited him to come forward and read.

Caleb was so excited because the man invited to read the Scripture was Mr. Jesus, his new friend. Caleb looked around the group of women to see if Mrs. Mary had noticed, but she was sitting still with her head bowed as if she were praying.

Mr. Jesus began to read from the scroll of Isaiah, but it sounded like he was just talking to the people. He said that God sent him to give good news to the poor, to set the prisoners free, and to heal the blind, and to care for those who were hurting. He also said that this was the year that God was going to bless his people.

Caleb thought Mr. Jesus' words were beautiful. So did all the other people. They all agreed that he had a beautiful voice and he spoke so well.

Seeing Mr. Jesus again made Caleb feel happy deep inside, and his words made him want to really be good and help other people.

He wondered if Mr. Jesus would visit with Mrs. Mary this afternoon and if maybe he could manage an invitation to visit, too. He liked Mr. Jesus and wanted to learn more about him.

Then Mr. Jesus:

> **...rolled up the scroll, gave it back to the attendant and sat down. The eyes of everyone in the synagogue were fastened on him. He began by saying to them, "Today this scripture is fulfilled in your hearing."**[1]

There was some whispering among the people. It seemed everyone was bragging about knowing Mr. Jesus and his family. Caleb felt happy inside because he, too, knew Mrs. Mary, and that made him feel close to Mr. Jesus. He knew that his own mother was friends with Mr. Jesus when they were growing up.

But then Mr. Jesus said,

> "...no prophet is accepted in his hometown."[2]

And that's when Caleb realized that something was wrong. His mother grabbed his arm and was pulling him down the stairs. He knew she was mad, but he didn't know what he had done. He was trying to ask, and she just kept yanking his arm toward home.

Caleb looked behind him and saw that everyone was just pouring out of the synagogue and it looked like the men were fighting. Caleb had never seen anything like this and wanted to watch. But every time he slowed down, his mother pulled his arm harder. He had no choice but to go home with her and hope his Abba would tell him what happened. Apparently, he had missed all the action.

He tried to play with his little sister and keep out of his mother's way. She still seemed really upset and he didn't want to displease her. He decided that asking his Abba would be safer.

It was quite a while after noon before his Abba came home and he looked more upset than his mother. *What is going on?* But he knew better than to ask. Mother was putting his little sister down for a nap when Abba's best friend Mr. Tyrek came over.

Now, Caleb learned that the commotion was because Mr. Jesus claimed to be a prophet when everyone knew that he was just Jesus, <u>and</u> he claimed that God loved other people just as much as he loved the Jews. Caleb didn't quite know what to think about either of those things, but they didn't sound so terrible to him.

Then he learned that the men of the synagogue had tried to kill Mr. Jesus by pushing him over the cliff at the edge of the town of Nazareth. Caleb was horrified to learn that his own Abba had participated in this action.

Caleb didn't want to hear any more. He rushed out of the house and into the garden. He climbed the apricot tree and looked over into Mrs. Mary's yard. There he saw her quietly sitting and watching the mother bird feeding her nest full of babies. She didn't look upset or sad. Caleb felt that he should leave her alone, but the longer he sat there, the more sure he became that maybe she could explain what was going on.

He slipped carefully down the apricot tree and over to the fence. There he very quietly whispered, "Mith Mary?"

She turned toward him and smiled a welcoming smile. "Come, Caleb. I would enjoy some company."

So, Caleb joined Mrs. Mary in her backyard and sat and visited with her. "Mith Mary, I thought your son read beautifully thith morning."

"Yes, he did, Caleb. God has blessed him with a good voice."

"Mith Mary, is Mr. Jesus okay? I heard what the men tried to do to him."

"Caleb, Caleb, Jesus is fine. Don't worry about him. His Father will protect him from any harm. Didn't you hear his message? He said he had been sent by God to preach and teach and heal. God will protect him from anything men will try to do to him. I promise."

"But Mith Mary, I don't understand why everyone got so mad at him."

"Well, Caleb, sometimes people get mad when you try to tell them something new." Caleb looked at Mrs. Mary and wrinkled up his nose. She knew that he didn't understand. She thought a minute and then said, "Caleb, you know the wagon that you pull your baby sister in?"

"Yeth Ma'am, she loves it when I give her a ride."

"Caleb, whose wagon is that?"

"It's my wagon."

"It doesn't belong to your little sister?"

"No, Ma'am. I've had that wagon since I was a baby."

"I see. So, as far as you know, it's your wagon."

"Yeth Ma'am. I <u>know</u> it's mine."

"Caleb, do you know where that wagon is right now?"

"Yeth Ma'am. It's in the back yard right by the back door. I park it there when I'm not using it."

"Caleb, go get that little wagon. I want to show you something."

Caleb ran to his own back door and got the wagon. His parents were still discussing the fight and didn't notice his coming and going. He pulled the wagon over to Mrs. Mary.

"Here it is, Mith Mary."

"Turn it over, Caleb, and look inside the rim of the right front wheel."

Caleb turned the wagon over and looked inside the rim.

He could see an "R" and a "Y", but he couldn't figure out the rest of the letters because there was some mud caked up under the rim.

R Y

Mrs. Mary helped him wash off the mud and there, plain as ever, was the word:

MARY

"Caleb, why does your wagon have my name on it?"

Now, Caleb was really puzzled. He scratched his head and admitted he didn't know.

"When I had baby James, my second son, my husband Joseph made that wagon. He put my name on it — because he said he wanted to have lots of kids, and he didn't want them fighting over it. So, that wagon really belongs to me — not you."

"Then how did I get the wagon?"

"I gave it to you to play with when you were very little — but it's not yours — it's mine."

Caleb sat quietly for a few minutes. "Thank you, Mith Mary, for letting me play with your wagon. I'll take extra good care of it."

"I know you will, Caleb. I only told you that story so that you would understand that sometimes people think they know the whole story — when they might not."

Caleb sat quietly and thought about what Mrs. Mary had told him.

"Mith Mary, Jesus said he was sent by God to do great things. Is that true?"

"Yes, Caleb, it is very true. He's been healing sick people, and preaching to people who were unhappy, and helping people to figure out how to please God."

"Mith Mary, Mr. Tyrek and my parents are very mad because Jesus said that God loves everyone — not just Jews. Is that true?"

"Oh, yes, Caleb, that is very, very true. God created everyone and loves them very much. In fact, he sent Jesus so that everyone in the whole wide world would know that God loves them."

"That's a good thing, isn't it, Mith Mary?

"Oh, Caleb, it's a wonderful thing to know that God loves you. And he loves every single boy and girl in the whole wide world. And he loves them even when they don't know it!"

"I love you, Mith Mary!"

Caleb heard his mother calling, "Caleb, where are you? It's almost supper time. I need you to watch your sister while I prepare supper."

"Coming, Mother!"

"I'll see you tomorrow, Caleb. Oops, don't forget your wagon!"

"My sister will enjoy a ride in <u>your</u> wagon. Thank you for letting me use it."

_____

[1] **Luke 4:20-21**
[2] **Luke 4:24**

Names of Jesus' Siblings
Matthew 13:55-56

Jesus Teaches in His Hometown
Luke 4:16-27

His Hometown Tries to Kill Jesus
Luke 4:28-30

Jesus Went About Doing Good
Luke 7:21-22

Chapter 8
THE STORY OF BENJI

Mother didn't have to wake Benji up this morning. It was the first day of summer break from Hebrew school and he could hardly wait for morning.

He was up before the sunrise and trying to be quiet and not wake the rest of his family. Today was the big day. His family ran a fishing business and Grandpa Zebedee said that he could officially start work today at sunrise. He could hardly sit still to eat his breakfast.

He and his Abba would walk down to the dock together. His Abba built fishing boats and would be working in his shop nearby. His Grandpa Zebedee ran the overall family business and made all the decisions. Grandpa Zebedee, his four sons and two nephews, and all Benji's older cousins worked there along with many hired helpers.

There was a boat building section that Benji's Abba ran, a fish processing plant, a fish market, and the fishing division. He couldn't wait to find out where he would be assigned, but he had told Grandpa that he would like to be a fisherman someday.

He was surprised to find Grandpa Zebedee fast asleep in his chair outside the shed that served as his office. There was no one else around. His Abba had already started work inside his shop. Benji wasn't sure whether to wake Grandpa, or wait until he woke up, or to maybe go and ask his Abba.

"Hey squirt! So, you think you're old enough to work with the big boys today?" Caleb whirled around to see his cousin Laban taunting him. *Oh, no! I hadn't thought about having to work with Laban. I thought I would be working with Grandpa.* He rushed to wake Grandpa up, but Laban grabbed his arm and stopped him. "I wouldn't advise doing that. He's been out fishing all night and doesn't need a snotty-nosed runt to deal with. Come on. I'm your boss, so get used to it."

Benji once again couldn't decide whether to wake Grandpa or run and find his Abba. Anything would be better than having 13-year-old Laban in charge of him. They had never gotten along, and Laban was just plain mean at times. But if Laban really was his boss, then he didn't want to mess up on his first day. "Okay," said Benji, "What's my job?"

Laban led Benji over to a pile of tangled nets. "First assignment is to get these nets untangled and then I'll show you what's next."

Both boys began to pull on the nets. They were indeed tangled. Each of these rectangular nets were about 200 feet long and 30 feet wide. Laban began pulling the nets toward the right and Benji decided to pull to the left to see if that would untangle the knots. Laban got angry and told him he would never learn the right way. He said he would never be a good fisherman. Tears welled up in Benji's eyes and he could tell that that just made Laban meaner.

And that made Benji mad.

Next thing you know, it was more than just nets tangled into a tight knot.

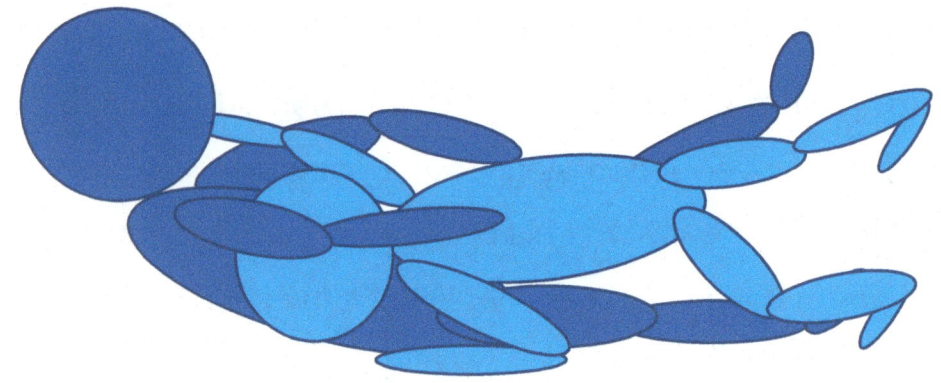

Benji heard Grandpa Zebedee yelling for him to stop and he felt himself being lifted off the ground by his right ankle. He was being carried upside down over to Grandpa's chair where he was dumped in the sand. The look on Grandpa's face was not good. Benji was still mad and determined to make Grandpa understand that Laban was being mean and ugly.

Grandpa just sat and looked at him without saying a word. Benji could feel his heart rate beginning to slow down and he bit his lip to keep the tears from coming. "Go home, Benji. You are not ready to work for me."

"But Grandpa, Laban called me names and said I was stupid!"

"Benji, go home. You need to decide whether you want to work for me and obey and respect the bosses I put over you — or whether you would rather do things your own way. Go home. You can come back tomorrow morning at sunrise, if you decide you want to follow my rules."

"But Grandpa! What about Laban?"

"No, Benji. You've got to learn to follow the rules if you want to work for me. Go home."

Benji decided not to bother his Abba and trudged home taking the longest route possible.

He got a little sympathy from his mother, but not what he expected. She just said that she felt he was too young to be starting to work anyway. She would be glad to let him spend the summer watching his younger brothers and sister. He dreaded telling his Abba what had happened.

At dinner, of course Abba wanted to hear all about his first day.

"Grandpa was asleep, and Laban was my boss. He was mean and unfair. He didn't like how I did anything. And he said... he said... I would never be a fisherman, and I punched him, and Grandpa got mad at me and sent me home. It's not fair! I wanted to work for Grandpa. I don't want to work for Laban! He's not my boss!"

Benji's Abba wisely let him tell his story, and just sat and listened before making any comments.

"Benji, you've wanted to be a fisherman since you were a little tiny boy. You wanted to be just like Grandpa. You love your Grandpa. But loving Grandpa and working for Grandpa are two different things.

"You see, for any business to work well — especially a family business — everyone must do his part, and everyone has got to learn to trust the other fellow to do his.

"If you had decided to come to work for me and help me to build boats, I couldn't just smile and be sweet to you if I asked you to bring me a 3-foot board and you brought me something different. It might look right to you, but you must learn to trust your boss to know what he needs.

"Now, I know that you and Laban don't get along outside of work, but I want to remind you that he has worked for Grandpa for a couple of years now. He had a job that needed to be accomplished today. He was probably pretty upset that you weren't listening to him and doing it the way he wanted it done.

"If you decide you want to work with Grandpa this summer — and that's totally up to you — you'll have to do things his way. If you decide you want to work with me this summer, you'll discover that you'll have to do things the way I want them done, too. I don't know any other way to say it. You may not like your boss, but he _is_ your boss, and your job _is_ obedience.

"Finish your dinner, and then take some time to think about what you want to do with your summer. You are still awfully young, and you may decide to stay home and help Mother again this year. That's up to you. Good night, Son."

Benji didn't need to think about it. He _knew_ what he wanted to do. He just didn't plan on it including Laban. He knew he needed to figure out how to be obedient to his cousin — who was intent on making his life miserable.

Benji took a little longer over his breakfast on Monday morning, and he and his Abba walked to the dock together. Abba didn't ask questions, and Benji didn't want to make conversation, so they walked in silence. "Have a good day, Benji," is all Abba said as he headed to the boat shop.

Grandpa was asleep in his chair and Benji knew to leave him alone. Soon, Laban showed up and the taunting began again. He called Benji a "quitter" and a "crybaby". But Benji managed to hold his temper. He asked questions and tried to do everything that Laban requested. They managed to get one of the nets untangled and stretched out on the sand.

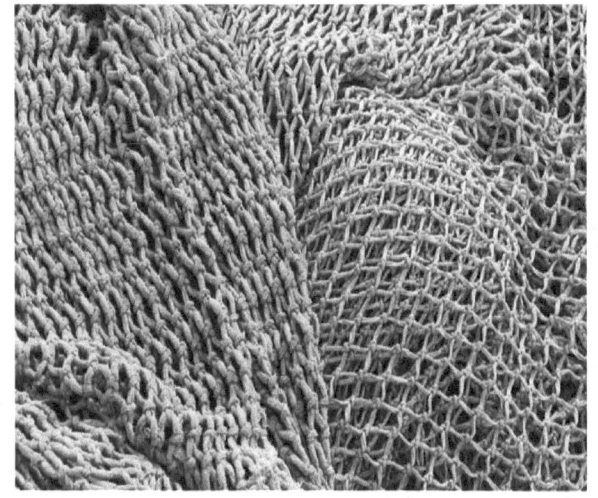

Laban showed Benji how to check the threads of the flax to make sure there were no weak spots that could break. When Benji saw torn threads, he was to mark it by tying a red piece of cloth around the spot so that the net repairers could mend it.

Laban eased up on the taunting when he realized that Benji was not going to fight back. But he continued to say nasty things to Benji at every chance.

When Benji finished a 10-foot section, Laban assigned him a new section and began to check Benji's work. Laban showed him a couple of loose threads that he had missed, and Benji felt his face turn red and his stomach tighten. He wanted to make excuses, but he reminded himself that he was here to learn the work — not fight about it. So, he apologized and promised to be more careful. Laban said he probably would never learn to be careful — but Benji was able to ignore it and keep working. He was determined to be more careful than ever.

It was hard work. Both boys were down on their hands and knees in the hot sand checking every single thread in the huge net. It was easy to become distracted, and Benji felt like every muscle in his neck was going to explode before Laban suggested that they take a break.

"Race you to the water!" And off they went. Of course, Laban, who was three years older won and called Benji a loser. But the cold water felt great on their hot bodies and tight muscles.

By the time they got back to work, Grandpa Zebedee was awake and checking their work. "Good work, boys. You should be able to finish this one today. There's four or five more nets that need to be checked, so that will keep you busy for a few days."

Laban and Benji went back to work and continued to check one section at a time until sundown. They occasionally took breaks to cool off, and mid-afternoon, Grandpa Zebedee brought them some juice to drink.

When Abba was ready to start home, he found Benji and Laban finishing the last section. Laban was trying to fold the net without re-tangling it. But Abba told Laban to lay it back out on the sand. Then he showed the boys how to roll it instead of folding it. This would keep it from getting so tangled. Benji was so proud of his Abba.

As they walked home, Benji asked, "Abba, how do you know how to roll the nets?"

"Don't forget, I worked for your Grandpa, too. Everybody starts at the bottom and works their way up."

It made Benji feel proud that he was following in his Abba's footsteps. And he had just completed his first whole day at work without losing his temper.

The next day, Laban and Benji found the net that they had marked yesterday already mended by the net repairers and ready for the next step. The men had removed the red ties and repaired each loose thread. Laban and Benji once again unrolled the net across the sand. But this time it was easier because it wasn't tangled.

Laban brought Benji a large bucket of rocks with holes drilled in them. He showed Benji how to carefully tie the rocks to the bottom of the net. All day long, Benji checked to make sure that the rocks were securely tied and replaced any broken ones. Laban worked on the top side of the net, tying pieces of lightweight wood to the top of the net.

It would take all day to finish this task since the net was over 200 feet long. Benji was grateful that Laban wasn't working right beside him, so there was less bickering. But Laban still took every opportunity to call Benji slow or careless or hopeless. Benji worked hard and didn't ask for breaks until Laban said it was time. Benji tried hard to let Laban be the boss and tried not to cross him.

As Benji walked home with his Abba, he had some questions. "Abba, today I tied rocks to the net along the bottom. I think that was to make it sink. But Laban was tying wooden pieces around the top, was that to help the fishermen get a better grip?"

"Well, it might help them to hold on better, but it's primarily to keep the net from sinking. The wood he was tying onto the top of the net floats and holds the net up close to the surface of the water. That way, you don't lose the net if the men have to let go for some reason. It will float near the surface. I would think that Laban should be teaching you these things."

"Laban really doesn't talk to me, except to tell me what to do and tell me what a failure I am."

"I'm sorry, Benji. Sometimes we all get bosses like that. I'm sorry it's your first one. But Grandpa tells me that you are doing good work, so I know that he's pleased."

"Thanks, Abba, that helps."

Most nights the fishermen left about sundown to start their fishing with the giant rectangular net. There were three boats, each with a captain and four oarsmen. The three captains directed the rowers to keep the boats in line to drop the giant net down into the water and then pull it slowly and carefully toward the shore. When they were close enough to the shore, the 12 oarsmen would jump into the water and haul the net full of fish up on to the sand.

Another crew of workers would sort the fish into barrels of water to keep them fresh. Depending on how many fish they caught on each trip out, they would do five to seven trips per night. They usually caught about 500 pounds of fish before morning.

But some nights, if they were not being very successful with catching the coastal fish, the three boats would spread out and each use a round net that one boat's crew could handle by itself.

Benji had learned how to check and repair both kinds of nets. It seemed that the better and faster Benji became, the meaner and more hateful Laban became. Benji was beginning to wish this summer was over!

It was on a morning near the end of the summer when Benji arrived at work and found all in disarray. Instead of the large rectangular net being laid out and ready to check, it was still dirty and filled with plants and sea creatures that were not fit to eat. The fishermen were all upset and Benji wasn't sure what to do.

Grandpa Zebedee looked exhausted as he spoke to the fishermen. "Rinse out the net so that the boys can get started checking it. Then meet me at the shed and I'll pay you for your night's labor even though we didn't catch anything."

Benji ran to Laban to see what was going on. Customers who had lined up to buy fresh fish were leaving. Usually, they sold fresh fish all morning and anything that was left over was sent to the processing plant where it was either smoked, dried or pickled.

They primarily caught four kinds of fish in the Sea of Galilee: Musht, which was usually about three pounds apiece, was their best-seller; biny, which could be between 20 and 50 pounds apiece and was used for feasts or large celebrations; catfish, which was considered unclean for the Jews, but was loved by the Greeks and Romans; and sardines. The sardines were only about three to six inches long and were usually sent straight to the processing plant.

But last night, they had caught nothing — not one single fish. The men were scared. This was their livelihood. They had to have fish, or they wouldn't have jobs. And the townspeople were upset at the fishermen for not bringing fresh fish for their families.

Grandpa Zebedee was trying to calm everyone down and maintain order. The men got the net rinsed and the boys set to work. Uncle John and Uncle James were double checking the boys' work to make sure they hadn't missed a rip that might have allowed the fish to escape.

Benji was determined to not miss a single torn thread and was concentrating so hard that he didn't notice a crowd gathering on the shore. When he looked up, there were over 100 people standing around a man who was teaching.

The teacher walked over to the fishermen and asked if he could use one of their boats. Benji's cousins Simon Peter and Andrew walked with the man out to their boat which was still floating not far from shore and pushed off a few feet. This allowed the teacher to be heard because the water magnified his voice. It also kept him from being crushed by people who wanted to meet him and touch him.

"Who is that man?" Benji asked.

"Jesus. He's a prophet and has been teaching around here," one of the fishermen replied.

"I heard that he can also heal people and make blind people see," another chimed in.

"I heard that he made a deaf man hear — and he had been deaf since birth!" said another.

"Shhhh! I wanna hear what he's saying!" said another.

Benji continued his work, but he began to listen.

> **"... I tell you, do not worry about your life, what you will eat or drink; …. Look at the birds of the air; they do not sow or reap or store away in barns, and yet your heavenly Father feeds them. Are you not much more valuable than they? Can any one of you by worrying add a single hour to your life?** [1]

> **So do not worry, saying, 'What shall we eat?' or 'What shall we drink?'…. Your heavenly Father knows that you need them.**[2]

That was good news. If the fish had disappeared there were going to be a lot of hungry people. Benji was just finishing checking all the rocks at the bottom of the net when he realized that Mr. Jesus had stopped teaching.

"Elias! Isaac! Abner!" Simon Peter called, "Jesus wants us to make one more quick run. Come on. Let's go fishing!"

Benji noted that none of his older cousins were very eager to get up and go back to the boat. But just like Benji, they had learned to obey their bosses whether they wanted to or not. Benji wished he was big enough to work the oars, but that would take a few more years.

Jesus waded back to the shore and stood watching as the men readied the boat and began rowing to the place that Jesus had indicated. It was a place where they had fished all night long and caught nothing.

It didn't take long for the men to row there. Instead of the rectangular net that was still drying, the men threw out the round net. The round net didn't need three boats to pull it to shore. It was about 25 feet in diameter. The fishermen dropped it into the water and let it sink to the bottom. Then using ropes, they pulled it quickly back to the surface. Any fish that couldn't swim away fast enough would be caught and brought to the surface.

Benji had forgotten his work and was watching just like all the other fishermen, workers, and the rest of the crowd. Benji watched as they dropped the round net and waited a few minutes to let the water calm down. Then the men began to pull up the ropes — except something seemed to be wrong.

Benji watched as they struggled to pull up the ropes. It was like they were hung on the bottom. Maybe they had snagged on something. The men pulled and strained. Grandpa Zebedee began to run toward his boat and yelled for his crew to join him.

Benji watched helplessly as the two boats tried to lift the net. Then they seemed to be taking smaller nets and dipping fish out of the larger one. They were dumping the fish in the floor of the boats, and the boats were sinking deeper and deeper into the water. Both boats were in danger of sinking when they were finally able to pull the round net close enough to the shore to empty it on the beach.

Benji saw more fish than he'd ever seen, and even though he had not been officially trained to sort the catch, Uncle John showed him how to safely pick up the musht fish. He carried them to the barrels of water that would keep them fresh.

It seems that the whole crowd was helping to sort the fish because they didn't want them to spoil on the shore and there were more fish than anyone had ever seen. Even Mr. Jesus was helping to carry some of the bigger biny fish. Some of them weighed up to 50 pounds and couldn't be handled by just one man. It was chaos.

Grandpa Zebedee was rolling out more barrels from the storehouse and directing them to be filled with water. Benji's dad and his crew of shipbuilders came out to help. People were buying the fish as fast as the sellers could take their money, and the tax collectors were busy counting the barrels and calculating their share.

As the round net's catch was almost sorted, Benji noticed that Mr. Jesus was talking with his Uncle John and Uncle James and his cousins Simon Peter and Andrew. They walked out to the two boats and all the fishermen ran out to help push the boats ashore so the rest of the fish could be sorted. Benji knew something was strange when he saw the four fishermen go and talk with Grandpa Zebedee and then leave with Mr. Jesus.

Benji wanted to ask questions but knew that it was not the right time. He just kept sorting fish until Grandpa Zebedee ran out of barrels.

Grandpa announced to the crowds that the rest of the fish were free for the taking. He had no more barrels to store them in. And what the townspeople didn't clean up, the seagulls enjoyed.

Benji walked home with his Abba who had missed all the earlier action. He wanted to hear what had happened and Benji told him the best he could.

"Abba?"

"Yes, Son."

"Why did Uncle John and Uncle James and Simon Peter and Andrew leave when there was still more work to be done? I don't understand. I thought that was a fisherman's rule to work until the work was done."

"Well, Son, it *is* the rule. But I believe they weren't quitting on the job.

"I believe that Mr. Jesus is the Messiah that was promised by God, and that makes his kingdom bigger and more important than Grandpa Zebedee's fishing business. And just like Grandpa tells you where to work and what to do, I believe that Mr. Jesus has called your Uncle John and Uncle James and Andrew and Simon Peter to work for him. He's given them jobs to do."

"Why didn't he give you a job to do, Abba?"

"Oh, he has!"

"I don't understand, Abba."

"God calls different people to do different things. He called me to be a boat builder. I tried to be a fisherman, but I got seasick every time I got in the boat. It became pretty clear that I wasn't going to be a good fisherman. But when I began to learn carpentry from a friend of Grandpa's, I realized that I could use my carpentry skills to build fishing boats for Grandpa. I believe that I'm serving God by being the best boat maker I can be — and the best dad and husband I can be.

"Your Uncle Jaden, my oldest brother, always knew that he wanted to be a fisherman. And he's a very good one. Someday, he'll take over for Grandpa. God will use him, like he uses Grandpa to help an awful lot of people.

"But Uncle John and Uncle James have been called to work for God in a special way. I don't know how God will use them, but I'm happy that they have found what they want to do. Someday, you'll find what you want to do — but I hope that you will always want to please God and obey God and be the very best man that you can be."

"This has been a crazy day." Benji said. "First no fish, then hearing Mr. Jesus say that we should trust God to provide for us, and then, wham! more fish than we know what to do with. I'm starving — but I hope it's not fish for dinner!"

"ABBA!"   Benji had not screamed like that since he was a little boy having nightmares — but this was worse than his worst nightmare. "ABBA!"

 His Abba quickly ran to Benji's side, holding a lamp. It was after midnight and Benji was crying and shaking in his blanket. "Benji, what's wrong? Are you sick?"

"Oh, Abba, I forgot the net! I left the net!"

"Benji, you left the fishing net? Where?"

"On the beach. I had just finished checking it and had finished all the rock repairs when Mr. Jesus sent the guys fishing. I went to watch, and I meant to come right back and pick up the net. But I forgot. I didn't pick it up. Oh, I know it's ruined! Everyone was walking there, and they dumped the fish right there. I know it's ruined! And Abba, when the tide comes in, it could wash away. Oh, Abba, I've got to go get that net before the tide comes in!"

"Let me tell your mother. Get your heavy poncho and take your lamp. I'll get the lantern and maybe we can find it."

"Oh, Abba, thank you for going with me, but it's all my fault. You don't have to come."

"Son, we'll go together. Get your lamp."

So Benji and his Abba hurried toward the dock in the wee hours of the morning. Of course, the minute they got close to the beach, Grandpa Zebedee stepped out of the shed to meet them. He was used to fishing all night so he was a light sleeper. "Who goes there?"

"Dad, it's me, Jonas, and Benji."

"Grandpa, I forgot the net. I had just finished it when everything got crazy, and I forgot to pick it up. I've got to find it before the tide comes in. I'm sorry, Grandpa. I know it will be a mess because people walked all over it. You can take it out of my pay. I'm so sorry. I'll work for free until it's paid for."

"Go home, you two, and get some rest. I found the net after everyone left. It _is_ a mess, but there's nothing you can do tonight. Get some rest and we'll deal with it in the morning."

"Yes, sir," said Benji, certain that he would be fired in the morning.

"I'll see you in the morning, Dad," said Benji's Abba.

He took Benji's hand as they walked slowly back home.

Benji was grateful for the warm blanket, but he couldn't get to sleep for a long time. He lay in the dark and blamed himself for being so careless. He finally cried himself to sleep just about the time Mother woke him up for breakfast.

Benji walked to work with his Abba, but he was grateful that Abba didn't try to come with him to talk with Grandpa Zebedee. He wanted to deal with Grandpa man to man — even though he was only 10.

Benji was surprised that Laban had laid out the circular net to be checked first. He would much rather have gotten the big net over with. He was eager to see how much damage was there and whether it would even be repairable at all. While they were checking the circular net, Grandpa Zebedee called Laban. Benji felt certain that Grandpa was telling Laban what he had done and then he would be sent home — he just knew it.

Instead, after talking with Grandpa, Laban just walked past him and said, "See you, squirt!" Benji watched as Laban headed to the processing plant. Benji's heart began to hammer inside his chest. The last place he wanted to work was the processing plant. He hadn't thought about that. That would be worse than being sent home!

"Benji!"

"Coming, Grandpa!"

"Benji, as you know a lot of things changed around here yesterday. Because four of my fishermen are gone, I'm rearranging some assignments. I am assigning you to be in charge of the nets. You'll need to train some new boys to help you. You'll be responsible to see that we have five large rectangular nets and three circular nets ready for use every night by sunset. That means that you've got to make sure to have extras in case some get torn and need repair. I'd like for you to keep about five extra nets ready at all times."

Benji could not believe his ears.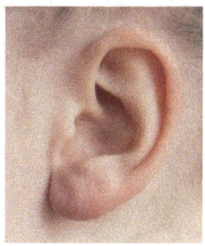

"But Grandpa, I messed up!"

"Yes, Benji, you messed up. We all mess up sometimes, but you did everything you could to make it right — even coming out in the middle of the night to try to fix the mistake. That tells me that you will take this job very seriously. I've watched your work and I'm proud of you. You are a team player and I hope that you will encourage those who work with you.

"Finish the round net quickly. I have hired some new boys for you to train later this morning. You've got a really messed-up net for them to learn on!"

As Benji worked on the round net, he remembered his Abba saying that he wanted to be the best boat builder he could be for God. Benji asked God to help him be the best net manager that Grandpa had ever had.

Something that he heard Mr. Jesus say yesterday was:

> **"... do to others what you would have them do to you....[3]"**

He knew that whenever he trained the new boys, he wanted to do it God's way.

---

[1] **Matthew 6:25-27**
[2] **Matthew 6:31-32**
[3] **Matthew 7:12**

Jesus Taught From a Fishing Boat
Luke 5:1-3

The Giant Catch of Fish
Luke 5:4-10

**Jesus Calls Peter, Andrew,
James and John to Follow Him**
Matthew 4:18-22

Chapter 9
THE STORY OF SAMSON & SOLOMON

"Where are we going, Samson?"

"I don't know. We've already asked at every place in town and no one will hire us. I don't know what to do." Samson honestly didn't know what was going to happen. He knew that if something didn't change soon, the entire family would be separated and sold as slaves. Their dad had become sick almost two years ago and had lost his job. They had used all their savings and Mother had stretched the food as far as she could — but this morning, there was no breakfast and there would be no dinner unless Samson could find work.

"Samson," Mother had said, "Even if I had flour, I don't have any oil or anything to go with it. We have absolutely nothing. Take Solomon and try one more time. Maybe go further away from town. Maybe some of the surrounding farms would hire you both."

Samson was 10 years old and his little brother Solomon was eight. They were both small for their age because they hadn't had much to eat for the past two years. All the farms said they were too young. They were just walking aimlessly along the beach, not knowing what to do next. They noticed a crowd was gathered around a man who was sitting in a boat teaching. Samson asked who the man was. "Shhhh!" was the reply.

A lady standing nearby whispered that his name was Jesus, and he was a prophet from God. He was healing people and helping those in need. Samson's heart did a flip and he and Solomon moved in closer to see if they could hear what he was teaching. They sat down by the water's edge and listened. *His words are beautiful, but what does it mean that God will take care of our need for food? Doesn't God know that we are starving to death and that soon our family will be split up and sold into slavery because we can't pay the rent?*

Samson kept thinking about one thing that Mr. Jesus said:

> "So do not worry, saying, 'What shall we eat?' or 'What shall we drink?' or 'What shall we wear?' ... your heavenly Father knows that you need them.[1]"

Mr. Jesus seemed to be teaching that if people would do things God's way, then God would take care of everything else. Samson wondered what that meant. He wondered how he could do anything God's way when he couldn't find work and he couldn't protect his three little brothers or his mother. He felt the tears come to his eyes, but he brushed them away quickly. He didn't want Solomon to know how desperate things were, but he thought he saw Mr. Jesus look at him and smile. That was nice. Not many people smiled at him these days — not since he had been begging for a job. Most of them just told him to go away. Samson felt a glimmer of hope, something he hadn't felt in a long time.

They watched as Mr. Jesus got out of the boat and waded back to shore. He was mobbed by people wanting to talk with him and touch him. But Samson's attention was on a group of fishermen who were rowing out to sea. It was a strange time to be fishing and there seemed to be a lot of other fishermen standing around watching to see what would happen.

Then Samson saw another boat full of fisherman going out to help the first boat because it had caught more fish than it could handle. *What is going on?*

Samson and Solomon watched as the two boats gradually worked their way back toward shore. Other fisherman ran out to help get the round net up on shore and emptied. There were more fish in the net than they had ever seen, and the crowd was going crazy. Samson learned that Mr. Jesus had told the men to go fishing and it had resulted in this amazing catch. The fishermen all began to sort the fish into barrels to keep the fish fresh. Many in the crowd began to help sort, too.

Samson and Solomon looked at each other and knew that God had just provided for them. They slipped into the crowd and picked up several good-sized fish and then instead of putting them into the barrels, they began to walk down the beach and toward home as fast as they could.

At least, that was the plan. But by the time they had gone only a few yards they were met by Mr. Jesus.

"Hello boys. I saw you listening to my teaching and I was wondering if you understood what you heard. Is there anything I can help you with?"

Samson and Solomon both immediately confessed to stealing fish and promised to take them back. Mr. Jesus knelt down and looked them both in the eyes. He stated again one of the things he had been teaching:

> **"But seek first his kingdom and his righteousness, and all these things will be given to you as well.[2]**

"What do you think that means?" Mr. Jesus asked gently.

Solomon answered that he didn't know, but he sure would like anything that he could give him.

Samson saw the look in Mr. Jesus' eyes and felt that he could trust him. "Mister, we really need those things that you talked about — food, clothes and we need rent money real bad. But I don't know how to get it.

"I thought God sent that boat of fish so that we would have something to eat tonight. We're really hungry."

Mr. Jesus put his arms around both boys and said, "Well, one thing I didn't say was that it was all right to steal! What I meant was that if you will do things God's way, then he'll take care of everything you need."

"Mister, we've been trying hard for the past two years and it just doesn't work that way! My dad's sick, and my mother and three little brothers expect me to provide for them, but nobody is hiring a 10-year-old."

Mr. Jesus smiled and said, "Would you be willing to do things God's way and see what happens?"

"Yes sir, if you'll tell me what to do. We'll do anything!" said Samson.

"Yes sir," said Solomon.

"Okay. Get back up there in the crowd and start sorting fish. That's just the first load. They've got two more boats full of fish. They are going to be sorting for quite a while. Let me show you the kind of fish to pick up."

Mr. Jesus led them back to the edge of the pile of fish. He showed them how to pick up the musht fish without getting cut by the scales.

Then he showed them which barrels to put them in. "Do things God's way and see if God doesn't take good care of you."

Samson and Solomon worked all morning. One of the fishermen handed out juice and thanked all the helpers.

When Mr. Jesus left and took four of the fishermen with him, most of the crowd left, too. But Samson and Solomon kept working. They sorted until they thought their arms would fall off.

"Hey, you two boys!" The boss man yelled at them.

Uh Oh!

Samson and Solomon thought about running, but they remembered that Mr. Jesus had promised that good would come to them if they did things God's way. And they really hoped they would get some fish. So, they answered.

"Yes, sir," they both replied together.

"Whose boys are you? Do I know you?"

Samson spoke up, "Our dad is Uzziah, but he's been sick for a couple of years now. We were listening to Mr. Jesus and he told us to help sort the fish, so we did."

"So, you've been working for me all day?"

"Yes, sir."

"Let me find you some sacks. I'm sure your mother needs all the help she can get. Collect as much fish as you can carry, and here's some money for your pay as well. You have helped me out today, and I think you deserve a reward. I appreciate the help. Is there anything else I can do to help you boys?"

Samson swallowed hard and decided that God was opening an even bigger door for help. "Mister, we need a job. Our dad can't work, and we've got two little brothers at home. We need jobs real bad. We'd be glad to sort fish anytime you could use us."

"Well, I think that could be arranged. But would you be willing to do whatever I need you to do? I could train you to become fishermen or possibly boat builders depending on what you would enjoy."

"Oh, yes, sir!" they replied together.

"Okay, be here mid-morning tomorrow and I'll put you to work. And my name is Mr. Zebedee. Tell your parents I'll take good care of you."

"Oh, thank you, Mr. Zebedee. Thank you."

Mr. Zebedee noticed the tears in both boys' eyes, but he never knew how God had used him to save their lives.

Samson and Solomon carried their sacks of fish home, and then Solomon ran to the market to buy some olive oil to fry it in. He also bought some vegetables and a round of bread. They would have a feast tonight! They gave the rest of the money to Mother and they celebrated God blessing them and meeting their needs.

The next morning, Samson and Solomon could hardly wait to get to work. They reported to Mr. Zebedee and he introduced them to Benji. Because they had arrived early, Benji wasn't quite finished with the round net, but it gave him a chance to explain what he was doing and why.   The boys seemed interested and asked good questions.

Once Benji finished the round net and had it ready for the net repairers, the three boys started spreading out the huge rectangular net that had been trampled on yesterday.

Samson caught on quickly and was very thorough and careful in his work. But Solomon had a hard time paying attention. Benji had to show him over and over how to check the flax threads and he often found whole sections that Solomon had skipped over.

Samson kept trying to help Solomon because he feared that they would both lose their jobs if Solomon couldn't get it right. But Benji kept encouraging them both, and the boys were proud of their first official day of work. They had more fish for the family and coins in their pockets to help Mother pay the rent.

Each day the two boys worked on the big rectangular net until it was almost completely covered in red ties. Benji had to keep the current nets checked so that the fishermen would have all they needed. Then he would check Solomon and Samson's work.

By Friday, Benji had sat down and worked out a plan with Grandpa Zebedee that would help everyone. Benji spoke to Solomon quietly, "Solomon, I need to talk with you about your work. Would you like to talk with me alone, or do you want Samson to hear it, too?"

"I want Samson to hear it, too. I'm sorry, I'm not any good at checking the nets. But please don't fire Samson. He's good at it!"

Benji assured him, "I'm not firing anybody. I just think you would do better at another job.

"So, starting on Sunday, your new job will be to collect the rocks that we need for the nets. Here's two buckets. You will carry them all around the inlet and collect rocks. When the buckets are getting too heavy, bring them in and dump them here in this barrel. Do you think you can do that?"

"Oh, yes! I can do that. Just show me what size rocks you want!"

"When you finish cleaning up the beach after each tide, then you can come and help Samson and me with the nets. And you'll be my assistant when I need help with other things. But most of the time, you'll be busy collecting the rocks."

"Thanks, Benji, for giving him another chance — for giving both of us a chance," said Samson.

"Samson, you are both good workers and Grandpa Zebedee wants to make sure you both learn to be good fishermen or boat builders. Solomon is just not quite old enough to understand the importance of the net. But you are doing great and I'm already learning to trust you. That's a pretty good accomplishment for the first week of work."

Samson and Solomon helped Benji roll up the huge rectangular net and they put it on the pile to be mended. Then Benji told them to take off early since they had completed their tasks for the day, and it was almost the Sabbath.

On Saturday morning, as Samson was helping Mother get the younger boys fed and dressed for synagogue, his Abba announced that he was going to go with them.

"Uzziah, you are not well. You can't go to synagogue!" Mother tried to plead with him.

Samson tried. "Abba, you need to stay home and rest. You are not well. You shouldn't go to synagogue this morning."

They both knew it was no use to try to change his mind. Ever since he had become sick, he had been like a different man. He was mean and cruel and sometimes even beat his wife and sons for little things. She knew that he would do as he pleased.

Samson asked Mother if they could just stay home, but she said that God had blessed them so richly this week, she wanted to go and show her thanks. At least none of the boys were old enough to worship with the men, so they would be safe with her. They wouldn't have to be with their Abba.

They left the house together as a family, but soon Abba was wandering around and talking to imaginary people. Everyone in town called him "the crazy man" but Samson knew that he was sick. He loved his Abba, but it made him sad the way people looked down on them. He was secretly glad that his Abba had forgotten all about the synagogue before they had gone very far.

Mother and the boys arrived and went up into the balcony where the women and children worshiped. The men worshiped on the main floor. Samson and Solomon stood by the balcony railing so they could see what was happening on the main floor while Mother sat with their two younger brothers and visited with the other women.

They were excited to see that Mr. Jesus was teaching that morning. Maybe they could talk with him afterward and tell him what God had done for them. They wanted to thank him for telling them what to do.

Mr. Jesus was in the middle of his teaching when the Bible says that someone cried out:

> **"Go away! What do you want with us, Jesus of Nazareth? Have you come to destroy us? I know who you are — the Holy One of God!"[3]**

Samson and Solomon froze in fear because they recognized their Abba's voice. They heard Mother crying. They were bracing for the hateful words that they expected from the Ruler of the synagogue and from their neighbors.

But Mr. Jesus looked up and smiled when he caught Samson's eye. Then he turned to the man and said,

> **"Be quiet!" Jesus said sternly. "Come out of him!" Then the demon threw the man down before them all and came out without injuring him.[4]**

Samson and Solomon watched as their Abba fell to the floor and then began to cry at Mr. Jesus' feet. Mr. Jesus stooped down and talked with him quietly for a while. Then they watched as their Abba got up and walked slowly out of the synagogue.

Samson motioned to his mother that he was going home, and he told Solomon to stay with his mother. Samson walked as quickly as he could and caught up with his Abba. His Abba was quiet and calm.

He hugged Samson and told him he was sorry. They walked home together with Abba's arm around Samson's shoulder.

When Mother and the younger boys arrived home, they found Samson and his Abba talking and laughing like old times. Mr. Jesus had healed their Abba.

Samson and Solomon arrived at work early on Sunday. They had seen Benji at the synagogue, so they were curious to hear what his reaction would be. They were not disappointed. Benji was so excited and happy for them. Together they repeated to each other all the great things that had happened since the day they had heard Mr. Jesus on the beach.

Now that school break was almost over, none of the boys wanted summer to end. They would continue to work for Mr. Zebedee after school every day, but there would never be another summer like this one!

_____

[1] Matthew 6:31-32
[2] Matthew 6:33
[3] Luke 4:34
[4] Luke 4:35

Jesus Preaching on the Beach
Luke 5:1-3

The Miraculous Catch of Fish
Luke 5:4-7

Healing of the Demon Possessed Man
Mark 1:21-27

Chapter 10
THE STORY OF JUDITH

It was true: Judith was a "Daddy's girl." How she wished she was a boy so she could go with him into the woods. He chopped down trees, then used saws to turn the wood into usable lumber. He wasn't a carpenter. He was a lumberjack. He sold his wood to all the local carpenters. And Judith felt that her Abba was the strongest and bravest and best Abba in the whole world.

Every night after dinner, Abba would spend time swinging her around. Sometimes she would do backflips by walking up his legs while he held her hands tightly. She always felt safe in his arms. They made up new routines while her mother fussed that she was getting too old for such antics. She was only eight years old, but her mother said she should be behaving more like a lady and less like a monkey.

Judith knew that Abba loved all five of his girls, but she also knew that as the oldest, she was his favorite. She tagged along with him every chance she got.

Tonight would be special. Abba was chopping down trees in a new forest and would be extra hungry. Mother had let Judith make the bread all by herself. She had spent most of the day preparing it: mixing, kneading, and letting it rise. Now it was in the outside oven and would be perfect when Abba arrived for dinner. But her Abba didn't come.

Mother fed the little girls and encouraged Judith to eat, but Judith was old enough to know that something was terribly wrong. Mother said that the wagon had probably broken down and not to worry — but Judith could see that Mother's face was pale and she was trying not to show how worried she was.

Mother told Judith to watch her sisters so she could run to Uncle Nirel's house and ask him to check on Abba. It wasn't far and she was back quickly. She assured the girls that Uncle Nirel would go and help Abba get home. It was a long wait. Judith helped her mother get the little girls to bed, but Judith couldn't sleep. She brought her blanket into the living room and lay down, but sleep would not come. Now that the little girls were asleep, she and Mother both began to cry. But then they would wipe away their tears and say something like, "It's probably just a broken-down wagon. That wagon is really old."

It was after midnight when Uncle Nirel and three other friends carried her Abba into the house. A tree had fallen the wrong way and pinned him to the ground. He was in a lot of pain and they carried him to a blanket on the floor in the living room so that Mother could keep an eye on him. They had given him some strong wine to help ease the pain. Only time would tell whether his back would heal, and he would be able to walk again. There were no doctors back then who could help.

Mother sent Judith to bed and brought her own blanket to be beside her husband. She took care of him all though the night and prayed that God would heal her husband. *How can I raise five girls without a husband? And if he lives, will he ever be able to walk again?* So many questions, such a long night.

But that night turned into weeks and then into months as Mother and Judith took turns nursing him. They took turns rubbing his legs and exercising them, but his legs continued to shrivel and grow weaker and his pain just seemed to get worse.

Judith had always been close to her Abba, but now she spent as much time with him as possible. He seemed to be in less pain when she would entertain him with stories or questions. One day she asked, "Abba, where was God when that tree fell on you? Why didn't he protect you?" And even though she was so young, he answered her as honestly as he knew how.

"Judith, I think that God was in Heaven just like he always is. He could have stopped that tree from falling, but I believe that both good and bad things happen, and we shouldn't blame God for them. I was the one who was careless and cut into a rotten tree so that it fell the wrong way. That's not God's fault."

"But why didn't he protect you?"

"Maybe he did! The tree could have landed on my head or my neck, and then I wouldn't be here listening to your questions, and your mother would be raising you girls all alone."

Another question that Judith asked during this time was, "Abba, what did you do to deserve this? Did you do something bad? Some of the ladies at the well told Mother that you must have done something bad for God to cause this to happen."

"Oh, Judith, I'm sorry that you and Mother have to put up with the gossips at the well. I don't think God caused this to happen. It was an accident. You need to not listen to those people. I hope you'll grow up to love God and know that he loves you."

Abba often entertained the girls with stories that he had learned at Hebrew school. He told them stories about God's love for his people Israel. He told them about Noah, and Abraham, and Joseph, and Moses, and Daniel. And he told them that someday God would send a Messiah to help them understand him better.

Judith loved learning about God and asked more and more questions. Her Abba didn't always know the answers, but he tried to help her understand that God loved her and cared about her. He cared about what was happening in their lives.

One way that Abba said he knew that God was watching over them was through their four closest friends. If it had not been for Uncle Nirel and Abba's three carpenter buddies, Mr. Haran, Mr. Mica and Mr. Isaac, Mother would have gone crazy with worry. But these four men and their wives would drop off food and provide help around the house. They took turns visiting Abba just about every evening and tried to cheer him up.

Abba had quite a bit of wood stored in his back yard that was ready for sale. The men sold it for him as he needed the money.

One morning, when Judith arrived home from the well, she found all four men talking with Mother. She knew that it was a workday, and she was terrified that Abba had died. She screamed for them to tell her what was going on. They assured her that they were just discussing a possibility for her Abba. They invited her to sit down and join the discussion.

Mr. Haran and Mr. Mica told Judith that they had gone to hear the new prophet Jesus yesterday. They listened to his teaching and were amazed that he had healed many, many people. So now they were trying to convince the others that if they could somehow transport her Abba to where Jesus was teaching, that Jesus would heal him. Mr. Haran and Mr. Mica had called them all together to talk with Mother and Abba. They needed Abba to decide what they should do.

Abba said he was willing to try anything. Mother was less supportive since every little movement seemed to make Abba's pain worse. The four men reminded her that they were running out of options since all the wood had been sold and there was no more income. When she reluctantly agreed, the next question was how to transport him.

The men decided the safest way would be to carry him on his blanket. They would use two or three blankets since he was a large man, and they didn't want the blankets to tear. Then each would carry a corner like a stretcher.

First, they needed to find out where Jesus was teaching that day. Since Mr. Haran and Mr. Mica knew who they were looking for, they set out to find where Jesus was. They quickly located him and came back to report that the house where Jesus was teaching was just a little more than a mile away.

The four men helped Mother stack three blankets so they wouldn't tear under his weight. Then the men lifted her Abba onto it. Judith covered her ears because she couldn't stand to hear her Abba scream out in pain. Then the four men lifted him up by the four corners.

"I'm going with them," Judith called to her mother. She didn't wait for a response. She walked alongside her Abba as the men carried him carefully on his blanket. Mother stayed home with the younger girls.

When they finally reached the place where Jesus was teaching, the house was packed and the yard was full. There was no way they could get close to Jesus. They laid the blanket down in the dirt and sat down to try to figure out the next step. Mr. Haran lay down to stretch out his back (carrying a full-grown man for over a mile was hard work — even for a carpenter). They could hear Jesus teaching inside the house.

Just then, Mr. Haran sat up and yelled, "I've got it!" The crowd around them all turned and stared, and he apologized for being noisy. He whispered, "Mica, your shop is closest to here. Do you have some rope? We would need four pieces. Each piece would need to be about 15 to 20 feet long."

"Yeah, I should have. Why?"

"Do you see that roof up there?" It was a flat roof where families would go to sit in the evenings. "I think we could tear out the tiles and let Ezra down through the roof. We're carpenters — we can fix the roof easily and there's no way that Jesus can miss seeing his need."

"Let's do it!" all four of them agreed. So, while Mr. Mica ran to his shop to find the ropes, Mr. Isaac, Uncle Nirel and Mr. Haran pushed their way through the crowd to the stairs and started quietly making a hole in the roof.

Judith stayed with her Abba. She wanted to cheer him up but couldn't think of anything to say because the movement had really made his pain much worse.

Finally, she asked, "Abba, do you really think this man could be the Messiah?"

"I don't know, Judith, but Mr. Haran and Mr. Mica think so, and they said that they saw him healing lots of people yesterday. I just know that I feel hope and I'm trusting that God is guiding us to the right place." That made Judith feel better.

When Mr. Mica got back with the ropes, he and Judith tied one to each corner of the stretcher. They tied it as tightly as they could, but it still looked like the blankets would slip off when they lifted her Abba. After some experimenting, they made it secure by tying the corners of the blankets around the ropes so that there was no way the blankets could slip off.

When the hole in the roof was large enough, the men came down and began to carry Judith's Abba up the stairs. That was the hard part! It was difficult to keep his bed level and every jolt was very painful. Then they very carefully let him down into the hole with the ropes. Judith had followed the men up the stairs and was peeking down into the hole.

She heard the crowd gasp when they realized that a man was being let down on a blanket. She watched as they began to push out of the way so that there was a place for him to land. When the blankets hit the floor, her Abba screamed in pain. Judith held her breath as Mr. Jesus stepped toward her Abba and said:

".... Get up, take your mat and go home.[1]"

Judith and her Abba's friends watched in amazement as he stood to his feet. He leaned over and picked up the blankets and ropes. He hugged Mr. Jesus and then the crowd parted to let him walk through. Everyone was amazed.

Judith raced down the stairs with the men close behind her.

"Abba, Abba, are you okay?"

"Okay?" Abba grabbed Judith and swung her around. "Yes, precious Daughter, but I'm better than okay!

"Come on, let's go tell your mother!"

Uncle Nirel and Judith tried to keep up with Abba as he practically ran home. Mr. Mica, Mr. Haran and Mr. Isaac went back to repair the roof before they joined them.

Judith and her little sisters were dancing and singing. Everyone wanted to hear over and over what Mr. Jesus had said and done. It was hard to believe that only hours earlier Abba had been in such pain and his legs so shriveled that it was impossible for him to stand. Now he was dancing with Mother.

It was decided that instead of working tomorrow, the entire family and the four friends and their families would go and listen to Jesus teach. They had questions about this prophet who could heal so completely. But Judith knew, without a shadow of a doubt, that this man was sent by God to heal her Abba.

---

[1] **Matthew 9:6**

Friends Bring a Crippled Man to Jesus
Mark 2:1-4

Jesus Heals the Crippled Man
Luke 5:20-25

Chapter 11
THE STORY OF JOEL

"I don't want grapes, I want pomegranates! And hurry back, I might need you."

Helak sighed as he took the grapes back to the kitchen and asked the servant for pomegranates instead. Everyone in the kitchen understood that Master Joel was just being Master Joel. They hurried to do his bidding, because he could have them beaten or sold if they displeased him.

When Helak returned with the pomegranates, Master Joel seemed satisfied, but declared that he needed help finding the ball he was playing with yesterday. Helak knew that Joel deliberately hid the ball because it entertained him to watch the servants try to find it. But he had no choice but to play along.

Joel was the son of one of the wealthiest men in town. His dad was Matthew Levi, a tax collector. Joel's every desire was met, and servants attended his every need. He didn't go to Hebrew school — Hebrew school came to him. He had a private tutor who tried to persuade him to learn, but Joel wanted someone else to do that for him, too.

All the servants agreed that Joel was on the fast track to total failure if his parents didn't make some changes soon. Joel was 12 years old and could not even dress himself — or so he claimed. About the only thing he had mastered was feeding himself and complaining about how everyone else did their work. Little did they know that even at this moment, Joel's dad was listening to Jesus and amazing changes were about to happen.

That night at dinner, Joel and his sister Janica were delighted to be entertained by their dad's description of a new teacher named Jesus that he had heard. Dad kept saying that he was more than just a prophet; Jesus was the Messiah sent from God.

Then he dropped the bombshell: "I have decided to follow Jesus. I will no longer be collecting taxes. There will be some changes around here. Your mother and I need to talk privately, so please go to your rooms and let us discuss some things."

"But Dad, we haven't had dessert!" whined Joel.

"How about if I have it sent to your room?" Dad gave the signal to the servants to do so and Joel and Janica were dismissed.

"What do you think that's all about?" Joel asked Janica.

"I don't know. I don't see how a new teacher could make Dad so excited. And what did he mean there would be changes?" Neither child realized that their lives were about to be turned upside down.

The next day all seemed as usual. Dad was gone all day and the household seemed to be running normally. But that night, Dad had a new announcement that sounded a lot more exciting.

They were going to throw a party for all their friends. It would be a grand event and everyone they knew would be invited. It was planned for Sunday night, and extra servants were hired to help with the preparations.

All week, Joel and Janica watched as the outdoor courtyard was prepared. Banqueting tables were lined along the walls. Servants were everywhere. Joel and Janica were glad that they had their private servants, otherwise no one would have had time to take care of their personal needs.

The Sabbath day was a day of rest, and mid-afternoon Dad said that he needed to talk with Joel and Janica. They both expected a lecture about being on their best behavior with their guests at the party and were not at all prepared for what their dad and mother had to say.

"I am totally convinced that Jesus is the Messiah promised by God. We have waited for him for over 1700 years. I have seen him heal the blind, make the deaf hear and the mute speak. I <u>know</u> he's no ordinary man and I have decided to follow him. If what I understand about the Scripture is true, then he will overthrow Rome and make Israel a free nation again. That means it could be a dangerous time before we get the victory, but I believe that God is on our side.

"I know that this will greatly impact your lives, and that makes it the hardest decision I've ever made. Your mother and I agree that we need to follow Jesus wherever he goes. It will be a great adventure. It will be hard. It will be fun. It could be dangerous. But it's something that we have decided we must do.

"Instead of being a tax collector, I will simply be following Jesus and learning as much as I can about him and about God's plan for the overthrow of Rome."

Joel and Janica sat in silence. They didn't know what to say. Finally, Joel asked, "Don't we have a say in this?"

His dad looked him right in the eyes and said, "You do not have a say in our decision to follow Jesus. And since you are not yet 13 years old, you are required by Roman law to be with us.

"I know that once you meet Jesus, you'll be convinced that this is the right decision. There's already a large group of men and women and their families following Jesus, so I know you'll make great friends. It will be a different kind of life — but it will be amazingly good. Just wait and see!"

But Joel was not convinced. "Is that all?" Joel asked rudely, then marched up to his room. He refused to come down to dinner and had Helak bring him a plate to his room. All day Sunday he stayed in his bed and pouted.

Early in the afternoon, Helak said that it was time for Master Joel to change into his party clothes. Helak helped Joel bathe and put on his fanciest clothes. Janica's servant was getting her ready, too. Soon the guests began to arrive. They were dressed in the finest and most fashionable dress available — much of it imported from Egypt. The finest foods and wines were served, and the musicians entertained superbly.

Dad brought Jesus over to meet Joel, and while Joel knew how to be socially polite, he was not impressed with this commoner. Joel had been taught to judge a person by their clothing and jewelry, and Jesus just wore the simple cloak of a peasant. Joel made it clear that he was not interested in speaking with Jesus.

Dad introduced Jesus to the crowd and invited him to speak, but Joel used that time to make his way to the dessert table one more time. He really wasn't interested in anything Jesus had to say.

But after Jesus spoke, Dad announced to all his friends that he had decided to follow Jesus and help him with his ministry. He would no longer be collecting taxes.

Then he announced that his estate was for sale or rent, so if there was anyone interested, please see him afterward. The crowd went crazy with questions. Matthew Levi was one of their own and they were shocked that he was taking this step.

Joel ordered Helak to take him to his room and prepare him for bed. He didn't intend to be humiliated in front of his friends. *What is Dad doing? Where will we live? What will happen to me?* He had never lived anywhere but in this mansion and he couldn't imagine anything different.

Each day after that announcement was a new nightmare for Joel. Servants were let go, slaves were released, and household goods were being sold so that the house was stripped bare.

Helak was still in charge of helping Joel pack — but Joel refused to cooperate. So, Helak prepared a traveling bag for Joel. Dad had told Joel that he should only take one bag and that he would be carrying it himself. It should include a couple of simple robes and a blanket and any small treasures that he would like to take.

Dad and Mother and even Janica seemed to be very excited about this new adventure. But Joel spent most of his time in bed, crying over the clothes and toys that Helak was packing for sale.

Once the house was sold, Helak and the other servants were let go. Dad had made sure that they were placed in good positions. Then the family walked out of their now empty mansion. Three were looking forward with joy in their hearts and one was looking backward, crying his eyes out.

Joel had never carried his own bag and had not walked more than a quarter of a mile in his life. He had always been carried on a litter by servants. His feet hurt, his arms hurt, his neck hurt, the sun was hot, he was hungry, he was thirsty, and his feet <u>really</u> hurt bad.

"Joel, I think your feet wouldn't hurt so much if you would take off those ridiculous sandals. Walking barefoot is so much more comfortable and won't cause as many blisters," his dad suggested. But Joel insisted that only peasants went barefoot, even though both his mother and dad were now barefoot. He felt the sand would be too hot without his sandals. The truth was that his feet were so tender that the sand probably would have burned his feet, but the ornate sandals were rubbing blisters all over his heels and toes.

"How far is it and where are we going anyway?" grumbled Joel.

"We are going to the river today. It's not much further. There will be some shade and a place to sit while we listen to Jesus teach. I don't know where we'll stay tonight. We'll just follow wherever Jesus leads us."

When they finally arrived at the river, all the shady places had been taken and Joel found himself sitting in the dirt, thirsty, exhausted, and thoroughly confused. He had no intention of listening to Jesus and all he wanted was to put his feet in the river to cool them off. After a while, he decided that that's just what he would do.

He got up and made his way to the water's edge. He didn't know how to swim, so he very gingerly put first one foot and then the other into the water. It felt wonderful.

Other kids were playing in the shallow water to try to keep cool. They were splashing and laughing and having fun since they were far enough away to not disturb Jesus' teaching. Joel tried to carefully walk along the rocks, but his sandals were slippery, and without warning he sat down with a splash! The other kids laughed and that made Joel mad. He was embarrassed and didn't know how to deal with the other kids. He told them to go away and leave him alone. So, they did.

That night everyone was given a piece of bread and some cheese for dinner. And even though Joel complained, it really tasted good because he hadn't been snacking all day like he did at home. But when he was told to unpack his blanket and stretch out on the ground, he lost it. He was terrified of spiders or scorpions or snakes or fleas or whatever else might be in the dirt. He was sunburned, his feet were covered in blisters, he didn't have a bed or a pillow, and most of all, he was angry. And the person he was most angry at was Jesus. He was the cause of all this!

Jesus taught along the Sea of Galilee all that week and Joel spent most of his time sitting in the shallow water trying to keep cool and making sure he couldn't hear what Jesus was saying. But on Friday morning, Jesus announced that they were going to Cana for the Sabbath.

No!!!!!!!!!!!!!!!!!!!!

Joel didn't know how much more of this torture he could take. And he didn't know that it would get worse before it got better.

The blisters that were beginning to heal broke open and bled so that his feet were a bloody mess. The sunburn that had begun to peel reburned the fresh new skin. And the muscles that had never walked a mile now had to walk 16.

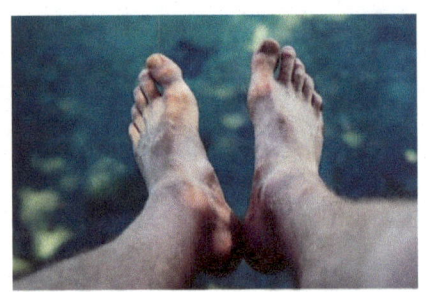

Let's just skip over the things that Joel had to say to his parents, his sister, and all those around him who would listen. We'll just say, he was one unhappy little boy.

Dad and Mother walked as slowly as they could so Joel wouldn't be left behind, but they knew that Joel would have to deal with his own anger. They couldn't help him with that, and they couldn't carry him. It was time for Joel to grow up.

Janica had already made lots of friends and asked permission to run ahead with them. Her parents were pleased with her attitude and prayed for the day when Joel would understand their decision to follow Jesus.

They had to admit that their feet hurt, too. They, too, had led a cushy life and walking 16 miles in a day was not their habit. Dad usually sat at his tax collecting booth and Mother had servants to do all her housework. She had mostly socialized with friends or busied herself with sewing projects.

By the time they arrived in Cana, they were late for dinner, but their host graciously made a plate for each of them and helped them to find a place to throw their blankets. When Dad saw Joel's bleeding feet, he found a pan of water and washed them gently. He finally convinced Joel to throw away his fancy sandals and let his feet heal naturally. But nothing he could say or do could ease Joel's anger.

On the Sabbath morning, the disciples that were following Jesus crowded into the local synagogue to hear Jesus teach, but Joel refused to get up. He pulled his blanket over his head and stayed put. By mid-morning he realized that he was very hungry, but there was no one around to prepare him breakfast.

As the people began to return from their worship time, Joel just pulled the blanket over his head tighter and tried to pretend he wasn't there. Over and over, total strangers would ask if he was okay, or if they could bring him something. Joel just pulled the blanket tighter over his head and refused to answer.

By mid-afternoon he was so hot and thirsty, he knew he had to get up and get a drink of water. When he tried to walk, the pain was unbearable, and he sat back down.

"Hey, is there something I can get you?" asked a young man that didn't look much older than Joel.

"Yeah, a new life!"

"My name is Yanis. Let me bring you a cup of water. Maybe that will make you feel better." And before Joel could think of a nasty retort, Yanis was gone.

In a few minutes he returned with a cup of water and a couple of apricots. He plopped down beside Joel and took a bite of the fruit. "Man, your feet look terrible!"

"Thanks! Do you have any other helpful comments?" retorted Joel.

"Hey, I didn't mean to offend you. I remember how bad my feet felt when I first started following Jesus. But it gets easier. What's your name?"

"Joel and no. There's no way <u>this</u> will get easier. Jesus has totally wrecked my life. My family has gone berserk. The only home I've ever known has been sold. My personal servant is not here, and I'm supposed to follow Jesus around and wear peasant clothes! And my feet hurt!"

Usually people took the hint and moved away from Joel, but not Yanis. Very quietly he said, "My story is very similar to yours. My dad is a priest. My four brothers and I were all studying to be priests. But I heard John the prophet preaching and I was there the day he baptized and introduced Jesus as the Messiah. I got so excited. I couldn't wait to get home and tell my dad. He wasn't happy. He ordered me to quit going to listen to Jesus teach, but as I searched the Scripture, I just became more and more convinced that Jesus really was the Messiah.

"On my 13th birthday, what should have been the happiest day of my life, my dad told me to choose between him or Jesus. I said that I believed that Jesus was the Messiah. I won't bore you with the details — but I was kicked out of my house and my dad said to never come back. My mother secretly gave me a blanket and a bag of food. I didn't know what to do. I wandered around town for a couple of days thinking that they would change their minds.

"But then I decided to go to Jerusalem. Man, my feet hurt. I had to beg for food, and sleep wherever I could. When I got to Jerusalem, I went to the olive garden and there I met this group of Jesus' disciples. They took care of me. Jesus healed my feet and has been providing for me ever since. I miss my family, but Jesus has given me a new family and a new purpose that I never felt when I lived at home.

"Hey, Esau, what's up? Come meet Joel." And with that another boy who looked a little younger than Joel plopped down on the other side of him.

"Where'd you get the apricot? I'm starving!" asked Esau.

Yanis replied, "I've got my connections."

When Esau agreed, Yanis added, "Just go to that door right there and ask. They just about always have something if you are hungry."

When Esau left to check out the snack, Yanis told Joel, "We stick together here and help each other."

Soon Esau was back with yet another friend. He was introduced as Enid, and the four boys sat and talked and got acquainted as only boys can. At dinner time, the boys brought Joel a plate and sat down to eat together. At bedtime, they brought their blankets and surrounded him with the first real friendships he had ever known.

The next morning, they helped Joel walk to where Jesus was teaching and for the first time, Joel really listened. He heard Jesus teach:

> **"Do not store up for yourselves treasures on earth ... where thieves break in and steal. But store up for yourselves treasures in heaven ... where thieves do not break in and steal. For where your treasure is, there your heart will be also.[1]**
>
> **No one can serve two masters. Either you will hate the one and love the other, or you will be devoted to the one and despise the other. You cannot serve both God and money.[2]"**

After Jesus finished teaching, crowds of people gathered around, and he began healing the sick. Joel was amazed at what he saw. This was no magic trick. These were hopelessly sick people that were being made well. He saw a man whose arm was shriveled, and Jesus made it whole again — just like brand new. Joel was shocked. I guess his face showed it because when Jesus got a break, he walked over to where the boys were sitting.

He plopped down beside them and called each one of them by name. When he looked at Joel, he said, "Welcome Joel, son of Matthew. I'm glad you have decided to follow me. Now I think we'd better take care of those feet before they get worse, don't you?"

And before Joel could think of a reply, Jesus touched his sore feet, and they became strong. The blisters were gone, the bloody places were gone, and in their place was strong, sturdy skin that looked like he had walked barefoot all his life — instead of the sickly white tender skin that was there before.

Then Jesus talked to the four boys as if nothing significant had just happened. "We're leaving for Jerusalem tomorrow. I want you boys to stick together and teach Joel some of the fun stuff along the way. I don't believe he's ever been fishing or eaten what he's caught. Take care of each other, have fun, but take it slow. Joel's muscles aren't quite as strong as they will be in a few weeks."

"Yes, sir," they all replied.

"Is Phillip going with us?" asked Yanis.

Phillip was one of the followers of Jesus. He was married, but he often hung out with the younger guys and was a lot of fun to be with.

"I'll see if he wants to go with you guys or whether he thinks you four can handle it alone," said Jesus.

Joel couldn't wait to try out his new feet — because that's what they felt like. He could run and jump, and they didn't hurt. He searched to find his parents to tell them the good news. They were thrilled, not only with the change in his feet, but also the change in his attitude. And they quickly gave him permission to travel with "the boys" tomorrow.

Early the next morning, each boy was given an extra bag to carry containing bread and fruit and cheese and Yanis' bag contained a frying pan to cook the fish they hoped to catch along the way.

Philip joined them and brought his young son, Jordan. It took a week for them to reach Jerusalem, but Joel could not remember ever having so much fun. He learned about God's creation and being a part of the family of Jesus. Each day he grew stronger physically and emotionally. What a difference Jesus brought into his life! And how grateful he was that Yanis and his friends had not avoided him for his bad attitude.

---

[1] **Matthew 6:19-21**
[2] **Matthew 6:24**

Jesus Called Matthew
Luke 5:27-28

Matthew Threw a Party
Luke 5:29-32

Jesus Healed the Sick
Matthew 4:23-24

**Jesus Taught About
True Treasure**
Matthew 6:19-24

Chapter 12
THE STORY OF LAILA

"Laila!"

"Coming, Zaydee," replied Laila. (Zaydee is the Jewish word for Grandmother.)

"I need you to go back to the market and see if you can still find some good radishes. I know that your Abba loves radishes and I forgot to get them.

"And while you are there, see if Mr. Raul has more pomegranates. He was out this morning but said his son would pick more later today. I hope he's not sold out again."

"Is there anything else, Zaydee? Everything smells so good in here. You are cooking a feast for Abba and Mr. Jesus! How many people will be coming for Sabbath dinner?"

"I don't know, Laila, but run to the market quickly and we'll talk later."

"Yes, Zaydee, but I will need coins to purchase things."

"Forgetful, forgetful. I can't seem to remember my own head! Here's the coins. Now hurry."

"Laila, can we go with you?" called her two little brothers.

"Not this time, I've got to hurry or the market will be closed. I'll try to take you next time." Her little brothers loved going to the market with her, but didn't get to go often now that they were in Hebrew school. "Be good while I'm gone and don't bother Zaydee."

"We won't," they replied together.

Laila wondered whether they were saying they wouldn't be good, or that they wouldn't bother Zaydee — but she had to hurry, so she let it go.

Laila was thrilled to be out of the house and pretending to be the woman in charge. She was 11 years old and would probably be married and have her own home in a couple of years, but she liked to dream that that day had already come. With the shopping basket over her arm, she hurried to the market and quickly found the radishes, but Mr. Raul had already packed up and gone home. There would be no pomegranates today. She decided to purchase some dates and hoped that Zaydee would not be too disappointed.

Zaydee was pleased with the radishes, and thanked Laila for buying the dates. At least they would have some fruit to share with the guests. Laila was putting away the shopping basket when Zaydee called again, "Laila!"

"Yes, Zaydee. What do you need?"

"Laila, I just put the butter out for the bread. I forgot to churn more this morning. There's not enough butter! Would you have time to churn more before sundown?"

"I think so, but we would need fresh cream. The morning milk is spoiled by now."

"Run over to Mr. Jacobson's and see if he has any. They milk their goats twice a day so he should have some that's fresh. I'm so sorry, I'm so forgetful."

"Zaydee, it's no problem. Just let me get my jar, and I still have enough coins." Laila grabbed the milk jar and quickly ran out the kitchen door and across the pasture to Mr. Jacobson's house.

It was perfect timing because he was just finishing milking his goats and had fresh cream to pour into her jar. She thanked him, paid him the coins, and walked carefully back home so she wouldn't spill a drop.

When she got home, Zaydee was busy slicing the radishes and all seemed to be under control.

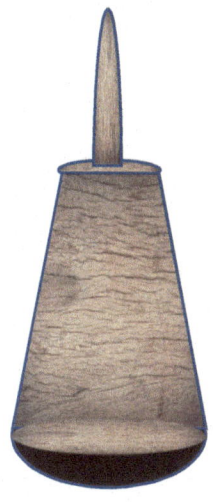

Laila quickly poured the cream from the goat's milk into the butter churn. Churning was hard work. She had to push the paddle up and down, and up and down, and up and down, until the milk thickened like whipped cream. She was out of breath and her hair kept falling into her face as she pumped. But finally, she felt the cream begin to thicken.

She decided to take a quick break and stepped outside to cool off her face. Then she had to finish the butter. She would need to continue to churn it until it became firm — which would take another 10 minutes of churning. But it was not close to sunset yet, so she knew she still had time before the Sabbath. When the butter was firm, she took it out and put it into the butter molds so that it would look pretty for their guests.

Then she could breathe.

She had just sat down when she heard, "Laila, come help me get the cucumbers sliced and I think we will be all done."

"Coming, Zaydee. Have you already sliced the onions?"

"Yes, I did them earlier — that's what made me remember the radishes. What would I do without you, Laila?"

"What would we do without you, Zaydee? You have helped so much since you moved in with us." Laila quickly sliced the cucumbers and set them on the table. Now, they would just wait until Abba and Mr. Jesus and the others arrived. Then the house would once more be filled with laughter and fun.

Laila sat down again and remembered that morning a few months ago, when her Abba had told her that things were going to change. She had been so scared.

Her two little brothers were at Hebrew school and her older brother, Laban, was at work. Abba asked her and Zaydee to join him and Mother in the living room. He said that he had been listening to Jesus, and Jesus had called him to be one of his disciples, to follow him and learn from him. And Abba had said yes.

He told them about the miracle catch of fish, and how he was convinced that Jesus really was the Messiah sent from God. Now, he wouldn't be living a fisherman's life and leaving each night at sunset and returning each morning to spend his day with them. He would be gone for weeks at a time and would only see them when Jesus was teaching in Capernaum.

He promised that when Hebrew school was on break, the whole family could come and travel with him if they wanted to. They had a lot of questions, but Laila could tell that Abba was very happy. This would be a great opportunity for Abba because Mr. Jesus was apparently a very important man.

Then last night, Abba had stopped by the house to warn Mother that he had invited Jesus and all the disciples to eat the Sabbath meal with them the following night. He didn't know how long they would be in Capernaum, but he hoped he could spend a few days with them.

Mother was grateful for the warning because it allowed her, and Zaydee, and Laila, time to get enough food prepared for the group of disciples. Abba had already ordered fish from Uncle Zebedee, and he promised to be home early enough to cook it before the Sabbath started. Laila glanced out the door and realized he had better hurry! Since no one ever knew whether there would be 20 or 120 disciples traveling with Mr. Jesus, it was hard to know how many to prepare for.

Mother had baked bread all day today and was lying down resting while Zaydee and Laila finished the preparations. Laila went over in her head all the things that they had ready to serve. Mother had prepared the bread, and she and Zaydee had prepared the fish sauce, and the plates of vegetables, and the dates, and finally the butter.

"Laila!"

"Coming Zaydee. What did we forget?"

"I was just thinking that I had some grape jelly put aside. It would be nice to serve with the bread and butter. But I can't find it."

"Scoot back and let me look, Zaydee," said Laila. "I don't see it. Didn't we move that out to the storeroom? I'll run out there and check." She grabbed a lamp and went outside to the storeroom. Sure enough, there were several jars of grape jelly. She grabbed one, since that's all she could carry with the lamp in her hand. She called for her brothers to come to help, but they didn't respond. Maybe one jar would be enough. *But where are the boys? They should be in the courtyard.*

Just as she entered the house, Abba burst into the kitchen with his gigantic smile and hug for her. He kissed Zaydee gently on the cheek and then headed to the bedroom to find Mother. Thankfully, the boys had only moved to the front yard to wait for Abba. Laila took them with her to the storeroom to get more jelly. It looked like there would be a huge crowd tonight.

Soon the house was filled with people. The men were busy frying fish in the back courtyard, and everyone was helping to move the food outside. What fun it was to have Abba home. His boisterous laughter could be heard over everything else.

"Laila." Laila thought she heard a faint call from the house. She left the group and found Zaydee sitting alone in the kitchen. "Laila, I'm so tired. Could you help me get to my blanket? I feel too tired to walk. I'm afraid I'll fall."

"Of course, Zaydee. You've overdone. You've been on your feet all day and I should have helped you more. Here, take my arm."

Laila was worried because Zaydee usually had more energy than both Laila and her mother put together. And Zaydee loved being with Mr. Jesus. It seemed strange that she was choosing to rest instead.

"Did you eat something, Zaydee?"

"No, I just want to sleep."

So, Laila helped her to bed and offered to bring her a plate of food. When Zaydee refused, Laila promised to check on her to make sure she didn't need anything after she had rested a while. But when Laila went back to check on Zaydee, she was sleeping soundly. So, she left her and went back to the party that was in full swing in the courtyard.

Some of the followers of Mr. Jesus spent the night in the courtyard, while others went to Mr. Jesus' house and slept there. Some had relatives that they stayed with, and others still owned homes in Capernaum.

On Saturday morning, Abba and Mother were surprised to not find Zaydee in the kitchen setting out breakfast for the family. When Mother went to check, she found Zaydee still asleep, but something didn't look right.

Mother saw that Zaydee's face was flushed and she had thrown off her covers. She had a high fever and was mumbling about something that her husband had done. Since her husband had died many years earlier, Mother was rightly concerned.

"Laila!" called Mother. "Run to the well and bring me a jar of water and some cloths. Zaydee has a fever and we must get it down. All I know to do is to put cool wet cloths on her. And tell Abba I won't be able to go to synagogue with him. He'll have to leave the boys here since I'll need you to bring me water, and the boys can't go to synagogue unsupervised."

Abba and Mother whispered at the door and agreed that he would go on to synagogue for worship but would check on them afterward.

So instead of going to synagogue to hear Mr. Jesus teach, Laila found herself carrying jars of water to her mother who was taking care of Zaydee. And Laila was in charge of two very energetic little brothers.

She kept them busy cleaning up the courtyard even though it was the Sabbath. She told them it wasn't work — it was a game to see who could get their side the cleanest. It worked.

Each time she checked on Mother and took her fresh water, Zaydee looked worse. Laila was old enough to know that high fevers often led to death and she could tell that Mother was afraid. She gave her a hug and then returned to keep an eye on the boys.

About mid-afternoon Abba and Mr. Jesus returned from synagogue. Abba took over entertaining the boys, and Laila went with Mr. Jesus to Zaydee's room. Mother was crying and Zaydee looked awful. Mr. Jesus simply touched her hand and commanded the fever to leave. That was it. Zaydee opened her eyes, the natural color returned to her face, and the fever was gone.

Before Mother and Laila could speak, Zaydee was out of bed and asking Mr. Jesus if he was hungry. They all headed to the kitchen and Zaydee was pulling out the leftovers for anyone who needed a snack before dinner. It was as if the fever had never happened.

Here's what the Bible says happened:

> **When Jesus came into Peter's house, he saw Peter's mother-in-law lying in bed with a fever. He touched her hand and the fever left her, and she got up and began to wait on him.**[1]

Laila and Mother hugged, and Laila asked her mother if it was okay if she slipped away for just a few minutes. She wanted to walk along the beach and think. Her mother assured her it was okay but reminded her not to be gone too long or she would miss out on time with Abba and Mr. Jesus.

Laila walked down to the beach, and since it was the Sabbath, it was mostly deserted. No fishermen were at work, and other than a few others who wanted to be alone, she could walk in peace. *Who is this man that Abba follows? Abba said he was the Messiah. How did he just command the fever to leave? Who can do that? If he were really the Messiah, wouldn't he be somber and serious all the time like the priests and Pharisees? Mr. Jesus is more like Abba — always laughing and joking and teasing. He is a fun man to be around and so very, very kind. I have never met anyone like him.*

She realized that the sun was getting lower in the sky, and they would need to eat dinner before the sun set because usually Mr. Jesus was ready to travel once the Sabbath had ended. She knew she would be needed to help serve the food, even though they would do no cooking on the Sabbath.

When she arrived home, she found that several of the other disciples were already helping Mother and Zaydee set out the leftovers. Zaydee was peppering Mr. Jesus with all kinds of questions about God and Heaven and he seemed to be delighted to answer her questions.

How does he know the answers? Laila wondered.

> **At sunset, the people brought to Jesus all who had various kinds of sickness, and laying his hands on each one, he healed them. 2**

They were bringing sick people to Mr. Jesus, and right there in Laila's own backyard Mr. Jesus began to heal them. One by one, he touched men and women who had leprosy — a disease that destroyed the skin and nerves and was very contagious. Laila realized that she had never seen anyone <u>touch</u> a leper. That was unheard of. But Mr. Jesus did. And he made the blind to see, and the deaf to hear, and the mute to speak, and he made crippled legs strong, and crippled arms straight. And he ordered the demons to leave people alone and they became sane and whole. It took Laila's breath away.

"What are you thinking, my precious daughter?" Abba asked as he put his arm around Laila.

She turned her eyes to meet his and he saw the tears in her eyes. "I believe he must be God himself. No one can do what he does."

Peter squeezed his daughter and his heart felt that it would burst. First his wife had believed, then her mother, and now his daughter. How he prayed that his three sons would soon decide to follow Jesus.

_____

[1] **Matthew 8:14-15**
[2] **Luke 4:40**

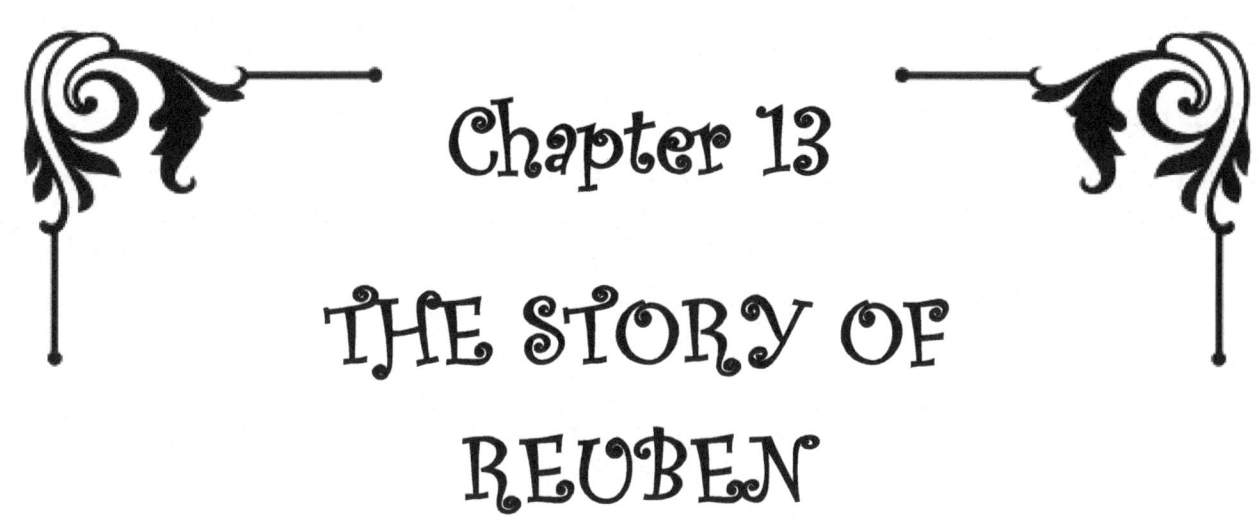

Chapter 13
THE STORY OF REUBEN

"Reuben, I would like to speak with you after class."

"Yes, Rabbi," replied Reuben, wondering what that was all about. He couldn't recall messing up on anything — at least not recently. He had given a report on the teachings of Jeremiah yesterday, maybe he had spoken incorrectly on something. For the rest of the day, his mind continued to wonder why the rabbi would want to meet with him. But finally the school day ended, and Reuben was left alone with Rabbi Adar.

"You wanted to see me, Rabbi?" Reuben asked politely.

"Yes, Reuben, but I assure you it is all good. I just wanted to know what your plans are for the future. You are one of the finest students I have ever taught, and all the other rabbis agree.   You are almost through with your studies here. Remember that you will be expected to announce your plans for your future on your 13th birthday. I'm not pressuring you — you still have some time to decide — but I was just wondering if I could answer any questions or help you in any way. Have you given it some thought?"

"Yes, Rabbi. I feel strongly that I would like to continue my studies and become a scribe. I love studying the Jewish Scripture and my heart tells me that I would be happiest doing that full-time. I don't know whether that will be possible, I mean, I will need to secure a rabbi to teach me, but...."

"Reuben, there will be no problem with you finding a rabbi to teach you. You are an outstanding student. Your study on Jeremiah was very thorough and I must say, I learned more from you than I have taught you.

"Your dad and I talked a few days ago about your Bar Mitzvah (a special party for Jewish boys when they turn 13). That's just a few months away. Have you chosen the Scripture that you will recite?"

"Yes, Rabbi Adar. I have chosen Psalm 119. Every verse is about King David's love for the Holy Scriptures, and I want to express that at my Bar Mitzvah."

"But Reuben, there are 150 verses! You have chosen a very difficult passage to memorize. You could choose something simpler and still fulfill the requirements."

"But, Rabbi, I've already got it memorized. It is so beautiful to me and I've been working hard on it."

"Then, I have no doubt, it will be perfect. I just wanted to speak to you about these two things so that you will be ready for your special day."

"Thank you, Rabbi Adar. I believe that I will be ready."

"Have a good night, Reuben. You have made me very proud."

Reuben and his mother were alarmed that Bartholomew, Reuben's Abba, had not arrived for dinner. They had finally decided to eat without him. When he arrived, he apologized for being late and quickly joined them.

"I saw the most amazing thing a while ago. I can't get it out of my mind. I've actually been walking around to try to clear my head. I had finished repairing a wagon and decided to come home early when I ran into a rather large crowd down by Mr. Abel's house. I was just standing there waiting for them to pass when a leper came out of nowhere and bowed down at a man's feet. The leper didn't cry, 'Unclean, unclean!' but he was terribly deformed by the leprosy. He was obviously in the final stages because there wasn't much left of him. His nose and lips and ears were all eaten off by the leprosy. His fingers were just bones. It was hideous.

"I jumped back and so did everyone else in the crowd. But he was bowing at the feet of a man named Jesus — at least that's what someone told me."

"Abba, I've heard about this man! He's a fake claiming to be the Messiah!" exclaimed Reuben.

"Son, let me tell you what I saw with my own two eyes."

"Yes, Abba, I'm sorry for interrupting you. I do want to hear what happened."

"I was shocked that Jesus didn't move away from him and he didn't stop him from worshiping him. But I was trapped by the crowd and couldn't move away — and besides, I wanted to know what would happen."

> A man with leprosy came and knelt before him and said, "Lord, if you are willing, you can make me clean."
>
> Jesus reached out his hand and touched the man. "I am willing," he said. "Be clean!" Immediately he was cleansed of his leprosy. [1]

"I was so shocked. Jesus reached out and touched him. And when he spoke, the leprosy just disappeared. This man's face returned; his hands returned right there before my eyes. He was completely healed. His nose and lips and ears looked perfectly normal. His fingers and hands were just — just normal looking.

"I didn't know what to do. The crowd was getting bigger, and very excited. I finally broke away from them so that I could think more clearly. I walked down to the beach because I needed some quiet. I've never seen anything like this!"

"Bartholomew, was it some kind of trick? Could it have been staged?" asked Mother.

"I don't see any way that it could have been. My eyes and my heart tell me that I saw something that was from God."

"Abba, don't say such things!"

"Son!"

"I'm sorry, I was wrong to speak to you that way." But Reuben was concerned that his Abba had been deceived, and he loved him and wanted him to be safe.

The last few months before Reuben's 13th birthday were strange and stressful. His Abba was going to listen to Jesus teach as often as he could slip away from his business. Rabbi Adar was afraid that Reuben was being influenced by his Abba and Jesus' teachings. So, Reuben was being watched closely at school. All the rabbis were questioning him and demanding that he defend his beliefs. They didn't want Reuben to start following Jesus when he had such a promising future as a scribe and teacher of the Law.

One evening about a month before the big event, Abba announced at dinner, "I have decided that once you have turned 13 and are settled under your new rabbi, I will sell my shop and follow my new rabbi, Jesus. Mother has decided that she will travel with me, and together we will follow him wherever he leads us."

Reuben's heart sank. He felt that he had lost both of his parents to a false religion that would destroy their relationship with God. Nothing could have made him sadder — and yet, his parents didn't seem sad. If anything, his Abba was happier than he had ever seen him. He was filled with a peace and joy that was real and made him seem more alive than ever.

Reuben was grateful that at least the move would not happen before the Bar Mitzvah. He was looking forward to that special celebration. Everyone from the local synagogue was invited, and all his relatives.

The month passed quickly and Reuben's birthday and last day of school arrived. When he got home that Thursday, the house was a beehive of activity. Servants had been hired to help set up the courtyard for the party, and the kitchen was filled with all kinds of wonderful treats being prepared. Bread and meat were being cooked outside and everything smelled wonderful. Reuben felt like a king getting ready for his coronation — until Mother asked him to make sure the ceremonial water jars were filled.

Soon after noon on Friday, the guests started to arrive, servants were setting out the food, and the party began. When some of his school friends arrived, Reuben organized a ball game off to one side of the courtyard.

Families from the synagogue arrived and the courtyard was almost filled with the rabbis from his school and their families and Reuben's relatives from all over Galilee. One aunt and uncle had traveled all the way from Jerusalem to be there. When Jesus arrived with seven other disciples that were close friends of his dad's, there was a distinct murmur in the crowd. But Jesus was a delightful guest and soon had everyone relaxed and laughing again. Even the rabbis and Pharisees found him a delightful man to be around.

After dinner, Rabbi Adar led the ceremony, and several of Reuben's other teachers spoke about his excellent study of Jewish Scripture. When Reuben was called upon to recite his Scripture, he was able to do all 150 verses without stumbling (actually, he missed a couple of words — but no one noticed except himself and maybe Jesus).

Then Rabbi Adar announced to the crowd that Reuben, son of Bartholomew, was officially a man according to Jewish law. He asked Reuben to declare what he had decided to do with his life.

Reuben cleared his throat and suddenly felt incredibly nervous. All night it had been a fun celebration, but now the seriousness of the moment hit him, and he couldn't get his throat to work.

The crowd seemed to sense that something had changed in Reuben and they became very quiet. That made Reuben feel even more nervous. But as he accepted the cup of water his mother handed him, he steadied himself and addressed the crowd.

"Family and friends, I hereby declare that to the best of my understanding, God has called me to be a scribe. I want to continue my studies of God's Word for the rest of my life and I hope to someday teach it to others."

The crowd broke out in approval, clapping and cheering. The rabbis looked relieved that they had successfully taught this one well.

But Reuben was not finished, and he held up his hand asking for quiet.

"I have made another decision that I also want to announce. I feel that as a student of God's Word, it is my responsibility to check out this one who claims to be our Messiah. So, Jesus, Sir, if it is all right with you, I would like to travel with you and hear your teachings so that I can compare them to our Jewish Scripture. I am asking the rabbis to allow me a break in my studies while I investigate your claims. It is my intention to continue my studies no later than one year from today."

There was no applause, only a quiet gasp and then just quiet talking among themselves. Jesus and his friends were polite enough to not make a scene. But Reuben found himself being nearly squeezed in two by his Abba and Mother. He knew that they were pleased with this decision that he had kept a complete surprise.

The rabbis assured Reuben that he would always be welcome to resume his studies but expressed their displeasure at his decision to take such a break.

The party broke up fairly soon afterward, but Jesus and his friends stayed and talked to Reuben and welcomed him. They invited him to explore and ask any questions he desired. And he felt certain that he had made the right decision. He must find truth and the only way he knew to do that was to study the Scripture and investigate for himself.

During the next week, it was decided that a cousin who had trained under Reuben's dad would take over the shop and also rent the house since he was planning to be married soon. With that taken care of, there was nothing left to do but to pack a traveling bag and begin their new life.

Jesus and his disciples were on their way to Jerusalem and had already left. Reuben was not used to long walks and neither was his mother, so they took it slowly. It was a very sweet time of companionship for the three of them. Reuben felt freer to ask questions about his dad's beliefs now that he was 13 and was considered to be a man.

They talked about many things, but also just enjoyed this time away from work and school and responsibilities. It took them a whole week to get to Jerusalem and they found the disciples camped in the olive garden. The next day they were able to follow Jesus around the city.

That morning, Jesus led the group to the Pool of Bethesda.   There were many crippled and sick people gathered around the pool. Most believed that the water of the pool would make them well. Even though there were lots of people there who needed help, Jesus went to one man and healed him.

Here's what the Bible says:

> **Here a great number of disabled people used to lie — the blind, the lame, the paralyzed. One who was there had been an invalid for thirty-eight years.   When Jesus saw him lying there and learned that he had been in this condition for a long time, he asked him, "Do you want to get well?"**
>
> **"Sir," the invalid replied, "I have no one to help me into the pool ...."**
>
> **Then Jesus said to him, "Get up! Pick up your mat and walk." At once the man was cured; he picked up his mat and walked....[2]**

Reuben looked at his dad and his dad shrugged his shoulders but didn't say a word. He wanted Reuben to come to his own conclusions. Reuben found John, one of Jesus' closest friends and asked if he had time to answer some questions.

"Sure, what's up?"

"I guess I just saw my first healing. I've got some questions," admitted Reuben.

"Yeah, it's a little shocking at first. But you'll see lots more!" assured John.

"But why did Jesus heal this man? I mean, he didn't seem to be a follower of his. There were lots of other people who needed to be healed. Why did Jesus heal this guy? And he didn't even say thank you!"

"Well, you'd have to ask Jesus. But what I've learned is that Jesus has compassion on all people. He's not just good to Jews or those that love and trust him. He's good to everybody.

"I think it broke his heart to see this guy in pain for so long. So, he made him well.   And he's not looking for *thank-you's* even though he appreciates them. He does good things because he's good — not because they are. Does that make sense?"

"I guess so. I've just never met anyone who cares like that," said Reuben.

"You'll see a lot more! And welcome to the group," said John.

After the festival in Jerusalem, Jesus and his disciples traveled out into the mountain area surrounding Jerusalem. Reuben enjoyed this time to just relax and be alone with God. But he also enjoyed getting to know the followers of Jesus and asking them questions. He loved doing research and studying, so he was always asking questions.

One day he noticed that Jesus was missing from the group and he asked one of the disciples where he might be. *Has he deserted us here in the mountains?* The man explained that Jesus often went into the mountains to be alone and to pray and sometimes would be gone all night long.

"He's back today, though. He seems to be having one-on-one conferences with some of the men in the group. I don't know what that is about, but he's probably teaching them things they need to know."

As Reuben began to pay attention, he noticed that one man would return to the group and tag another man who would leave. After a period of time, that man would return and call for another man to go and talk with Jesus alone. This continued most of the day. Reuben saw his dad being called out and he wondered if Jesus would call for him. Maybe Jesus would have time to answer some of his questions.

As the disciples gathered together for the evening meal, Jesus announced that he had chosen 12 men who would be his apostles. They would be his special students and would learn how to carry on the work after he was gone.

Reuben's dad was one of the 12 chosen to be an apostle and Reuben felt proud of his dad. Then he immediately began to struggle: *If Jesus is not the Messiah, then he is a liar and a fraud, or just plain crazy. Why should I be glad that Abba is following a madman? And why does it feel so right?* He felt confused but decided to congratulate his dad and figure it out later. He could at least be happy that his dad was happy.

Reuben enjoyed traveling with the group and felt that it was a wonderful vacation from his years of study. His body was growing healthy and strong from all the walking and outdoor living and healthy lifestyle.

He listened closely to Jesus' teachings and compared them to what he remembered about the Jewish Scripture. He was becoming more and more convinced that Jesus just might be the Messiah.

But one day as they were entering Capernaum, Reuben saw something that shook his belief. He saw Jesus help a Roman soldier. You see, Israel was an occupied nation. That means that the Romans had taken over their country and ruled it. They set the rules and collected the taxes, and they were hated for their cruelty to the Jews. Every Jewish family knew someone who had been either killed or made a slave by the Romans. And there were crosses in every town where those who didn't obey the rules were crucified. No, Reuben couldn't follow someone who helped the Romans.

Jesus not only healed this Roman soldier's servant, but then he praised him for having faith. He even said that this Roman's faith was greater than most Jews. That made Reuben mad. But when Jesus said that at the Great Feast in Heaven with Abraham and Moses, there would be some Romans and other outsiders present, while a lot of Jews would be thrown out — well, that settled it.

Reuben had been taught that the Jews and the Jews alone were God's chosen people, and that God had no love for anyone else. And Reuben liked it that way.

Reuben began to think about his next step. He decided to stay with Jesus until he could secure a position as a student with a rabbi who would teach him. But something didn't quite seem right about going back to Rabbi Adar. Reuben hated to admit it, but he really felt that he already knew more than Rabbi Adar about the Scripture. No. He wanted to study under someone who <u>really</u> knew the Scripture. He wanted to know the <u>truth</u>.

Reuben decided that he would stay with Jesus' group until they returned to Jerusalem. He didn't want to travel alone, and he was certain Jerusalem would be the best place to find a rabbi to teach him. Also, in Jerusalem he would be close to the temple and would have continual access to the Holy Scriptures. So, without telling anyone, he made his decision and felt relief that it was settled.

As the group began traveling south again toward Jerusalem, they were passing through the city of Nain. They stopped to let a funeral procession pass. Reuben was shocked to see that the dead man was no older than he was — just a very young man beginning his life.

Here's what the Bible says happened:

> **As he approached the town gate, a dead person was being carried out — the only son of his mother, and she was a widow. And a large crowd from the town was with her. When the Lord saw her, his heart went out to her and he said, "Don't cry."**
>
> **Then he went up and .... said, "Young man, I say to you, get up!" The dead man sat up and began to talk, and Jesus gave him back to his mother.[3]**

Reuben felt that his head would explode. *What have I just seen? I know the Scripture. I know that only God can raise the dead. Now I'm confused all over again.*

He pulled away from the other disciples and camped alone that night. He wanted time to think and to pray. They would be in Jerusalem within a few more days. *What should I do? What do I believe?* He didn't know. And He didn't know who to ask.

Early the next morning, he woke to discover Jesus sitting quietly near his blanket. He sat up startled.

Jesus said very quietly, "I'm sorry to startle you. I was on my way to pray and saw you and thought I would encourage you. I know you are feeling confused.

"I suggest you contact Rabbi Nicodemus when we get to Jerusalem. He is not a follower of mine, but he is a serious student of Scripture, and I believe that he is searching for <u>truth</u> just like you are. He would be a great mentor for you and a place where you could grow and ask your questions."

And before Reuben could respond, Jesus was gone.

Reuben rubbed his eyes and wondered if it was a dream. But he knew it wasn't, and the name Rabbi Nicodemus was very clearly in his head. *But how does Jesus know that I was planning on looking for a rabbi when I get to Jerusalem? And how does he know that I am feeling confused? And how does he seem to know so much about my desire to know the <u>truth</u>? There is something about this man Jesus that I just can't explain.*

Reuben decided that he would stay with the disciples until they arrived in Jerusalem. Then he would check at the temple to see if anyone knew a Rabbi Nicodemus. So, once again, Reuben felt his life settle down, and he relaxed and just enjoyed listening to Jesus' teachings and watching him heal as they journeyed toward Jerusalem.

Rabbi Nicodemus came highly recommended by every priest and Pharisee that Reuben consulted. Apparently, he was a very highly respected rabbi and member of the Sanhedrin.

He made an appointment to meet with Rabbi Nicodemus and the rabbi granted him a one-week trial to see what kind of student Reuben was. When Reuben proved his excellent work habits and quick understanding of the passages, Rabbi Nicodemus agreed to mentor him.

It was hard to say goodbye to Jesus' disciples, and especially to his parents, but he knew that he had found the place where he needed to be. Rabbi Nicodemus had several other students, so Reuben soon found himself immersed in his studies and surrounded by fellow students who enjoyed digging into God's Word to find <u>truth</u>. Reuben was clinging to this promise from Jewish Scripture:

> **You will seek me and find me when you seek me with all your heart.**[4]

---

[1] **Matthew 8:2-3**
[2] **John 5:3-9**
[3] **Luke 7:12-15**
[4] **Jeremiah 29:13**

Jesus Heals a Man with Leprosy
Luke 5:12-13

Jesus Heals Man at Pool of Bethesda
John 5:1-9

Jesus Calls the 12 Apostles
Luke 6:12-16

Jesus Heals the Roman Soldier's Servant
Matthew 8:5-13

Jesus Raises the Widow's Son from the Dead
Luke 7:11-15

Chapter 14
THE STORY OF DINAH

"Mother, does God love everybody?"

"Of course, dear."

"But does he love everybody the same?"

"Of course, dear."

"But does he love Junos and Cronus?"

"Of course, dear."

"But they aren't Jewish!"

Sometimes Dinah drove her mother crazy with questions. Dinah's head was filled with questions, and no one would take her seriously because she was a girl. Girls in the first century weren't supposed to think. Girls were supposed to cook and sew and raise children and say, "Of course, dear."

Because she was a girl, she wasn't allowed to go to school and learn like her older brothers. But Dinah liked to think, and she had thousands of questions.

Dinah got up from her sewing and went to the back courtyard. She had questions and she wanted answers.   But she didn't know where to find them.

She went back into the house to talk with Junos. She wasn't much older, but she knew so many more things.   Junos was Roman and believed there were many gods, and she knew what to do to keep them happy. Maybe Junos would know the answer.

She found Junos sweeping out the living area and dust was flying everywhere. "Junos, I have a question."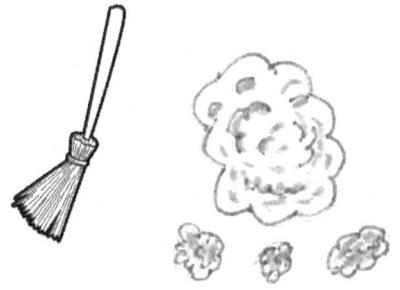

"Not right now, little one, I've got to get this room cleaned before your father brings guests home tonight. Later."

It was middle of the afternoon before Dinah caught Junos making bread and free to answer her question. "Junos, does God love everybody?"

"Well, different gods love different things. Let me think. I'm not sure that the gods love anybody except themselves. I mean, they don't love people — they expect us to love them. Is that what you are asking?"

"No. But that's an interesting thought. Thanks."

Dinah slipped off her stool and went back outside to think some more. Now she had even more questions. She had been taught that God loved her, but Junos said that her gods didn't love people.   That was curious.

She wondered if her Abba would know the answer. But she knew he would tell her not to worry her little-girl-head with questions.   What she really wanted to know wasn't whether God loved people other than Jews — she already knew that he didn't, or at least that's what she had been taught.

What she really wanted to know was if God loved some Jews more than others and ... would God still love her even if she disobeyed him.   And she didn't know quite how to ask that question without getting into a <u>lot</u> of trouble.

You see, it all started about a month ago with a simple trip to the well with Junos. They had filled their water jars and then Dinah had asked Junos if she could stay and talk with her cousin Abigail for a while. So, Junos had allowed her to stay at the well. But when Abigail left, another girl had come to draw water from the well and Dinah had said hello. She learned that the girl's name was Naomi. They began talking, and ever since that "hello," Dinah's questions had multiplied.

Dinah and Naomi both discovered worlds they never knew existed. Dinah learned that some Jewish families didn't have enough food to eat, and some slept outdoors. She was shocked to learn that some Jewish girls her age were sold into slavery. Naomi learned that some Jewish girls had closets full of clothes and actually slept in beds and had servants to take care of all their needs.

For the past few weeks, Dinah had been slipping out of bed much earlier than the rest of her family and going to the well to meet Naomi. She always took a water jar so that she could pretend she was just "helping" Junos.

She <u>knew</u> that slipping out of the house and talking to Naomi was not honoring her parents' wishes. So, there was that question again: *Will God quit loving me if I am disobedient? And why is it wrong for me to be friends with a person who is a fellow Jew, but who happens to not be rich?*

Naomi was not only Jewish, but Dinah felt that she was more careful and thorough in following God's Law than she was. Yet, Naomi was poor. *Does God love rich people more than he loves poor people? And why?*

Dinah thought that as she grew up, she would get answers to her questions, but she was discovering that the more she grew, the more questions she had.

Then last Wednesday, she had arrived at the well and found Naomi crying. Dinah rushed to her friend, calling, "Naomi, what's wrong? Are you hurt? What's going on?"

Naomi pointed to the pieces of what was left of her water jar.

"What happened? Oh, Naomi, don't cry. Your mother will just buy another one. She'll understand. Don't cry. And are you hurt? Your knee looks scraped." Dinah was trying to be helpful.

Naomi looked at Dinah in disbelief. "<u>You</u> don't understand! There's no money to buy another jar. <u>This</u> is our water jar. I have broken it. I don't know what will happen."

Dinah just sat and looked at her in silence. She let her mind try to comprehend a world like that. She thought of the shelf in her kitchen where there were 10 or 12 water jars just sitting and collecting dust.
"Here," she said, "take my water jar."

"Oh, no. I couldn't take yours," whispered Naomi.

"Then I will 'accidentally' forget my jar and you can take it," said Dinah.

"Oh, no! That would be stealing. I would never steal someone else's jar."

"Then you will have to accept it as a gift from me. You are my friend, and I will tell Junos that I fell and broke my jar."

"Dinah, that would be lying! I will not let you lie in order to help me."

"Naomi, you are my friend and I want you to have this water jar. Your family needs it. If Junos misses it, I will tell her the truth."

Naomi was such a good friend, and they had discussed Dinah's questions of whether God loved all Jews the same and whether his love changed if they were disobedient. Naomi felt that God's love was secure, but she still wanted Dinah to obey God's Law.

She wasn't sure whether it was okay to accept Dinah's gift. They discussed all the pros and cons and lost track of time.

Suddenly, Dinah realized that she would be missed at home. She pushed the jar into Naomi's hands and ran home as quickly as possible.

"And where have you been so early this morning?" Junos greeted her at the door as she entered the kitchen.

"I went to the well and got busy talking — you know how I like to ask questions! I just lost track of the time."

"You went to the well? Where is your water jar?" asked Junos.

(Can you hear the sinister music playing in the background?) *Caught! Now what?*

Dinah took a deep breath, and in that moment, she knew that she wanted to tell the truth and quit hiding her friendship with Naomi.

"Junos, I gave my water jar to a friend who broke hers. Was that a terrible thing to do?" And with that Dinah burst into tears.

"I think it was a very kind thing to do, but why would she need your water jar? Couldn't she just go home and get another one?"

"That's the problem, Junos. She couldn't. In the first place, she doesn't have a home. And her family doesn't have enough money for a new water jar."

"Did she ask you for your water jar?"

"Of course not. She did not want to take it, but I insisted."

"Dinah, you know that I will have to tell your mother."

"Yes, Junos, I know. I hope that she will not make me give up my friendship."

"So, you admit that you have made a friend that your mother will not approve of?"

"Yes, Junos."

"What kind of girl is this?"

"She's Jewish. She loves God very much and she obeys his Law and she insisted that I tell you the truth and not lie to you. She's a good friend, but she and her family are very poor. In fact, if her Abba doesn't get well soon, she and her entire family will be sold into slavery to pay their debts."

Junos' eyes softened as she remembered when she was taken as a young girl and sold on the Roman slave auction because her dad could not pay his taxes.

Junos looked intently at Dinah, "Give me time to think. Eat your breakfast and go to your room. I'll speak with your mother about it. You know that I have to tell her."

"Yes, Junos, I know." She slowly ate her breakfast and had just arrived in her room when her mother came in. Dinah could tell from the look on her face that her mother was not happy.

"Dinah, Dinah, what am I going to do with you? What do you have to say for yourself?"

"Mother, I gave my water jar to Naomi because she broke hers. I thought it would be the kind thing to do. I was only trying to be helpful."

"Dinah, you know good and well that that is not the problem! Who is Naomi? Who are her parents? Is she the right kind of young lady for you to be friends with?"

"She is Jewish, and she follows God's Law. I have not met her parents," replied Dinah.

But Mother continued, "Junos tells me that her Abba is sick, and they are poor and homeless. How do you think that looks for you to be friends with such a person?"

"Mother, doesn't God love all Jews?"

"Dinah, don't start that with me. I'm tired of your questions. You know that you disobeyed. You will not leave this house unsupervised again. You are getting too old to be allowed to wander around like a heathen (someone who doesn't believe in God). Until you are safely married, you will be chaperoned at all times. Do you understand?"

"Yes, Mother, I understand." Dinah was determined to not cry. Even if she never saw Naomi again, at least her family had a good water jar!

She wondered if she would be allowed to go to the well with Junos. Maybe she could at least wave at Naomi. But Dinah decided that she would not disobey her parents again. It was wrong and she knew that God was not pleased with it.

 Her mother worked quickly and by mid-afternoon had secured a Jewish servant named Yavonna who would be Dinah's personal attendant (and watch dog). She had supervised several young women in the area and came with excellent references.

To Dinah's great delight, she discovered that Yavonna was quick-witted and an excellent debater. The afternoon passed quickly as they got acquainted. Yavonna helped Dinah choose a dress for the dinner party that her Abba was giving that night.

Dinah loved the parties that her parents hosted on most Sabbath evenings. It gave her a chance to meet new people and to learn new things. Her Abba, Simon, was a Pharisee and so invited other Pharisees and their families.

Pharisees were the spiritual and political leaders of Israel. After the women and children had gone home, the men usually stayed and talked about the political situation. They didn't know that Dinah stayed up, hid and listened. She wondered if that was another thing that would make God not love her. *Maybe secretly listening is disobeying. Oh, all this thinking makes my head hurt. I need to get ready for dinner.*

Yavonna filled a pan of water and helped Dinah refresh her face and smooth back her dark hair. She seemed more like a friend than a servant and that made Dinah happy.

She discovered that they were eating in the front courtyard. The front courtyard was used for larger crowds and more important people so that everyone in town could see who the guests were and what they were serving. It was exciting to be surrounded by people watching — like being a princess.

The servants were busy seating guests, and because it was so hot, there were servants everywhere waving giant palm leaves to keep the guests cool.

She wished she could be seated at the main table with her Abba and his special guests. When she was little, she used to hide under the main table to hear what was being said. But now that she was 10, she had to settle for a table of girls near the center. *Oh, well,* she thought. *Maybe I can get a better view from here.*

Dinah reclined on what looked like a low couch. The "head" end was pushed up to the table and Yavonna stood behind her. Several of the other girls also had attendants.

The girls were jabbering on and on about clothes, and sewing, and cooking, and certainly about getting good husbands.

Dinah found her mind still thinking about her questions. Her heart was wondering what would become of Naomi and whether her family had enough to eat. The question just kept pounding in her head: *Does God love all Jews — or just some of them? Just look at this courtyard,* she thought to herself, *even it reflects a difference between Jews.*

The main table was filled with Abba's Pharisee friends. Around the table were the couches where each man would recline and eat from the table. They were dressed most elegantly and were certainly considered to be proper Jews.

Mother was reclined at her table with a group of the Pharisees' wives. They were dressed perfectly and were showing off their jewelry and new robes. They talked of nothing but their children and grandchildren like good Jewish mothers.

The Pharisees' children were reclined at two tables right in the middle between their parents — one for boys and one for girls.

All these tables for the important Pharisees, their wives, and children, were on a platform so that they were elevated above everyone else.

The other tables were placed in a circle around the center platform. These tables were for the guests who were not quite so important. Dinah's mind demanded to know why there were "outer circle" people and "inner circle" people. *They are all Jews. Why is there a difference?*

Beyond that, there were the spectators. Most of them were also Jewish, yet they were not invited, and never would be. That reminded her of Naomi, and Dinah wondered again if she was okay.

Is God's love like that? Does he love some Jewish people more than others? And why should it matter to God whether you were born rich or poor? And doesn't he control that? When will I get answers? Or will I just grow up and become an "of course, dear"? She visibly shuddered at the thought.

As she looked around the room that evening, she noticed a young man reclining at one of the outside tables. She didn't recognize him. He really wasn't dressed properly. But there was something else about him that attracted her attention. She couldn't take her eyes off of him.

Her mind began to race and ask questions. *Why is he not dressed appropriately for such a fancy dinner? And why doesn't he care that he's not dressed up? Why does he look so comfortable and calm? He doesn't look at all nervous like the other people in the courtyard.*

There was something about him that made her feel that she could ask him any question in the world, and he would know the answer. *How can that be?* Most of her Abba's friends acted like they knew everything about everything. This man was different. She couldn't put her finger on it — except for the words "confident" and "peaceful."

She turned to talk with the girl seated beside her and asked if she knew who he was. "He looks like a peasant to me," she said with disdain.

Dinah knew that she couldn't just stare at him all evening, but every chance she got, she turned to see what he was doing.

Once when she turned to look at him, Yavonna leaned down and whispered in her ear. "His name is Jesus and I'll tell you about him later. Don't keep staring, it's not correct behavior for a young lady." Dinah resented being told how to behave — but when her eyes met Yavonna's, she knew that Yavonna was a friend who had information that she wanted desperately.

"Thank you, Yavonna," she said, and she tried to keep her attention on her own table guests.

Jesus was apparently charming his table mates and making lively conversation. In fact, his table seemed to be doing more laughing and having more fun than anyone else in the courtyard. It was hard to not turn and look when his table erupted with genuine laughter.

At that moment Abigail, her cousin who had just turned 12, announced that her parents had chosen her husband and that she would be espoused (engaged to be married) soon. All the girls were discussing the lucky man and plans for the wedding.

Suddenly there was a deathly silence over the entire courtyard.

> **A woman in that town who lived a sinful life ... came there with an alabaster jar of perfume. As she stood behind him [Jesus] at his feet weeping, she began to wet his feet with her tears. Then she wiped them with her hair, kissed them and poured perfume on them.[1]**

No one in the whole courtyard was breathing. Everyone was waiting to see what their host, Simon the Pharisee would do. Simon was horrified. First, he was horrified that one of his guests had been touched by this sinful woman. And secondly, he was horrified that Jesus did not seem horrified by it!

Then a strong but kind voice rose over the crowd as Jesus said,

> ... "Simon, I have something to tell you."

> "Tell me, teacher," he said.[2]

> ... "Do you see this woman? I came into your house. You did not give me any water for my feet, but she wet my feet with her tears and wiped them with her hair. You did not give me a kiss, but this woman, from the time I entered, has not stopped kissing my feet. You did not put oil on my head, but she has poured perfume on my feet."[3]

> Then Jesus said to her, "Your sins are forgiven."[4]

The party broke up pretty quickly after that. Everyone seemed to be upset. And for once, Dinah didn't even consider hiding and listening to her Abba's conversations. She was eager to get to her room and hear what Yavonna knew about Jesus.

Yavonna cautioned her to remain quiet until after Junos had turned down her bed and helped her change into her night clothes. Once Junos was gone and the door was closed, Yavonna told Dinah that she would try to answer any questions she might have.

"I have more questions than will fit into my head. It feels like it will explode. Where do I start? But I guess my most pressing question is, 'Who was that man?'"

"That's an excellent place to start, because once you figure that out, then all your other questions become easier. He is a prophet sent by God and I have been listening to him teach for almost a year now.

"I am a follower of Jesus. I keep it quiet so that I will be allowed to work here and answer your questions. If Jesus were just a prophet, that would be exciting and wonderful. But I personally believe that he is who he says he is: The Messiah."

"The Messiah? Like <u>the</u> Messiah? The one everyone is waiting for?"

"Yes. Except there's a problem. A lot of those who said they were waiting for him are not happy with him and don't believe that he is the Messiah."

"I'm confused. Either he is or he isn't, right?"

"Yes."

"And you believe that he is the Messiah?"

"Yes."

"Why?"

"You saw him tonight. What did you think and feel?"

"I felt that he was wise and good and loving and caring. There was something about his eyes that made me feel safe. And he had an incredible sense of confidence — but it wasn't cocky like my Abba's friends. He was just confident. I couldn't put my finger on it.

"And then there's the way he treated that woman. If indeed he is the Messiah, it answered my question."

"What question is that?"

"I've been wondering if God loved all Jews just the same — or whether there were different levels of Jews. And I've been wondering if God would still love me if I messed up and was disobedient to his rules."

"And what do you think now?"

"I think that God loves all Jews regardless of whether they are rich or poor, and I think he was criticizing my Abba for treating people differently based on wealth."

"You are quite a thinker! I'm so glad that God has sent me here to teach you."

"Do you think God has sent you here?"

"I certainly do! When someone begins to ask questions about God and what he desires and wants, <u>he</u> <u>answers</u>. It may not be in the way we expect, but he always answers those prayers. He wants us to know him and know that he loves us."

"That's super cool!"

"I think it's bed-time for a tired girl. This has been a long day and we've got plenty of time to answer the rest of your questions. But you need to promise me one thing. Don't tell anyone that I'm a follower of Jesus or I will be asked to leave, and you will not learn the answers to your questions."

"I promise. I'm so glad you came to help me, Yavonna. And boy, do I have a long list of questions for you!"

"Tomorrow, little one, tomorrow."

---

[1] Luke 7:37-38
[2] Luke 7:40
[3] Luke 7:44-46
[4] Luke 7:48

Jesus Forgives Sinful Woman at Simon's House
Luke 7:36-50

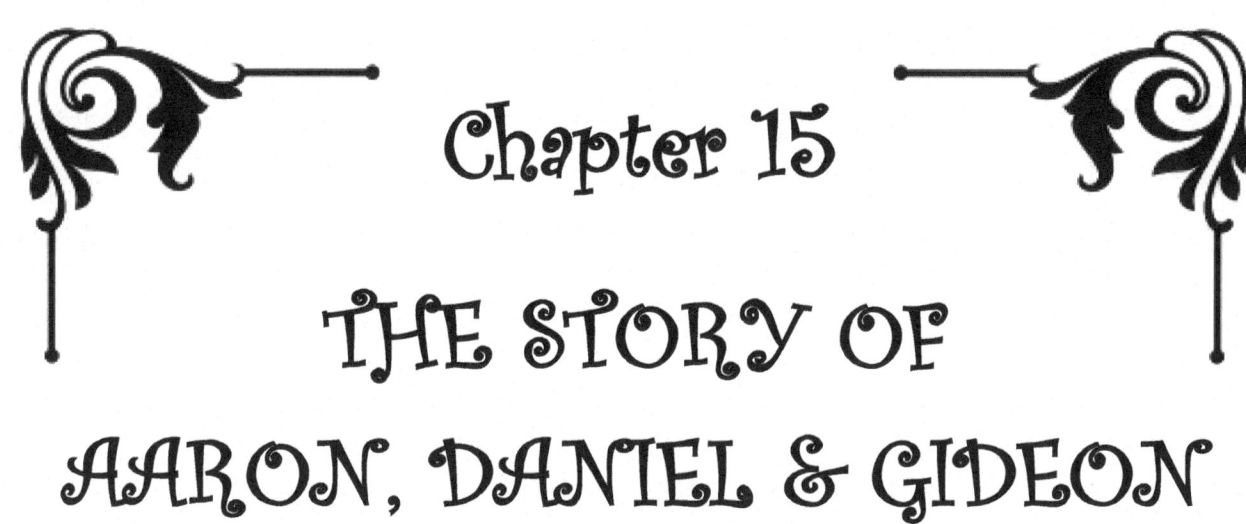

Chapter 15
THE STORY OF AARON, DANIEL & GIDEON

"Did not!"

"Did, too!"

"Did not!"

"Stop it, you two. We've got to get this barley planted today. We don't have time to fight.

"Daniel, take your sack and go to the right side, Gideon, take your sack and go to the left side and I'll work in the middle. We'll see which of you can make it to the middle first." Aaron knew that they would work better apart and that they couldn't resist the competition. He also knew that they were careful workers and would do a good job.

It was hard being the older brother, especially now with Dad gone most of the time. Aaron was only 14, but he was in charge of the farm and his brothers knew that they had to obey him. Sometimes it took a wrestling match to prove to them that he was the boss, but most of the time, they cooperated. His brothers, Daniel and Gideon, were 10-year-old twins.

Aaron had always known that he would stay on the farm when he turned 13, but he assumed he would work under his dad, just like his dad had worked under his dad. The farm had been in the family for many generations. But just before his 13th birthday, Aaron's dad, Thomas, had met Jesus and started going to listen to him every chance he got. It meant a lot of the work fell on Aaron, but he loved the farm, and didn't mind hard work. He was up before dawn taking care of the animals. Then he would eat breakfast with the family and afterward head for the fields. They grew wheat, barley, and rye. Galilee was a well-watered and well-fertilized farmland, and Aaron had thought that he and his dad would farm it together until someday it would be his. Now, at 14, he was running the farm while his dad followed Jesus, and he wanted to make sure that everything was taken care of.

Today, they would finish sowing the barley fields and he could give the younger boys a couple of days off before the wheat needed to be sowed. (Sowing meant planting the seeds by throwing it onto the prepared ground by handfuls.)

Tomorrow, he would take the oxen and plow up the fields and get them ready for sowing the wheat. His brothers weren't strong enough to handle the oxen just yet.

His mind was planning ahead so that every crop would benefit from the rains and seasons. With good planning, in Galilee one could always have a crop in the field, harvesting in both the spring and the fall.

Gideon was getting close to finishing his section, but Daniel would need a little help, so Aaron stepped toward the right and started sowing toward him. Sowing was an art. You picked up a handful of grain and threw it as you walked through the soft prepared soil. If you threw too little, the crop would be small. If you threw too much, the crop would also be small — because it would be too crowded.

Sowing was definitely a skill that took a lot of practice. It had to be done just right. All three boys knew just the right amount of ground that their sack should plant. It was a satisfying feeling. They had farming in their blood.

As they headed toward the house, they noticed that a group of men were approaching from the road. Daniel and Gideon took off running. They were sure that it was Abba and they wanted to be the first to greet him.

"I got here first!"

"Did not!"

"Did so!"

"Boys! Boys! Is that any way to act in front of our guests? This is Yanis, Joel, Enid, and Esau. And this is Daniel and Gideon, my younger sons. And this is Aaron, my first-born, and the one in charge here."

Aaron blushed at the praise from his dad.

"You boys go to the back yard and get acquainted while I check on Mother."

The boys greeted each other, but Aaron felt that instead of the back yard, they needed to go to the well and let him and his brothers wash up for dinner. They led the visitors down to the well. When you put seven boys all together around a well of water, they will soon be "well" acquainted, somewhat clean, and quite wet.

The farm boys were amazed to learn that these four young men had all been raised in and around Jerusalem and had never really been on a farm. Aaron's dad had invited them out for a quick visit with his family since Jesus was in Capernaum which was only a day and a half away.

All through the dinner, Daniel and Gideon pestered Abba to let them travel with him for a couple of weeks. But Aaron was opposed to the idea because it would leave him alone to do all the work on the farm. Already, Aaron was worried about whether he would be able to get the plowing done that he had planned, or whether he would be expected to entertain the guests.

He shouldn't have worried, because at sunrise the next morning his dad was up and had one team of oxen already harnessed to the plow. Aaron quickly harnessed the other team and headed for the farthest field.

Several times during the morning, the visitors checked on Aaron to see if there was anything they could do to help, but they knew they couldn't handle the oxen. They watched as Aaron and his dad expertly broke the hard soil into smaller and smaller chunks until it was soft and moist and ready for the wheat seeds. With Dad's help, they would be ready to plant wheat tomorrow. That would be a relief and would catch Aaron up.

But at dinner, strange talk was floating around the table. Abba was actually talking about taking Daniel and Gideon with him and leaving Yanis and Joel to help Aaron on the farm. As Aaron looked over his now revised schedule, he felt that it might be possible _if_ Yanis and Joel were really serious about working, and not just taking a vacation. They assured him that they were.

Mother was not at all sure she wanted Abba taking the twins so far away from home without her, but in the end it was decided.

Early the next morning, Aaron found Yanis and Joel eager to see what farm life was all about. Aaron felt proud of "his" farm. He took Yanis and Joel to care for the animals and had never laughed so hard watching them try to milk the goats. He showed them how to care for the animals and explained their specific needs. The more he taught Yanis and Joel, the more sure he became that the farm was where he belonged.

The boys returned to the house for breakfast with Abba and the other guests. Abba had some final instructions for Aaron and then they were off.

Aaron took Yanis and Joel out into the newly plowed fields and taught them how to sow the seeds evenly over the field. Joel had a better rhythm for it than Yanis, and he claimed that singing as he worked made his movements smoother.

Aaron told them that no one would know what kind of job they really did until the wheat started growing. Then the whole world would be able to look and say, "Oh, look — this sower had a steady hand — and that sower made clumps!"

That afternoon during a rest time, Yanis shared with Aaron and Joel that for the first time he really understood what Jesus was talking about when he told the parable of the soils.

"I haven't heard that story. Why don't you tell me while we sit here and catch our breaths?" said Aaron.

Yanis told it just the way Jesus did:

> **"Listen! A farmer went out to sow his seed. As he was scattering the seed, some fell along the path, and the birds came and ate it up.**

> "Some fell on rocky places, where it did not have much soil. It sprang up quickly, because the soil was shallow. But when the sun came up, the plants were scorched, and they withered because they had no root.
>
> "Other seed fell among thorns, which grew up and choked the plants, so that they did not bear grain.
>
> "Still other seed fell on good soil. It came up, grew and produced a crop, some multiplying thirty, some sixty, some a hundred times.[1]

"Now I can see what Jesus meant by 'prepared soil.' Without it, the seed would have a really hard time taking root and growing," said Yanis.

"I hear what you are saying, but I don't understand why Jesus was teaching about seeds," said Aaron.

"Well, it really wasn't about seeds — it was about hearing the truth and being ready to accept Jesus as the Messiah. Some people are better prepared than others. And some are just downright rocky!"

"So, you guys believe that Jesus is the Messiah?"

"Yes," they responded together.

"Well, we've got three fields to plant in wheat today, and the sooner we get it done, the sooner we can call it quits. But I'd really like to know what makes you believe that Jesus is the Messiah. I mean, I've heard my dad's beliefs, but I'm just not sure."

Yanis said, "Let's get busy and I'll be glad to share my journey with you later."

Aaron was pleased that they got all three fields of wheat planted. It would have been a little quicker with his brothers, but he enjoyed the friendship of Yanis and Joel and teaching them about farm life. He had never really been around boys his own age.

And of course, after they were through in the fields, the animals needed to be cared for again. This time, Yanis seemed to be catching on to milking the goats, but Joel preferred feeding them.

That night as they sat in the back yard after dinner, Yanis and Joel both shared their stories of getting to know Jesus and realizing that he was the Messiah. You read their stories in Chapter 11.

"I feel a lot more secure in believing that Jesus is the Messiah now that I've heard your stories. I hope he is the Messiah.

"But tomorrow is another long day. We need to repair a rock fence before that wheat comes up, or the animals will do the harvesting! At least we can talk while we work.

"Are you sure you guys aren't sorry that you decided to stay here? It's a lot of hard work!"

"What? And miss your mother's cooking? No way!"

After breakfast that morning, Thomas had kissed his wife goodbye and taken their two young sons with him for a few days. Esau and Enid enjoyed having the two younger boys with them. Daniel and Gideon had never been away from the farm, so they were excited about every turn in the road.

Thomas thought they could probably meet up with Jesus in Capernaum, but sometimes Jesus changed plans, and it could take a while to locate him. The boys had no problems keeping up with their dad like some of Jesus' new followers. They were sturdy 10-year-olds who had worked on the farm all their lives, so they were strong and healthy.

They were a little surprised to be sleeping on the ground with just a blanket, but quickly decided that lying under the stars was a grand way to spend the night.

It was a good experience for Enid and Esau to see Thomas as a dad and not just some man who followed Jesus. They recognized what a hard sacrifice it was for Thomas to leave his wife and children behind to follow Jesus. He had indeed left everything, and their admiration of him grew.

As they approached Capernaum the next morning, they learned that Jesus was teaching near the Sea of Galilee. Thomas and the boys joined the rest of the disciples there. He left Daniel and Gideon with Enid and Esau, while he went to speak with Jesus. He wanted to let him know he had brought his sons with him and would need to be available as a dad.

Jesus was delighted and came over to meet Daniel and Gideon. The boys became very quiet and shy in Mr. Jesus' presence because they knew that he was a great man. But he soon had them relaxed and was laughing with them. He asked them how they thought the two "city slickers" were getting along trying to do all their work. Then he went back to teaching the crowds and healing. Daniel and Gideon were fascinated to see how many people came to see Mr. Jesus. They didn't know there were that many people in the whole world.

Enid and Esau assured Thomas that they didn't mind keeping an eye on the twins, so he could do his duties in working with the crowds.

By mid-afternoon, Enid and Esau could tell that Daniel and Gideon were tired of listening and needed to move around, as 10-year-old boys do. Esau asked, "Are you guys getting hungry?"

"Yeah!" was their joint response. So, Enid and Esau led them away from where Mr. Jesus was preaching and teaching. There they found the camp of followers who were beginning to prepare the evening meal. When Enid and Esau introduced Daniel and Gideon, they were given some fruit and instructed to collect driftwood for the fire. A lot of firewood was needed to keep the ovens baking bread and to be able to cook the fresh fish they had caught.

Sometimes, when Jesus traveled, they just ate fruit and bread that they cooked at home. But along the Sea of Galilee, Jesus' followers usually fried fish and cooked fresh bread in rock ovens. Tonight, there would be a feast — that is, if you liked fish.

The smells were wonderful, and Daniel and Gideon wondered if they would starve to death before Mr. Jesus finally came. He finished healing all the people and sent them to their homes. Then he came over to the camp with all the disciples and they enjoyed the meal together.

Daniel and Gideon were able to sit near their dad and be introduced to all the apostles and their families. The twins felt very, very far away from the farm.

It was a perfectly clear night, and the moon was just coming up over the horizon when Mr. Jesus called for certain of his disciples to prepare for a ministry trip with him. The others would wait here and get some rest. They had three boats: one that would hold 15 people, and two small boats that would only hold six each.

Mr. Jesus called out the names of those to go in the two small boats. Then he began to call out the names of those to go in the large boat with him. Suddenly, Daniel and Gideon's eyes popped open, wide awake. Their dream has just come true. Mr. Jesus called their dad's name, and then he said, "and Daniel and Gideon." Mr. Jesus had included them, too!

So, the 27 named people found their traveling bags and were told to pack some bread and some dates because there probably wouldn't be food the next day. They lined up to receive these items from the cooks and then boarded their boat.

For two little farm boys, they were beyond excited. Abba showed them how to throw their blanket down between the benches so that they could get some rest. They lay in the floor of the boat watching their Abba take his turn rowing. The stars were magnificent overhead and the gentle swaying of the water quickly put them right to sleep.

On and on the rowers rowed. Mr. Jesus was headed to the land of the Gadarenes across the Sea of Galilee. He, too, stretched out on his blanket and quickly fell asleep after a hard day of ministry. The rowers took turns waking up the next team of rowers, and then there would be a shuffle in the boat so that the exhausted men could change places with the more rested ones.

Have you ever been sound asleep and had someone throw a glass of water in your face? Well, that's sorta what happened.

Daniel and Gideon were sound asleep. They were lulled into a deep, deep sleep by the gentle rocking of the boat and the rhythmic sounds of the oars, when all of a sudden, they not only had water in their faces — they were thoroughly soaked.

Their robes and their blankets were soaked with ice cold water. And the water was almost a foot deep right where they had been lying. The boat had turned from a sweet cradle to a roaring roller coaster. They were going up one side of a wave and crashing down the other. At times it seemed the boat would just flip over and dump everyone out into the sea.

Both boys were screaming, but they couldn't be heard over the sound of the wind and the pounding of the waves onto the boat. They were hanging on, but were sure that this was the end of their short lives.

Here's what the Bible says:

> **A furious squall came up, and the waves broke over the boat, so that it was nearly swamped. Jesus was in the stern, sleeping on a cushion. The disciples woke him and said to him, "Teacher, don't you care if we drown?"[2]**

Now you need to realize that not only were these two little boys scared to death, but everyone on that boat was scared — except for one person. Many of these men were professional fishermen and <u>they</u> thought they were about to die — so don't be too hard on Daniel and Gideon for feeling frightened.

But Mr. Jesus wasn't scared. He was sleeping like it was still a gentle cradle. Why? Because he knew the plan. Let's look at what happened.

> **He got up, ... and said to the waves, "Quiet! Be still!" Then the wind died down and it was completely calm.[3]**

Daniel and Gideon looked around amazed. The sea was perfectly quiet and still as glass. The sun was just beginning to come up and that was a good thing, because they were wet and cold. Even though they were 10 years old, they appreciated Abba offering them the warmth of his hug. The three of them sat together with teeth chattering until they reached the shore. Then they started racing around collecting driftwood to make a fire.

When they had their arms full of wood and turned back toward the group, Mr. Jesus was wading toward the shore. There was a crazy man running toward Mr. Jesus. They knew he was out of his mind because he wasn't wearing any clothes and his hair was all matted and dirty looking.

The boys couldn't decide whether to run to find Abba, or to run as far away and as fast as possible. *But what if this strange land is filled with crazy men?* They certainly didn't want to run away from the disciples. So, they just stood still and watched.

The man bowed at Mr. Jesus' feet and yelled,

> ..."What do you want with me, Jesus, Son of the Most High God?...."[4]

Mr. Jesus talked quietly with the man and the boys couldn't hear what was happening. Then Mr. Jesus pointed to a large herd of pigs that were feeding in a pasture.

Daniel and Gideon watched as the entire herd of pigs ran off the edge of a steep cliff and drowned in the sea. The Bible tells us that there were about 2000 pigs that died that day.

Daniel and Gideon just watched with their mouths hanging wide open. They had wanted an adventure away from the farm, but this was more than they had ever anticipated.

They fearfully brought their firewood to the pile, but kept their eyes on Mr. Jesus sitting and talking with the crazy man. Someone had given him a robe, and he was talking quietly with Mr. Jesus.

The disciples began to stretch out around the fire and eat breakfast. The bread was soaked, but the dates made a decent meal. They were preparing for a full day of ministry when a large group of townspeople arrived.

Then all the people of the region ... asked Jesus to leave them, because they were overcome with fear. So he got into the boat and left.[5]

Everyone loaded back onto the boats and started home. Daniel and Gideon wanted to ask questions and discuss what they had seen, but Abba asked them to hold their questions until they were alone. He promised to answer every question that he could. He told them to just enjoy the boat ride and relax.

The boat ride may have been uneventful for the adults in the boat, but for the two boys who had never seen the Sea of Galilee during the day, it was a fantastic journey. The sun was dancing on the waves. They saw sea birds and jumping fish.

They enjoyed listening to the disciples laughing and talking. It took about two hours to reach Capernaum, and everyone was ready for a snack when they arrived.

"I think it's time for us to start home," Abba said after they had filled up on fruit and bread and cheese. "If we start now, we can probably make it home for supper tomorrow night.

"Daniel and Gideon, empty the sand out of our packs, and then Daniel, take your pack over there and ask that lady for three rounds of bread and some fruit for a day's journey for the three of us. Gideon, go ask Mr. James if we can borrow three dry blankets. Ours will need to dry out before they will be much good. I'm going to go talk with Mr. Jesus and I'll be right back."

Soon they were ready to start their walk. For the first time they could ever remember, Daniel and Gideon had their Abba's full attention. They had always shared him with their older brother, Aaron. They walked steadily and easily — no one wanting to break the silence.

Finally, Gideon asked, "Abba, if Mr. Jesus knows everything, then why did he take us all the way over to the other side of the Sea of Galilee?"

"And almost kill us in the process!" added Daniel.

"We've got a long journey and I'm glad you've got questions. But let's try to do them one at a time, okay?"

"Okay, so mine first," said Gideon.

"Okay, think about it. Did Mr. Jesus accomplish anything at all in the land of the Gadarenes?"

"He killed a lot of pigs!" volunteered Gideon.

"He made a lot of people mad at him!" added Daniel.

"Anything else?" prompted Abba.

"Oh, yeah, he made that crazy man well."

"Do you think Mr. Jesus would have gone all the way across the Sea of Galilee just to make that one man well?" asked Abba.

"Why did he need three boatloads of people to do that?" asked Gideon.

"Let's stick to one question, but we'll come back to that one."

"Mine's next."

"Okay, boys. Don't fight. It's time you learn to quit that bickering. It's not something that would please Mr. Jesus and it doesn't please me."

"Sorry, Abba," said Daniel.

"Sorry, Abba. I'll try to remember," said Gideon.

"So, the question is: do you think Mr. Jesus would go all the way across the Sea of Galilee just to heal one sick man?" asked Abba.

"I guess so, but he's a really busy man."

"All I can tell you is that I've been following Mr. Jesus for just about a year now. I've seen him do amazing miracles, but they are always for the benefit of individual people. He never heals a whole town. He often takes the person aside and heals them privately. He really loves people.

"I feel like he loves me, and I feel like he loves you, Daniel, and you, Gideon. I personally believe that he traveled all the way from Heaven to come down here and teach me how to follow and please God. And I believe he traveled all the way across the Sea of Galilee just to heal that one man named Legion.

"Daniel, I see a well up ahead. Let's stop and take a rest and get some water and then we'll be ready for your question."

After a quick rest and some cool water from the well, Daniel wanted to know why Mr. Jesus took three boatloads of people to go to heal one person.

"Mr. Jesus says that he is training us to do his work," said Abba. "He says he won't always be around, and that we'll be in charge. We need to learn that people are important, so he takes a group of us on just about every ministry he goes on."

"So…. That's why you follow him? To learn how to take care of people?"

"Yes. And I think he's teaching me to love people in a way that I've never done before. I mean, I've always wanted to help my friends, but I've never been very loving toward the sick, the poor, or those who are not Jewish. I think Mr. Jesus is growing my heart."

The boys thought about that for a while.

"Are you going to come back to farming?" Daniel asked next.

"I don't know, but I don't think so. The plan, the way I understand it, is for Mr. Jesus to take over the city of Jerusalem, and I will probably be an officer in the kingdom. So, I'll probably move your mother to the palace, and she'll live like a queen. Do you think she would like that?

The boys' eyes got big at that idea as they nodded.

"So how come we almost died in that storm last night?"

"Did you die?"

"No."

"Were you harmed in any way?"

"We were wet and cold," said Gideon.

"And we were scared to death!" said Daniel.

"But I don't guess we were harmed," Gideon added.

"Did you learn anything?" Abba asked.

"Duh! Mr. Jesus is so powerful. He told the winds to stop and they stopped. The waves just stopped when he told them to. That's powerful!" exclaimed Gideon.

"That proves that he really is God, doesn't it?" Daniel asked.

"Over and over, I've seen Mr. Jesus show his disciples that he really is God in the flesh.

"Sometimes the lessons are a little hard, but I'm trying to learn to trust him. It was hard for me to trust him last night when I saw you boys terrified. I was just about as frightened as you — because you were with me. I didn't want anything to happen to you. But think about it: Mr. Jesus was in the boat with us. Nothing bad was going to happen!"

"Whose turn is it?" asked Daniel.

"I don't remember. Is it okay if we just talk like three men and not take turns?" asked Abba.

That made Daniel and Gideon feel extra special.

"Sure!" they agreed.

"So, do you have a question, Daniel?"

"Yeah, who is Poseidon?" asked Daniel.

"Where in the world did that come from? I mean, I see the connection to the storm, but I'm just wondering who is teaching my boys," asked Abba.

"I just heard a man praying to Poseidon when we were in the boat. It sounded like he was talking to God, but he was begging him to save him from the storm."

"Okay. I understand. Daniel, Poseidon is a myth or an imaginary god of the Greeks. Some of the disciples are still struggling to understand God and Mr. Jesus, and when they get scared — they go back to their superstitions.

"Maybe Mr. Jesus deliberately put that man in the boat so that he could see that it is Mr. Jesus, not Poseidon, who controls the wind and waves."

"So, who sent the storm?" asked Daniel.

Abba thought for a minute because he didn't want to give the boys any wrong answers, and then began.

"I believe that the storm could have had two sources. First, the storm could have been sent by God himself to teach us all a lesson in trust, and to open our eyes to really see that Mr. Jesus is the Messiah and Creator.

"But you boys are old enough to know that God has an enemy named Satan. And Satan could have sent that storm to try to destroy Mr. Jesus.

"But you don't have to worry about that — God is so much bigger and stronger and smarter than Satan. There's nothing that Satan can do that God can't straighten out and make even better. So, I'm not going to tell you that I know the answer to that one — because I don't."

"Thanks, Abba. I understand," said Gideon.

"Me, too," said Daniel.

They walked along quietly for a while before they came to a shady spot. They stopped and ate some bread and fruit and rested their legs. They found a creek behind some trees and were able to get a good drink of cool water. It was so relaxing to just be together.

"So, I think it's time for me to get to ask a question," said Abba.

"Okay, what do you want to know?" replied Gideon confidently.

"How is it working out having Aaron as your boss?"

The boys thought about it just a minute and then Daniel said, "Pretty good. Sometimes we give him a hard time, but he's really fair and he works harder than anybody."

"We miss you, but we understand, and Aaron's a really good boss and he's a good teacher," said Gideon.

"And patient," added Daniel.

"Sounds like I have three sons to be proud of!" replied Abba. "I'm proud of Aaron for being a good teacher and good boss, and I'm proud of both of you for recognizing it and honoring him. That makes a dad just about as proud as he can be. Let's get back on the road and get in another hour before dark. Okay?"

"Sure!" agreed both boys.

"Abba, why did all those pigs jump off the cliff? Did Mr. Jesus cause that?"

"Well, yes and no. Satan had attacked a man with a bunch of demons. Mr. Jesus sent the demons out of the man and into the pigs. The demons controlled the pigs and caused them to jump off the cliff. Satan wants to hurt people and any of God's creatures. I've seen demons do really horrible things to people. But Mr. Jesus heals them and sets them free."

"Abba, what are demons?" asked Gideon.

"Well, from what I understand, they are a little like angels — only they are evil and work for Satan."

"Then why were the townspeople mad at Mr. Jesus?"

Abba replied, "We're all afraid of things we don't understand. I guess they thought Mr. Jesus came to hurt them — that he was an enemy."

"That's sad. He came all that way to help them," said Daniel, "but he didn't get mad. He just left."

"I thought he looked sad," said Gideon.

"Me, too," said Daniel.

"He was sad. But when someone asks him to leave — I've never seen him argue. He just leaves."

"If I traveled all the way over there to help somebody, I think I would make them let me stay and help them!" said Gideon.

Abba laughed and said, "I can see it now. Gideon arrives to help, beats up all the people, and then heals them."

They all laughed as they thought about how different Mr. Jesus was from them.

"I'm fairly sure there's a well just ahead. If I remember right, there's a nice grassy area behind it where we can camp for the night."

As they stretched out in the grass and looked up at the stars, they remembered being rocked to sleep in the boat, and they felt that warm secure feeling of being safe in Mr. Jesus' care.

They didn't have many questions for Abba the next day. They walked and talked about many things. Abba told them about some of the things he had seen and done since following Mr. Jesus. They told him things that had happened on the farm.

 By mid-afternoon, the boys began to recognize neighbors' farms and they knew they were getting close to home.

When they could see their own barn, Gideon yelled, "Beat you!" and off they ran. Thomas wasn't far behind them. He was glad to be home, too, even if it was just for one night.

They shared a lively meal with Gideon and Daniel wanting to tell everything they had seen and done, and Yanis and Joel wanting to tell everything they had learned and experienced on the farm. It was a happy reunion, but one that everyone knew would be too short.

Yanis and Joel had promised Aaron that they would come back and help with the harvest because they wanted to see the result of their hard work. Aaron assured them their help would be welcome.

The next morning, as Yanis and Joel walked away with Abba, the three boys left behind felt a little sad. They wished they could travel with Mr. Jesus.

Aaron put a hand on each of his little brothers and told them what Yanis had told him: "When you work hard doing what Mr. Jesus wants you to do, then you are being obedient. Not everyone can travel with him, or else who would grow the food?

"Come on, I saved the fun stuff for you two. We need to muck out the barn today!"

---

[1] Mark 4:3-8
[2] Mark 4:37-38
[3] Mark 4:39
[4] Mark 5:7
[5] Luke 8:37

Jesus Stops Storm at Sea
Mark 4:35-41

Jesus Heals Demon-Possessed Man
Luke 8:26-37

Chapter 16
THE STORY OF ARIAL, HAVA & MIRIAM

It was one of those strange things that sometimes happen in small towns. The three spiritual leaders at the synagogue in Capernaum, who were best of friends, and all three married within months of each other, were now all three anxiously awaiting the births of their first-born sons any day now.

But as strange things tend to not go as planned, all three men each ended up with the most beautiful little girl that they could imagine.

Twelve years later, the three girls, born within a week of each other, considered themselves to be an inseparable trio. Arial, Hava and Miriam were the wealthiest girls in town as their dads were the spiritual leaders of Capernaum. Arial's dad was the Ruler of the synagogue. Hava's dad was the Ruler of the Hebrew school there. And Miriam's dad taught at the Hebrew school and was a member of the Sanhedrin, the governing body of the Jews.

The girls had every right to be spoiled rotten but had somehow managed to be the pride of Capernaum. Everyone loved "the trio." They were the friendliest, kindest, and most caring of young women. If someone was ill, they dropped off bouquets that they picked in the woods. If someone was lonely, they made fancy breads and stopped by for a visit. They were a joy to be around and were loved by all.

Their latest project had made them more loved than ever. They were using their musical talent to entertain the little children of Capernaum. Twice a week, 15 to 20 little children would come to Hava's back courtyard and there the girls would teach them songs.

Hava played the harp and sang. Arial played the lute and sang. And Miriam taught the little ones worship songs based on King David's Psalms.

The girls spent much of their time writing their own music and rewriting the words so that the little ones could understand and participate. All three loved the Psalms, and when they found words they didn't understand, each one had a doting Abba who would help them interpret the Hebrew.

They had created a hide-away in the woods behind Arial's house, and their dads had helped them to place rocks in strategic places so that they had the perfect rehearsal studio. You could find them there most every afternoon where it was nice and shaded.

The trio was also very well informed for girls of that time period. They each had been taught to read the Hebrew Scripture and they knew about Jesus, the man who claimed to be the Messiah.

They knew that their dads' positions as Jewish leaders forced them to be against Jesus. Yet, they also knew that their dads were torn and troubled. The trio often heard them discussing the healings and miracles and wondered why everyone was so stressed over a man who was doing so much good.

When Jesus first moved to Capernaum, he was often invited to read the Scripture and teach at the synagogue, but now it seemed that he wasn't being allowed to teach there. The girls discussed what was going on and why orders were being given to stop Jesus' ministry.

They wondered what would happen if Jesus really was the Messiah and overthrew the Roman government. They wondered what life would look like when the Jews were free from Rome.

Last week Jesus had been teaching along the Sea of Galilee. They had also heard that he had taken some of his followers across the sea to the land of the Gadarenes, but had left most of his followers still camped outside of Capernaum.

Yes, they were well informed young Jewish girls who were quickly approaching the age for marriage, a subject that often came up in their discussions. They hoped that whoever their parents selected for their husbands would always live close enough to keep the trio together.

"Let's go down by the creek and pick a bouquet for my Aunt Sharon. She's getting so discouraged," suggested Miriam.

"Isn't she getting any better? I thought she saw a new doctor last week," asked Hava.

"If anything, she seems worse. I think he just took her money and did nothing. I don't know how she stands being cooped up in that house all the time."

"Let's not only take flowers, but let's serenade her."

"Oh, that would be fun. Let's pick out a Psalm."

"I love the harmonies when we do this one:

> **Shout for joy to the L**ORD**, all the earth.**
> **Worship the L**ORD **with gladness;**
> **come before him with joyful songs.**
> **Know that the L**ORD **is God.**
> **It is he who made us, and we are his;**
> **we are his people, the sheep of his pasture.**
>
> **Enter his gates with thanksgiving**
> **and his courts with praise;**
> **give thanks to him and praise his name.**[1]

"I know that she'll love it. We'll pick a bouquet and then go to her house to sing."

They found the flowers they wanted and arranged them into a nice bouquet. Miriam knocked on Aunt Sharon's door and one of the servants, Rayna, answered. She took the bouquet to Aunt Sharon and helped her move to the window.

In a few minutes, Aunt Sharon was waving down to the girls and the girls began to sing their song for her. The trio could tell that it cheered her up, and they were glad they could do something to help.

They waved goodbye and Arial hugged the other two girls and said she needed to run to help her mother. They agreed to meet at the regular time to prepare for the children's worship tomorrow morning.

Hava and Miriam walked slowly toward their own homes. They were trying to work out the harmonies for one of the children's songs.

Early the next morning, Miriam arrived at Hava's and they started setting up for the children. It was not like Arial to be late. When it was only a few minutes before time for the children to arrive, Hava's mother volunteered to run to Arial's home and see what was wrong. When she returned, the children had already arrived, and she just whispered to the girls that Arial was sick, and they would have to do it without her. The two girls sang with the children for a little while, but then sent them home early because they were so worried about Arial.

"Why didn't she send word to us that she couldn't come?" asked Hava.

Hava's mother told her, "I think that Arial is a lot sicker than that. In fact, I think we should be going there now."

Miriam, Hava, and Hava's mother all walked quickly to Arial's house. News traveled quickly in Capernaum, especially when it concerned the Ruler of the synagogue and his lovely daughter. The yard was filled with neighbors and friends. Hava and Miriam managed to get inside the front door where they saw Arial lying in the living room. They ran to her and kissed her, but she was too sick to know.

The girls were sent back outside so that the three mothers could tend to her. There was little that they could do except to keep applying cool wet cloths and pray that the fever would go away.

Hava and Miriam waited out in the courtyard with the other friends and neighbors. They learned that during the night, Arial had started running a very high fever. Hava and Miriam just sat and cried and waited with the others. All they could think about was singing together yesterday and picking flowers and the fun they had had ministering to Aunt Sharon. So many happy memories. *How can Arial be dying when she was so alive and happy yesterday?*

Suddenly, Rabbi Jairus burst out of the house. "I'm going to find Jesus. Jesus can heal her!" He took off at a run toward the Sea of Galilee.

That caused quite a stir among the crowd. The crowd was divided among those who felt it was the right thing to do, and those who felt that it was the worst thing their Rabbi could do. But everyone felt nothing but sympathy and concern for their Ruler regardless of their belief.

After another 30 minutes of waiting, it was announced that Arial was dead. The crowd was totally silent with shock. A group of men went to find Rabbi Jairus.

Within a few minutes the mourners began to arrive with their flutes and lyres. They began singing sad, mournful songs called dirges.

Hava and Miriam asked to see Arial and were allowed inside the house with the family and close friends. It was a horrible time of grief and sadness. The trio would never sing again. How they hated the sound of the dirges. Would they ever feel happy again?

About an hour later, Jesus and three of his disciples arrived with Rabbi Jairus. He asked everyone to leave the room except for them and her mother. Hava and Miriam and others quickly moved outside to the yard with all the other relatives and friends.

Here's what the Bible tells us:

> **When he arrived at the house of Jairus, he did not let anyone go in with him except Peter, John and James, and the child's father and mother. Meanwhile, all the people were wailing and mourning for her. "Stop wailing," Jesus said. "She is not dead but asleep."**

They laughed at him, knowing that she was dead. But he took her by the hand and said, "My child, get up!" Her spirit returned, and at once she stood up. Then Jesus told them to give her something to eat. Her parents were astonished....[2]

Hava and Miriam waited outside. They couldn't believe their eyes when Arial herself came running outside to find them. She looked perfectly normal. They kept hugging her and couldn't believe their eyes. Jesus and his disciples went out the back way quietly and avoided the crowd. Rabbi Jairus and his wife stayed in the house and received their friends there.

"Let's sing!" said Arial.

"Oh, let's do the one we did yesterday," Hava said. So instead of dirges, the trio once again sang King David's Psalm in worship.

"That's the song you sang for me yesterday," said a gentle voice behind them. The girls were shocked to see Miriam's Aunt Sharon standing there beside them.

"Aunt Sharon, what are you doing here? It's great to see you and you look really good. But are you all right?"

"Not only has Jesus raised Arial from the dead, but he has healed my disease. I'm well — completely well! I'm trying to find your mother to tell her the news."

"Oh, Aunt Sharon, what happened?"

"Well, Rayna, my servant has been telling me about Jesus and how he's healed so many people. I didn't want to get in trouble with your dad, Miriam, but what Rayna said made sense. I had watched Jesus and his disciples go back and forth past my window and he seemed okay. Rayna kept begging me to just go down to the front door whenever he was passing and ask him to heal me. But I was afraid.

When you girls sang for me yesterday, I knew that God was telling me I should give it a try. If he really is from God, then that would be better than seeing another doctor. So, I told Rayna to be on the lookout for his disciples.

When she saw them coming this morning, she told me, and I went out the front door and met him. And here I am! I'll tell you the details later, I want to go find my sister."

"I think Mother and Abba are still inside the house with Arial's parents. Just go on in. They will want to hear your news too."

Rabbi Jairus was with Jesus when he healed Aunt Sharon. But in all the excitement over Arial, he had forgotten all about it.

And so, on one day, Jesus turned the little town of Capernaum upside down. The three Jewish leaders spent many evenings talking about and considering all that they had seen and heard Jesus do. They had seen firsthand his healing powers and knew that he was sent from God.

And the trio declared that they believed that Jesus was the Messiah sent from God. They would sing his praises every day for the rest of their lives.

---

[1] **Psalm 100:1-4**
[2] **Luke 8:51-58**

Jesus Heals a Woman
Mark 5:25-34

Jairus Asks Jesus to Heal His Daughter
Luke 8:41-42, 49-50

Jesus Raises Girl From the Dead
Luke 8:51-56

Chapter 17
THE STORY OF KOBE

> "Kobe, wake up!
> Kobe, wake up!
> I need you to wake up NOW!"
> Mother was shaking Kobe awake and he was trying to get his mind to function.

"Mother, what's wrong? What's happened?"

"I don't know. But you know what Dad's always told us. If he's not home by the third watch (about 2 a.m.), we should get out and hide.

"We've got to hurry. I'm not sure what time it is, but it's nearly sunrise. I overslept. Get up and get your bag packed. You know the plan."

Jana had woken up a few minutes earlier and realized that her husband was not home. She had started packing a food bag when she realized that the sun was beginning to rise. She ran to wake up Kobe and get him started.

They had to get out of the house before the Roman soldiers arrived. Something had gone wrong last night, and they had to get out. But there were things she needed to pack.

Kobe appeared looking disheveled but alert. He had his bag packed. "Grab the skillet out of the courtyard and go to the hiding place. Can you carry this food bag, too? I've got to get myself packed," said Mother.

"Sure," said Kobe, as he took the food bag and his personal bag that included a blanket and a heavier robe. He grabbed the skillet as he ran to the back of the chicken coop. They would stay there to wait and see if the Romans would come and ransack the house. *But what is taking Mother so long? She knows the rules.*

He heard horses' hoofs pounding up the street when he finally saw her coming out of the house. She was trying to salvage too much, and they would be caught. He ran out of hiding to grab a couple of her bags and hurried her to the hiding place just as the soldiers arrived and began knocking down the front door.

Kobe was only 12, but his father had drilled him repeatedly on what had to be done if something went wrong.

Kobe's dad was a Zealot. Zealots were an organized group of men who opposed the Roman government's rule over Judea. They often went on raids to attack the Roman forces and were always plotting ways to make life miserable for the Romans. In return, they were hated by the Romans. And if they were caught, there would be no mercy.

Not only would Kobe probably never see his dad, but the Romans would destroy their house and imprison or enslave both him and his mother if they were caught.

So, once she caught her breath, she and Kobe moved to the second hiding place deeper in the woods. "Mother, you brought too much stuff!"

"I know, and I didn't have time to change. Let me hide behind this tree and change and then we can throw away this outfit."

Kobe agreed and stood guard while she slipped her beautiful blue robe off and put on a plain black robe that symbolized mourning.

It was true that she was mourning — but it was also her protection, because more than likely the Roman soldiers would not question her being alone on the main highway without her husband. They would assume she was moving because of his death. Hopefully, the soldiers wouldn't identify them.

Once Mother had changed into her mourning clothes, she discarded the other clothes behind the tree and her load was a little lighter. "Mother, you know that Dad said to only take two bags apiece. I'll take the food bag and my personal bag. I can pack the skillet in my bag. But you still have four bags. That's going to call attention to us. What did you bring that wasn't on the list?"

"I don't know. I just grabbed things. I'm so sorry I overslept. I just couldn't think."

"Mother, you did the right thing. You got out just in the nick of time. But we need to repack things so that we don't make people think we're rich. If we are rich enough for all this stuff, then we should have servants to carry it. We don't want to look like robbers! Remember, we need to look like two very poor people in mourning."

"I think I grabbed everything," said Mother.

"I think you did, too."

"Okay, here's your blanket. What other robe do you want?" asked Kobe. "Did you get the money and the jewels?"

"Yes, they are in that box."

"Let's tie them in a cloth and they won't take up so much room," said Kobe.

"Oh, but isn't the box valuable?"

"Of course, but it's too big. It's got to go. And all this kitchen stuff has got to go. I'll get a job and buy you new stuff when we get a kitchen to put it in."

"Oh, Kobe, I'm so sorry. I tried to talk your dad out of going on this raid. I had a bad feeling. Now, I don't know what we'll do."

"Mother, you know the plan. We need to get to Galilee, and that's going to be a long walk. We need to stay hidden in Jerusalem for a couple of days, but then we can start walking. We'll go to Uncle Amal's house in Tiberius. He'll take us in and take care of us.   I'm sure he'll know where I can get work and we'll be fine. And if Dad can, he'll meet us there."

"Oh, Kobe. I'm glad that you are so brave. I'll be brave if you are!   Let's move to the third hiding place and then we can stay put for a while."

The next hiding place was a lot more pleasant, as it was near a stream and there were plenty of trees. They could hide their packs and just relax near the water. No one would suspect anything other than a poor, mourning mother and son spending the day seeking peace. But no one discovered them, and they began to relax.

Mother had grabbed plenty of bread, pickled fish, and cheese, so they just made a quick dinner and didn't light a fire. It wasn't terribly strange for them to throw their blankets on the ground and sleep under the trees since they had often traveled with Kobe's dad on his missions.

But Kobe found it hard to be brave once the sun went down. He couldn't remember ever sleeping outside without his dad. He was 12 years old, and he knew that he would try to protect his mother from any danger — but he sure hoped there wasn't any. They were still inside the city of Jerusalem, so the only real danger was being discovered by the Roman soldiers. Kobe knew he was no match for one of them, and they didn't usually travel alone.

Kobe and his mother stayed in their hiding place for two more days, but early on Thursday morning they packed their two bags apiece and started out of Jerusalem. They walked along the back roads, and while it took longer, doing so avoided anyone that might recognize them.

Soon they found themselves headed downhill and surrounded by beautiful mountains and scenery.

They had traveled many times to visit Uncle Amal, so they knew what to expect along the way.

It took them almost a week to arrive in Tiberius, but it was a pleasant trip for the most part. They fished and cooked their meals like Dad had taught them. But of course, everything they did reminded them of Dad. They tried not to think about what had happened to him. They had to keep their minds focused on getting to Uncle Amal's. Maybe he would have news. Maybe Dad was already there.

Maybe they would just start a new life in Galilee and Dad would focus on being a jeweler again and not be involved with the Zealots. Yeah, right! Kobe knew that his mind was playing tricks on him. He tried to focus on the details around him and listen for Roman horses.

Before they left the main road and entered Tiberius, Mother changed out of her "mourning" clothes and back into a brown robe. They didn't want to call attention to themselves in any way. She decided to keep the black robe just in case she wanted to wear it while at Uncle Amal's. She shuddered as she thought about having to face the facts if her husband was dead. But she quickly put on a cheerful face for Kobe.

"Kobe, you have been so helpful for this hard journey. I've enjoyed getting to know you in a new way. You are growing into a fine young man."

"Thank you, Mother. I know it's been hard for you. I'm glad I've made it easier. How much farther is it to Uncle Amal's? I'm looking forward to a home cooked meal and sleeping indoors for a change."

"It's only about three miles from here, so we'll be there shortly." She winked at him, and added, "Plenty of time for them to prepare a feast for dinner!"

Kobe couldn't remember the directions to Uncle Amal's, so he was glad that Mother was so familiar with the area. She and Dad had lived there before moving to Jerusalem, so she felt comfortable navigating the winding streets.

"Just around this corner and we'll —"

Mother gasped and caught her breath as she and Kobe stopped still in their tracks. Uncle Amal's home was totally destroyed. Parts of it had been burned and all the windows and doors had been broken.

They forced themselves to walk past it without looking too interested. But inside they were screaming. The damage looked recent, so he assumed that Uncle Amal was somehow included in the same raid his dad had been on.

They just kept forcing their feet to keep walking. *What will we do? Where will we go?* There was no plan now. It was just the two of them with no home and no place to go.

Mother led them down to the beach where they could at least sit and watch the fishermen heading out for the night. Kobe had never seen the Sea of Galilee at night and would have enjoyed the sights except that he had never felt so scared in his whole life.

He was only 12, so he knew it would be impossible to find a real job for at least a year. He knew they had some money and some jewelry, but he was pretty sure it wouldn't last that long. Mother had been strong until now, but with the sun going down, she was crying as he had never seen her cry. He knew he had to be the strong one — but how?

He was suddenly aware of a group of people walking along the beach. He put his arm around his mother and warned her to compose herself until they were past. But as they passed, one of the women in the group stopped and asked if they were okay. When Mother looked up to assure her that everything was fine, their eyes met, and the woman recognized that something was wrong. She genuinely wanted to help. Dad had always warned them never to talk to anyone. But Dad was no longer guiding them. Mother took one look into the eyes of the woman and knew that she had to trust someone.

"My husband died in Jerusalem, so when my mourning was complete, my son and I came to my uncle's home here in Tiberius. He was our only relative and now we've just discovered that he has recently died. We are alone and don't know what to do. I don't have any idea what to do."

"Oh, I'm so sorry for your loss. But you mustn't stay out here alone. If you'll come with me, you'll be welcome to stay with us until you can decide what to do. My name is Lois, and we are followers of Jesus. What is your name?"

"My name is Jana, and this is my son Kobe."

Kobe was horrified that she gave their real names in case the Romans were still looking for them. But he knew better than to make a fuss and call attention to the mistake. So, he smiled his greeting.

Mother seemed to be gathering up her bags as if to follow this lady, so Kobe did the same. It would probably be safer than sleeping out on the beach. He didn't know who this Jesus was, but there were many groups who followed a mentor or rabbi. He assumed that they were a similar religious group. So, they followed Lois for a few blocks and entered the courtyard of a large home overlooking the sea.

Lois introduced them to a few people, but Kobe's mind was a blur. There were at least 100 people there. They were shown a place to stash their bags and blankets and then invited to wash up and prepare for the evening meal.

Kobe couldn't believe their luck. This was too good to be true. They could safely hide <u>and</u> be provided with food. He wondered what kind of price they would have to pay for the food — but tonight, he didn't care. He was just grateful for the plate that was placed in his hands. He and his mother went back and sat on their blanket and ate their meal in silence.

Everyone was friendly, but didn't push for information, and he was grateful for that. After eating, they stretched out on their blankets, and while some in the crowd were singing pleasant songs about God, they cried themselves into a deep sleep.

Kobe and his mother continued to hide in their little world of pain and grief. The strangers around them were kind and caring but let them take their time to adjust to their surroundings. All his life, Kobe had been taught to hide and now he found his heart desiring to be a part of this new thing called friendship. He watched the other boys play ball and laugh and tease. He watched them going out in teams. Different boys would invite him to join them, but he always said, "No, thank you."

He had never been allowed to attend Hebrew school because they moved so frequently, and his dad said it was too dangerous for him to be known. Now, he was feeling strange new feelings inside that yearned for friends.

After they had been at the courtyard in Tiberius for about a week, Philip, one of the apostles who often mentored the young men, came and sat down beside Kobe.

"Kobe, I need some help. I was wondering, if it's all right with your mother, if you would go with me to deliver some food to a family in need."

How could Kobe say no when they had been given so much for free? He felt he should say yes. He looked at his mother and she nodded her permission.

"Sure," said Kobe as he got up to follow Philip.

"We'll be back in a couple of hours," Philip told Kobe's mother.

"We need to go to the market and pick up some food for a family. The dad is sick and not able to work and there's six little ones at home. Here, grab three or four of these bags and we'll fill them with food." Kobe and Philip both grabbed bags and Philip led them to the market.

Philip soon had the bags filled with fresh food, and Kobe watched as Philip paid at each tent. Their arms were filled with all they could carry as Philip led them to the home of the family in need. Philip talked with the woman of the house and encouraged her, and Kobe watched as Philip prayed with her. He knew there was a God, but he had never seen anyone talk to him as if he were really listening.

When they got back to the courtyard, Philip thanked Kobe for his help and told his mother she should be proud of him. That made Kobe feel really good. He was glad to help. Philip also told them that Jesus would be teaching down by the beach tomorrow if they wanted to come down and listen. Mother asked what time and Philip told her.

Kobe and his mother talked about what he had seen. He told Mother how Philip had treated the woman kindly and how he had paid for the groceries himself and given the groceries to the woman for free. That really impressed him. Mother could tell that Kobe wanted to learn more about this group, and she agreed that they, too, had been treated very kindly. She said they could go to the beach to hear Jesus for a little while tomorrow. She, too, wanted to know more about this group.

It was good to get out of the courtyard, and the beach was beautiful overlooking the Sea of Galilee. They listened as Jesus taught.

One of the stories that Jesus told really touched Kobe. Jesus said,

> "Therefore everyone who hears these words of mine and puts them into practice is like a wise man who built his house on the rock.

"The rain came down, the streams rose, and the winds blew and beat against that house; yet it did not fall, because it had its foundation on the rock.

"But everyone who hears these words of mine and does not put them into practice is like a foolish man who built his house on sand.

"The rain came down, the streams rose, and the winds blew and beat against that house, and it fell with a great crash."[1]

Kobe just kept thinking that all the efforts of his dad had ended in nothingness. He had spent his entire lifetime chasing a dream that had ended with nothing to show for it. And it had left Kobe and his mother crushed like the sand.

Kobe wondered if Jesus really could offer a better way of life. He certainly liked the love and kindness that he saw within the group. He liked how they cared for everyone and helped each other. If he were 13, he would be ready to choose, but right now he had to be obedient to whatever his mother wanted him to do.

After dinner, everyone in the courtyard was called together for a meeting. Jesus explained the plan for the coming days. He announced that a prophet named John the Baptizer had been murdered by King Herod, and that he wanted to spend some time alone with his apostles to grieve and hear their report of a recent ministry trip. He announced that the rest of the disciples would be moving back to Capernaum, and that he would meet them there in a few days.

The meeting was dismissed, and Kobe and his mother were wondering what this meant for them. *Will we be welcome?* They didn't have to worry for long. Jesus himself came to their area and sat down to visit. He said that he was glad that they were with the group and hoped that they had been well treated. Kobe and his mother assured him that they had been.

Then Jesus said something that surprised both of them.

Jesus asked, "Kobe, would you like to go with me on this ministry trip? I don't know how long we'll be gone — not over two or three days at the most. I believe that you will learn a lot. There will be the 13 of us and Matthew's son, Joel is going with us. Do you know him?"

"No, sir. I haven't gotten to know any of the boys. But I would like to. I want to learn more about what you are teaching. I didn't go to Hebrew school, so all of this is very new to me."

"Yes, I know," Jesus said kindly. Kobe had never felt so loved or understood, and he didn't know why.

Jesus turned to Kobe's mother and asked, "Would you allow me to take your son with us for a few days? We'll be crossing the Sea of Galilee and I'm not sure how long I'll need to be in Bethsaida. Then we will join you and the other disciples in Capernaum. Would you trust me to take care of your son?"

Kobe's mother swallowed hard. Kobe was all she had left, but she, too, felt that she could trust Jesus. She said, "Yes."

Philip and his wife came over a little later and brought their young son and newborn baby girl. Kobe's mother, Jana, was thrilled to get to hold such a little one. Philip asked her if she would mind helping his wife as the group moved to Capernaum. He promised to keep a close eye on Kobe.

So, for the first time that Kobe could remember, he and his mother would be separated. They had never been apart overnight, and with their losses being so fresh, it was stressful for both of them.

At sunrise the next morning, Jesus and the apostles and the two boys headed to the shore. The other disciples gathered all their belongings and prepared for the short hike back to Capernaum.

Kobe had never been on a boat before and was excited and nervous about being out on the sea. Philip pointed to a bench and he sat down and watched as the men took turns rowing. Six men would row while the others rested — but the entire time was spent in laughing and talking and enjoying each other's company. They talked about their recent ministry trip and Kobe enjoyed getting to know them better.

"Kobe, I think it's your turn to row!" said Philip as he finished his turn.

"I've never done it, but I'm willing to learn."

"That's all I ask. It really isn't hard. You just hold this end of the paddle and pull the other end through the water. There's a rhythm to it that will take you a few minutes to catch on — but you'll do fine. In. Pull. Up. Push. In. Pull. Up. Push. See, you've already got it."

For the first time in Kobe's life, he was participating, cooperating, being a part of something, and he could hardly believe how good it felt. All the men were encouraging him, and he felt something inside that craved this approval and attention.   He had always gotten approval from Mother, but this was different, and he couldn't quite put his finger on what it was. He finally came up with the word "teamwork."

He also noticed that Jesus was relaxed and just as friendly and welcoming as the other men. He took his turn rowing and didn't behave the way Kobe thought of priests or Pharisees back in Jerusalem.   They were going to Bethsaida. The apostles said that this was a secluded place where they could be alone with Jesus. Everyone looked forward to times when they could ask questions and learn from him away from the crowds.

But as they got closer to shore, they could see that crowds had already formed and were getting larger by the minute. There would be no peace and quiet here. Some boats that passed them earlier must have announced their coming, and people packed the shore. Kobe wasn't sure he had ever seen so many people except maybe at Passover time in Jerusalem.

As they waded to the beach, Jesus began to teach, and the apostles dispersed among the crowds to answer questions and to help with crowd control. Kobe found himself alone with Joel. They sat on the beach and listened to Jesus and found themselves gradually getting acquainted.

When they decided to take a walk along the beach to stretch their legs, Joel told Kobe about the first time he heard Jesus teach and how he had left to go and sit in the water so he wouldn't have to hear him. Kobe laughed and discovered that it was easy to share with Joel.

Kobe told him how worried he was about his mother being worried about him since she had just lost her husband and uncle. "So, what made you change your mind about Jesus, or have you?" asked Kobe.

"Oh, yes, I've changed my mind and he's changed my heart and life. You would not have wanted to be around me before he changed me." And then Joel told him the story of his becoming a follower of Jesus. You read Joel's story in Chapter 11.

"Do you mean to tell me that Jesus just touched your feet, and they were made well?" asked Kobe.

"Yeah. It's hard to believe, but you'll probably see him healing people tonight. I've seen him heal the blind, the crippled, the deaf, the mute and the leper."

"No way!" said Kobe. "No one can do that!"

"Let's go back to where Jesus is teaching. Usually at the end of his teaching, he starts healing people."

"<u>This</u> I want to see!" agreed Kobe.

And that's what he saw. Jesus healed the blind, the lame, the deaf, the mute, the lepers, the crippled, and those with fevers. It was amazing and Kobe was in shock. People were crowded all around Jesus asking for his healing and he was talking with each one individually and meeting their needs.

"Man, I'm starving," said Joel. "I wonder when Jesus is going to finish healing these people and send them away.   We usually cook fish when we're by the sea, but I don't see anybody working on it."

As the sun began to set, the people were told to sit down in groups of 50's. Joel and Kobe asked Philip what they should be doing, and he told them just to find a group and sit down. So, they did.

They watched as Jesus took five rounds of bread and two small fish and asked God to bless it. Then he began to tear the bread and fish into smaller pieces, and the apostles began to pass it around to the hungry people. Kobe couldn't take his eyes off of Jesus. He kept breaking the bread and fish and kept filling the disciple's packs so that they could pass it around to the people. Kobe's head felt like it would explode. This was not possible! There was only enough food for one grown man and yet Jesus was feeding thousands with it.

Kobe looked at Joel and said, "I'll be right back!" He got up and walked around the area. If indeed everyone was seated in groups of approximately 50 men — and most of those men had wives and multiple children — that meant that just about every group was at least 100 people. And Kobe lost count.

Here's what the Bible says:

> **The number of those who ate was about five thousand men, besides women and children.**[2]

Kobe found his way back to Joel and began to eat the bread and fish. He discovered that he had all the bread and fish he could eat. "How?" he kept asking Joel.

"What do you think?" asked Joel.

"I think that he's the best magician I've ever seen. But this food is real, and it's good. There isn't anything fake about it. What does that mean?"

"I think it proves that he is the Messiah, sent by God. He's a supernatural being living in a human body. And he can do supernatural things — like heal and produce food," replied Joel.

Kobe didn't know what to think. He knew that God existed, but he assumed he was distant and unapproachable. Not like this.

After the boys had helped the apostles clean up the area, they got back into the boat. Once again men took their turns at the oars, and this time Kobe volunteered for his turn. But after a while he noticed that Jesus was not in the boat. When he asked, he was told that often Jesus would give them orders that they did not understand. Their job was simply to obey.

Philip told Kobe that Jesus had said that he needed time to pray and wanted them to go on to Capernaum without him. He would probably spend a couple of days in prayer and then walk to Capernaum just for the peace and quiet.

The wind seemed to be rising on the sea and the waves were getting choppier. Kobe was feeling a little seasick but managed to keep his stomach. He took several turns at the oars, but it seemed the harder they rowed, the slower the boat went. They rowed and rowed and rowed. The fishermen in the group kept checking to make sure they were going the right direction, but the wind was just getting stronger and stronger and they seemed to be making no progress. The men were exhausted, and it was almost morning.

"What's that?" asked Joel who was catching his breath on a bench near the front of the boat, watching the rowers, and looking behind them. Within seconds, everything was chaos. Grown men were screaming and Kobe tried to scream but nothing would come out. They were certain that they were seeing a ghost. What else could explain a human shape walking on the water toward them? They were three or four miles from shore, near the middle of the Sea of Galilee.

Some men were searching for weapons to defend themselves, others were just collapsed in heaps, crying from exhaustion and fear.

Kobe was frozen to his seat. Then the "ghost" spoke, and they recognized Jesus' voice. He said,

... "Take courage! It is I. Don't be afraid."[3]

Peter had a request. What do you think he asked Jesus?

Here's what the Bible tells us:

> "Lord, if it's you," Peter replied, "tell me to come to you on the water."
>
> "Come," he said.
>
> Then Peter got down out of the boat, walked on the water and came toward Jesus. But when he saw the wind, he was afraid and, beginning to sink, cried out, "Lord, save me!"
>
> Immediately Jesus reached out his hand and caught him.... [4]

All the men helped pull Jesus and Peter into the boat.

The Bible tells us that three things happened when Jesus got in the boat.

 The wind stopped blowing and the waves died down.

 The men worshiped Jesus and declared again that he was the Son of God.

 And suddenly, they were at the shore.

Kobe just sat stunned. His mind kept going over what had happened. They had rowed and rowed and rowed and were only halfway across the sea. Jesus had <u>walked</u> three or four miles on the water through the storm and now, instantly, they were at the shore. *How did the boat travel the remaining three or four miles?* Kobe felt his head would explode. As the men were getting off the boat, he felt numb not only from exhaustion but from his amazement.

The apostles were laughing and talking about how scared they were, and Jesus was teasing them, but Kobe just felt dazed. Nothing seemed real until he heard these words:

"As a Zealot I have known a lot of fear, but I don't think I've ever been <u>that</u> afraid!"

Kobe's mind came alive as he looked at the speaker of those words. *What had he said? What did it mean? Who is that man?* He had to know.

But his body was too tired. They arrived at an unfamiliar courtyard and his body had to sleep. He threw his blanket down in the first available spot. Tomorrow...

Kobe lay on his blanket blinking his eyes in the bright sunlight. It took him a few minutes to figure out where he was since they had arrived before dawn and he had never seen this place. Later he found out that he was in Jesus' courtyard. As he lay there, he felt the urge to pull the blanket over his head and go back to sleep, then he remembered that he needed to find his mother and assure her of his safety. She would be worried.

He asked around and found out that most of the other disciples were camping at another house nearby. He found his mother there and was pleased that she had made new friends and volunteered to help in the kitchen. She seemed to be doing fine. They sat and ate breakfast together and he tried to explain some of the things he had experienced. But he kept asking himself if maybe it was just a dream.

His mother encouraged him to get some more rest, and he agreed that it would probably be best since he'd only gotten less than an hour's sleep before the sun woke him up. He threw down his blanket and was asleep before she could tell him to sleep well. Now with a mighty adventure, lots of exercise rowing a boat, a full tummy, and a blanket to keep out the light, Kobe slept until early afternoon.

This time he woke up clear-headed and eager to find the speaker who said he was a Zealot. He didn't want to alarm his mother though, so he just said he was going to walk back over to Jesus' house and see what was happening. She was glad that he had made some new friends and encouraged him to go and have fun.

Kobe wasn't sure what he wanted to say or what he wanted to know, but he knew that he needed to talk with the man who claimed to be a Zealot.

When he arrived at Jesus' courtyard, he found that most of the men were just waking up and were searching for food. They welcomed Kobe and offered him some fruit. He sat down and enjoyed their friendship, but his mind was focused on how to talk with the man and how to do so without revealing too much of his own history. As he sat and listened to the talk, he discovered that the man he wanted to talk with was named Simon.

Kobe kept watching for his chance to speak with him alone. Finally, that opportunity came when Simon took a water jar to the well to refill it. Kobe grabbed a nearby water jar and followed him to the well.

"Mr. Simon, my name is Kobe —"

"Yes, Kobe, I know you. You went with us on our adventure yesterday."

"Yes, sir. I was wondering —"

"You probably haven't seen that kind of adventure before, have you?" asked Mr. Simon.

"No, sir. I'm still trying to figure out if it really happened or if it was all a dream."

Mr. Simon laughed, "Oh, it happened, all right. I was there too, you know!"

"Mr. Simon, I was wondering if I could talk with you privately — I mean — I have a question about something you said, and I don't want to be heard by the others."

Suddenly Mr. Simon realized that Kobe wasn't just making small talk. "After breakfast, why don't we walk along the beach and stretch our legs? Would that work?"

"Yes, sir, and thank you very much."

They returned to the group and filled the water cups. Kobe still didn't know what he would say or even what he wanted to know, but he knew that he had to find out about Mr. Simon's being a Zealot.

"Kobe, come take a walk with me. This old man needs to stretch out his legs and I need some young ears to listen to me!"

"Oh, Kobe, I wouldn't go; he'll talk your ears off!" the group teased.

"I will be glad to listen, sir," said Kobe as he got up to follow Mr. Simon out of the courtyard.

They talked about the things they had seen yesterday as Jesus had fed the 5000 men, and how he had walked on the water. They laughed about Peter trying to walk on the water, too, but both admitted that it was a brave thing to try.

"Now, I've got a feeling you've got something more serious you want to talk about. Here's a couple of good rocks that will be perfect for a rest."

The beach was deserted since the fishermen wouldn't be arriving until around sunset. So, they could talk freely.

"Mr. Simon, I believe that I heard you say that you are a Zealot. I was wondering…."

"No. Let's get this straight. I <u>was</u> a Zealot. They still call me Simon the Zealot to keep me separate from Simon Peter, but I no longer follow that way of life."

"Okay… so you were a Zealot, but now you are not?" asked Kobe trying to put the pieces together.

"Kobe, I still have very strong feelings about the freedom of Israel, and I guess that's why I don't object to people calling me a Zealot. But I believe that Jesus is the Messiah, who has come to set Israel free from Rome. The very first time I heard Jesus teach, he taught:

> **'But I tell you, love your enemies and pray for those who persecute you.[5]'**

"I knew then that I had to get out of the Zealots and make some serious changes. Later, after I started following Jesus and hearing more of his teaching, I knew that I couldn't continue to hate. I had to learn to love. I watched Jesus heal Romans and love them and care for them. I knew that I wanted that kind of supernatural love.

"You've seen Jesus heal the blind and the crippled. Well, for this old man, he healed my heart. He set me free from hate and anger."

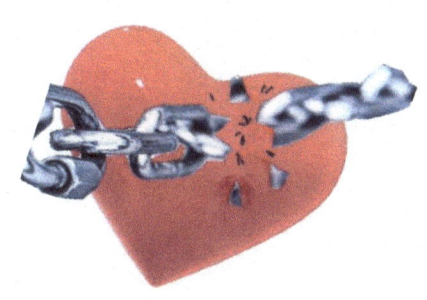

"Thank you, sir, for telling me. I just wanted to know."

"Kobe, I know that you've just recently lost your dad. Was he a Zealot?"

Kobe froze in fear. He had been taught to never reveal anything about his dad.

Simon put his arm on Kobe's shoulder. "Kobe, I'm sorry. I know that you haven't had an easy life. But you don't have to hide anymore. Are you a Zealot?"

"I've never thought about it. I don't think so. I hated the hiding and running all the time. When Mrs. Lois invited us to spend the night, I felt like there was nothing but peace and love and joy here.

"I would like to learn more about this New Way that Jesus teaches," said Kobe. "All I've ever known was hate. I've never felt this kind of love before. I think it's sorta like Heaven. I think that's why I was so surprised when you said you were a Zealot."

"Well, I was. But that is in the past. When Jesus really, truly changes your heart, you don't have to feel ashamed of your past — just sorry for the wasted time.

"Come on, let's go see what the guys are up to."

---

[1] **Matthew 7:24-27**
[2] **Matthew 14:21**
[3] **Matthew 14:27**
[4] **Matthew 14:28-31**
[5] **Matthew 5:44**

Jesus Takes Apostles for Private Retreat
Mark 6:30-34

Jesus Feeds the Five Thousand
Mark 6:35-44

Jesus Walks on Water
John 6:16-21

Peter Walks on the Water
Matthew 14:28-31

Chapter 18
THE STORY OF GERSHAM & MARIO

"Mario, do you see a piece of wood in the box that's just a little bigger than this one? This one isn't long enough."

"What about this one?" Mario asked as he handed the block of wood to Gersham, his brother.

"Perfect!"

Mario was glad to help his older brother Gersham with his projects. Gersham was blind, but he was able to carve beautiful things out of wood.

When Gersham was only four years old, his Abba took him to his carpentry shop and let him play with the leftover wood scraps. He would play contentedly for hours building forts and houses with the scraps.

Soon his Abba introduced him to tools and Gersham learned to shape the wood into balls and boats and blocks. Mother had her hands full with two more little ones at home, so Gersham spent most days with his Abba in the carpentry shop.

When Gersham turned eight years old, he was expected to go each morning to an area just outside of the temple to beg. His little brother Mario, who was six years old, walked with him there each morning on his way to Hebrew school. His Abba would come at noon and lead him to the carpentry shop to spend the afternoons with him.

Gersham hated just sitting and doing nothing, so he always had a block of wood and a rasp or file with him.

After school, Mario would come to the shop too, and together they would work on projects with Abba's scraps of wood. Gersham began to carve candlesticks and bowls from the wood. And he loved to make balls and boats for the little children who were brave enough to say hello.

Now that Gersham had turned 13, he was considered to be a man. But because of his blindness, Gersham needed his family to help him with everyday tasks. So, even though he was a man, life continued as usual for him. He begged at the temple each morning and worked at the carpentry shop every afternoon except for the Sabbath.

His woodworking continued to improve, and his dad was able to sell his candlesticks, kitchen tools, and bowls at his carpentry shop. This provided the money he needed to pay his parents for housing and food.

Sabbath days were the hardest for Gersham because he hated not being able to work with his hands. But they were profitable days for begging, so he usually spent the day sitting near the temple gate.

The Pharisees taught that people who were blind or crippled or sick were being punished by God, so Gersham had few friends. But Mario was not only a good brother, but a good friend. Often, he would walk down to the temple to talk with Gersham because he knew how boring the Sabbaths were for him.

He would sit beside him and describe the people who were coming and going into the temple. They often talked about the state of Israel, or what Mario was learning in Hebrew school.

One Sabbath afternoon, Mario decided to walk down to the temple and spend time with Gersham. As he got close to the temple gates, he saw Jesus and a group of his disciples leaving the temple. He heard them talking about his brother.

> ... "Rabbi, who sinned, this man or his parents, that he was born blind?"[1]

Mario felt his fist clench and his stomach tighten. All his life, he had been told that his parents were "sinners," or his brother would not have been born blind. His parents had been shunned and their business had suffered because they were not considered loved by God. Mario himself had few friends because his brother was blind.

Then he heard:

> **"Neither this man nor his parents sinned," said Jesus, "but this happened so that the works of God might be displayed in him."[2]**

Mario didn't understand what Jesus meant by displaying the works of God, but he sure did appreciate him teaching the crowd that Gersham and his parents didn't do anything wrong to cause the blindness.

Then as Mario watched, Jesus:

> **... spit on the ground, made some mud with the saliva, and put it on the man's eyes. "Go," he told him, "wash in the Pool of Siloam...."[3]**

The pool was close by the temple gate, so Gersham could easily get there by himself. Some of Jesus' disciples walked over with him, so Mario just stayed hidden in the crowd so he could see what would happen next.

Mario watched, amazed, when he realized that Gersham could see.

Gersham kept touching things and exclaiming over the beauty of the world. He loved the grass, the trees, the sky, and the people. He kept exclaiming over the variety of faces that he was seeing — all looking at him.

Mario couldn't stop his tears as he realized that Gersham was looking right at him — but didn't know him.   He had never seen his brother.

The crowd started arguing about whether this was really Gersham. They couldn't believe that he had been healed. But Jesus and his disciples had disappeared.

"Gersham," said Mario, and Gersham immediately ran to him and began to hug him. Mario and Gersham both assured the crowd that this really <u>was</u> Gersham, but the crowd wouldn't believe them.

Someone called the Pharisees, and they came and questioned Gersham. They wanted to know all the details.

Gersham told them about Jesus putting the mud on his eyes and telling him to wash in the pool. And now he could see! He was so excited — but the Pharisees seemed angry.

> **Some of the Pharisees said, "This man is not from God, for he does not keep the Sabbath." But others asked, "How can a sinner perform such signs?" So, they were divided.**[4]

The Pharisees angrily asked Gersham:

> **... "What have you to say about him? It was your eyes he opened." ....**[5]

And Gersham replied:

> .... "He is a prophet."[6]

Since the Pharisees were still arguing about whether this was really Gersham, they sent Mario for his parents so they could identify him. Mario ran all the way home and was so out of breath he could hardly speak.

His parents were frightened that something terrible had happened. Finally, he was able to tell them that the Pharisees wanted them to come and identify Gersham. He told them that they were mad because Jesus had healed Gersham so that he could see. But his parents were so upset about the Pharisees being angry that they didn't really hear the good news.

Mario's parents were not happy that Gersham had gotten the Pharisees and synagogue Ruler angry. They had tried hard to please them. They thought if they pleased the Jewish leaders, then God would be pleased with them.

When they arrived, the Pharisees demanded to know if this was their son.

They said, "Yes."

Then they asked if he was born blind and they replied, "Yes."

Then they asked how he could see. Mario's parents looked at each other and admitted that they had no idea. Mario's dad said, "He's of age, let him tell you!"

So, the Pharisees turned to Gersham again and demanded that he tell the truth. They said that they knew that Jesus could not have healed him because Jesus was a sinner who didn't even keep the Sabbath rules.

Then Gersham very boldly spoke:

> ... **"Whether he is a sinner or not, I don't know. One thing I do know. I was blind but now I see!"**[7]

The Pharisees kept questioning him about what Jesus did and why he could see.

Now at this point, Gersham probably was a little disrespectful, but he spoke the truth and it made the Pharisees really mad. He told the Pharisees that Jesus couldn't possibly be a sinner if he could heal a man born blind. Gersham told them plainly that Jesus had to be from God if he could do that.

The Pharisees became furious and told Gersham that he could no longer be part of the local synagogue. They went back into the temple and left Gersham and Mario and their parents standing alone.

"Come on," said Mario, "Let's go home." He knew that his parents were devastated that once again they were in trouble with the Pharisees. Mario wasn't sure what to do. The Jewish people believed that to be kicked out of the synagogue was like being kicked out of Heaven, and Gersham's parents were horrified. It should have been the happiest day for his family, but the Pharisees were angry, and Mario's parents hadn't even realized that Gersham could see.

Gersham was strangely quiet because he knew he had disappointed his parents. They walked home together slowly.

But as they were walking, Jesus came up from behind them and called Gersham by name. Jesus knew what the Pharisees had done, and he wanted to assure Gersham that it was okay.

The family stopped and turned toward Jesus. Jesus asked Gersham if he believed in the Messiah. Gersham said that he wasn't sure because he had never seen him.

Jesus laughed and said:

> ... "You have now seen him; in fact, he is the one speaking with you."[8]

Gersham fell on his knees and worshiped Jesus.

... "Lord, I believe!" ....⁹

Mario fell on his knees, too, and worshiped Jesus.

His parents were still in shock. They watched their sons worship Jesus, but their Jewish religion kept them from worshiping him. They were too afraid of the Pharisees.

Now Gersham's joy was overflowing. He talked non-stop all the way home, dancing around and touching everything and exclaiming with delight over every little thing.

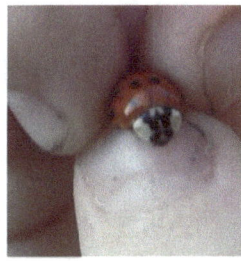

He had never seen a bird, or a bug, or a leaf, or the sunshine.

Gersham was filled with an incredible joy that was even greater because he had met Jesus, his Messiah. Mario, too, felt his heart would explode with joy. He had met the Messiah that the Jews had waited on for 1700 years. He knew without a shadow of doubt that Gersham's healing was from God.

Gersham and Mario just wished their parents could share that joy. It seemed to them that their parents were blinded by their religion and their fear of the Pharisees. They hoped that someday their parents' eyes would be opened, and they would see clearly that Jesus was the Messiah sent from God.

---

1 **John 9:2**
2 **John 9:3**
3 **John 9:6-7**
4 **John 9:16**
5 **John 9:17**
6 **John 9:17**
7 **John 9:25**
8 **John 9:37**
9 **John 9:38**

Jesus Heals Man Born Blind
John 9:1-38

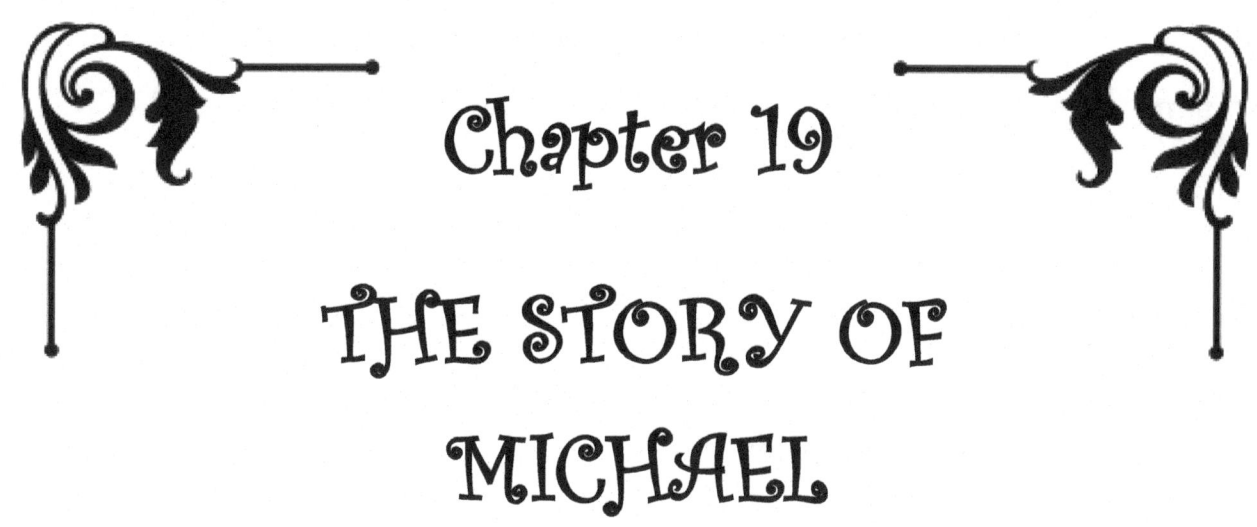

Chapter 19
THE STORY OF MICHAEL

Michael snuggled under his blanket for just one more minute before he threw off the covers and faced the day. Well, it wasn't exactly day yet. But ever since he and his mother had arrived, they had volunteered for the early morning shift. That meant they got up before sunrise and prepared breakfast for Mr. Jesus and all his disciples.

His eyes were adjusted to the dark enough to be able to find his way to the kitchen. The lamps were burning there, and the other helpers were beginning to set out the supplies they would need for breakfast. Usually there were 12 of them who prepared the meal.

Michael's job was simply to carry the food from the kitchen to the tables set up along the edge of the courtyard without waking up the sleepers.

Most breakfasts were easy meals — just rounds of bread and bowls of olives and olive oil for dipping and sometimes fruit.

This morning there were fresh apricots, and he knew that would make everyone happy.

His mother had baked the bread yesterday afternoon and wrapped it in cloths to keep it fresh. Michael started taking the cloths off and putting the rounds out on the tables. Because they were feeding about 100 disciples that slept in this courtyard and another 20 or 30 that slept at Mr. Jesus' house, a lot of bread had to be put out.

His mother was in charge of breakfast, and this morning she was looking frustrated. He stopped and gave her a hug.

"What's wrong, Mother? Are we missing something?"

"We're missing helpers! I only have half my usual helpers. Can you hurry up with the bread and start carrying water from the well? Just as soon as some of the others wake up, I'll send them to help you fill the water jars."

"Of course, Mother." Michael worked as quickly as he could to get the rest of the bread laid out. Someone still needed to set out the olive oil and olives and the apricots — but the water would be needed first.

So, he began to carry water. The well was about 10 minutes away, but he could only carry a two-gallon water jar. That would be enough for about 30 people. So, he was calculating how many trips he would need to make to supply enough water for 130.

He saw that the sky was already getting light when he was only on his second trip. And that's when he noticed it.

As he came into the courtyard carrying his second jar of water, he noticed that the courtyard was almost empty. He set down his jar of water and went into the kitchen.

"Mother, come here, please."

"Michael, you know I don't have time."

"Mother, it's important."

Mother knew that Michael wouldn't tease, so she dried her hands and stepped out into the courtyard. When she did, she gasped. *Where are the disciples?*

"Maybe Mr. Jesus sent them out on another ministry trip and forgot to tell us," suggested Michael.

Mother went back into the kitchen and asked the others if they knew where everyone was. They came out into the courtyard to look, too. Where there was usually over a hundred people sleeping crowded into the courtyard, there were just maybe six families scattered around and a couple of single young men and a few single women.

"Michael, go over to Mr. Jesus' house and see how many of them are coming for breakfast. There's no need to put out this much food if no one is here to eat it."

Michael ran as fast as his 10-year-old legs would run. He entered the courtyard quietly because he knew some of the disciples would still be sleeping if they worked late the night before. Everything looked pretty normal over there and he estimated approximately 20, but there would be some in the house. He ran back to report that they should set up for 30 people as usual from Mr. Jesus' house.

The crew began to put food away since they would obviously only be serving half the usual crowd. As others began to wake up, the shock rippled through the remaining disciples. Those who had heard Mr. Jesus teach yesterday reported that he had really upset some of the disciples with all his talk about death and dying. Those with young children seemed especially upset, and now it looked like they had left quietly during the night without saying goodbye.

When Mr. Jesus arrived and breakfast was served, he didn't seem at all surprised by the emptiness of the courtyard. He seemed sad, but not surprised.

☹

While the others cleaned up the breakfast and got ready for the day, Mr. Jesus met with his 12 apostles.

> **"You do not want to leave too, do you?" Jesus asked the Twelve.**
>
> **...Peter answered him, "Lord, to whom shall we go? You have the words of eternal life. We have come to believe and to know that you are the Holy One of God."[1]**

When the kitchen had been put back in order after breakfast, it was agreed that they needed to determine if there were enough volunteers to cover the evening meal. Some agreed to help who had not helped before.

Mother said that she could continue to prepare breakfast with the six volunteers who showed up this morning. And this afternoon, she wouldn't need to bake bread for tomorrow's breakfast because they had plenty of leftovers!

After the meeting, Mother said, "Michael, let's take a walk. I need to think, and you are my best listener!"

"Sure, Mother."

They walked quietly to the beach and found it mostly deserted. It was nearly noon and the fishermen were all home sleeping. The crowds that had earlier been purchasing fish had all gone home for the heat of the day.

"Michael, do you understand why the disciples are leaving?" Mother asked.

"Well, I guess they are scared of what the Pharisees might do to them," replied Michael.

"Yes, I think that's some of it. But I think some of them are disappointed that Mr. Jesus hasn't conquered Rome and set Israel free. Instead he talks more about loving Rome and being peaceful."

"Are you disappointed, Mother?"

"Yes, I guess I am. But I still think it could happen. I know without a shadow of a doubt that Mr. Jesus is sent from God. I just don't know what he's doing or going to do. That puzzles me."

"Are you thinking of leaving?"

"I guess I have to think about it. That's why I wanted to talk with you. I agree with many of the others that it could get pretty dangerous for all of us. I want to know what you are thinking. You are old enough to have a say in our decision."

"I agree with Mr. Peter! Where else would we go? If Mr. Jesus is from God, then we need to listen and obey and do what he says," said Michael.

"I like your faith! I think, as your mother, I get caught up in trying to figure out what's best to do and how best to protect you."

"But Mr. Jesus says that he's the Great Shepherd and he'll take care of us. I believe that."

"Michael, you are a wise young man. You'll never know how much I respect your opinion. And right now, I needed a healthy dose of your encouragement. Thank you."

"Anytime."

"You know that we could go to Uncle Enoch's in Bethlehem. He has told us we are welcome there, and you could go to Hebrew school with your cousins," said Mother.

"Mother, I will be obedient to you, whatever you decide. But if I were old enough to decide for myself — I would stay with Mr. Jesus. I know he is the Messiah and he'll take care of us. I know the Pharisees want to hurt us, but I don't believe they have any power as long as we let Mr. Jesus protect us."

"So, you are not afraid to stay with Mr. Jesus?"

"No, Mother, I'm not afraid. I know that bad things will probably happen, but Mr. Jesus is from God and I'd rather be with him than anywhere else."

"Michael, I want to stay with Mr. Jesus no matter what happens in Jerusalem. But I've got to admit that I'm afraid at times."

"Mr. Peter taught us that when we look at the waves — we sink. And when we look at Mr. Jesus — he lifts us up no matter how big the waves are, or how strong the wind is, or how deep the water is. I've learned a lot from Mr. Peter and the other guys teaching us."

"Then, let's keep our eyes on Mr. Jesus and follow him wherever he leads! I'm so proud of you, Son."

"Thank you, Mother. I'm proud of you, too."

---

[1] **John 6:67-69**

Jesus Teaches About His Death
Luke 9:22

Jesus Teaches That Following Him is Hard
Mark 8:34-35

Many Disciples Leave
John 6:66

Jesus Asks the Apostles if They Are Leaving, Too
John 6:67-69

Jesus is the Good Shepherd
John 10:11-15

Chapter 20
THE STORY OF GABRIELA

"Oh, Keturah, I came just as soon as I heard. I am so sorry. What can I do?"

"I don't know. I'm just in shock. What will happen now? How long will it take? Why Simon?"

"I know you have many questions. I don't know the answers. Leprosy is a terrible, terrible thing.

"Let me take the three older children and entertain them today. We'll go to the river or somewhere for them to play and let you rest. I would offer to take the twins, but they still need their mother. And it may help you to sit and nurse them. You won't feel so lonely."

Miss Martha gathered up the three older children. The two boys were six and eight years old and they understood a little more about what was happening, but Gabriela was only four and didn't understand why her Abba couldn't hug her and why he had moved out of the house.

Miss Martha walked with them to the small river that ran behind her house. The boys quickly began collecting rocks to skip across the water. But Gabriela just wanted to sit in Miss Martha's lap.

Miss Martha tried to explain to her what was happening and that her Abba loved her very much. Because Gabriela's Abba had become sick with leprosy, which was very contagious, he had to move out of his house. He would not be allowed to see his family except from a distance. That would be extremely hard for a little girl who loved her Abba dearly.

But that day was the beginning of a very special friendship between Gabriela and Miss Martha, who had never married. By the time Miss Martha took the children home, along with a meal for the family, she and Gabriela had become forever friends.

"Abba, Abba!" Gabriela called as she saw her father coming toward the front courtyard where she was playing. Usually he visited on the Sabbath and stayed far away. But this time, he opened the courtyard gate and came running to Gabriela. Tears rolled down both of their cheeks as he picked her up and held her close for the first time in three years.

Keturah and the two younger boys came running out to see what the commotion was about. "What happened?" she demanded. "Is it safe?"

"Yes, my love, it's safe. I'm safe. I'm well. I met a man named Jesus and he made me well. I went to the priest and he told me I was free of the leprosy and look — my hands are back. Jesus not only stopped the leprosy, but he gave me back my fingers and toes. I'm good as new." Everyone was crowded around Abba and wanted to hear over and over how Jesus had made him well.

Seven-year-old Gabriela was torn between wanting to never leave her Abba's arms and wanting to run and tell Miss Martha and her sister Miss Mary the great news.

Mid-afternoon, she asked permission to go and tell them. Abba was busy greeting his two older boys who were just returning from Hebrew school. So, it was a good time to leave without being missed.

"Miss Martha, Miss Martha!" Gabriela called as she arrived breathlessly at Martha's home.

"Goodness child, where's the fire?" exclaimed Miss Martha.

"Miss Martha, Mr. Jesus has healed my Abba! He's home! He's well! And all his fingers and toes are back just like new!"

"Oh, Gabriela, that is wonderful news. Mary, Lazarus, did you hear? Jesus has healed Simon, Gabriela's Abba." Everyone clustered around Gabriela and had her tell it again.

Gabriela had been coming over most afternoons so that Miss Martha could teach her embroidery. Gabriela wanted to learn to make beautiful things like Miss Martha, but her mother just didn't have time to teach her. Miss Martha loved teaching Gabriela, and was always patient as she learned to let the thread relax and not pull it too tightly. Over and over, they would undo the stitches and start again.

Today, she didn't have time for a lesson. She wanted to get back to her Abba and spend time with him. Miss Martha agreed, but made her wait until she could package up a basket of honey bread for her family to help with the celebration. Miss Martha was just like that — always caring for people.

Mother put Gabriela to work slicing the vegetables and everything seemed so different. They were preparing dinner for Abba and there was a joy that had been missing in this kitchen.

The next day, Abba went to check on his store. His managers had kept it running while he was away, but he was eager to see for himself how it was doing. The older boys were in Hebrew school, so Mother and Gabriela began cleaning things that had been neglected in their sadness. They wanted everything to be clean and shining for Abba. Both were humming as they worked, and the little boys caught the good mood and played happily.

In the afternoon Gabriela went to Miss Martha's for a sewing lesson and let Mother rest with the boys.

"Miss Martha, do you know Mr. Jesus? How did he heal my Abba?" asked Gabriela once they had gotten started on her project.

"Yes, I do know Jesus. I consider him a good friend. But he's more than that, Gabriela. I believe that he is the Messiah. Do you know what that means?"

"I know that the Messiah is the One we are waiting for to free us from Rome," answered Gabriela.

"The Messiah was promised to Abraham over 1700 years ago. God said that he himself would come and visit us."

"Wow! So, he's God?"

"I believe he is. You see we have over 300 prophecies about the Messiah, and so far Jesus has fulfilled many, many of them. He has healed your Abba — and he didn't do it halfway. He re-created his hands and feet. That's something only God could do. He has made blind people see and deaf people hear. He's healed broken backs and crippled legs and arms and all kinds of diseases. Those are all prophesies, or promises, that God gave to Abraham and to all the prophets since then. Every major prophet has told us about the Messiah so that we would recognize him when he arrived."

"That is so cool. So now that the Messiah is here, what happens next?" asked Gabriela.

"I'm not totally sure, but I know that he came to heal our relationship to God and teach us to trust him. And I know that my life has been different ever since I met him," shared Miss Martha.

"How, Miss Martha? How has your life been different?"

Miss Martha smiled and got a faraway look in her eyes. She said, "Let me tell you about the first time I met him. Lazarus, my brother, had started going to hear Jesus teach anytime he was around here. I think he first heard him teaching at the temple in Jerusalem about two years ago. He told Jesus that he and his group of disciples were always welcome to stop by for dinner, and that I loved to cook.

"One morning, a disciple of Jesus stopped by and asked if it would be convenient for Jesus and his group of disciples to come to dinner that night since he was teaching in Jerusalem that day. I asked how many people to prepare for and he said, 'Oh, there's usually about 100 to 120.' I thought I would faint, but then he added that many of them had family in Jerusalem, so there would only be about 30. I was so relieved to not be cooking for 120, I told him it would be fine.

"After he left, I started wondering how in the world I would feed 33 of us with only a few hours' notice. The courtyard would seat 20, but I knew that Lazarus could borrow some tables and couches from your mother — so I put him in charge of that. Mary and I went to the market and started shopping. There was so much to do, so much to prepare. Mary and I worked nonstop all day, and we had a wonderful meal prepared.

"All we really lacked was moving all that food to the courtyard. But when Jesus walked in, Mary forgot all about serving our guests.   She just plopped down at Jesus' feet and listened to all he had to say. And I got mad. Instead of kindly asking for help from some of the guests or even asking Mary for her help to get all the kitchen stuff out to the courtyard, I opened my big mouth and said,

> .... "Lord, don't you care that my sister has left me to do the work by myself? Tell her to help me!" [1]

Miss Martha put out her bottom lip like she was pouting, and Gabriela laughed. She could imagine Miss Martha doing just that.

"What did Mr. Jesus do? Did he make her get up and help?"

"No. He told me to leave Mary alone. He said that I was focused on the wrong thing and Mary was focused on the right thing. He was absolutely right."

"But it wasn't fair for you to do all the work!" exclaimed Gabriela.

"Maybe not — but it was what I had chosen to do, and I needed to let Mary do what she chose to do."

"So, if Mr. Jesus wants us to sit and listen to him, then who is going to do the cooking?" Gabriela demanded.

"Jesus changed my heart that day. I realized that the reason I love to cook and care for people is not to earn God's love, but because I want to show him how much I love him. Now, I can relax and enjoy showing my love to God and to people without getting in a tizzy!"

Gabriela giggled as she thought of Miss Martha in a tizzy. She always seemed calm and relaxed to her.

"Look how smoothly your threads are lining up today. You relaxed and sewed without pulling them so tightly. Maybe I should tell you more stories!"

"Thank you, Miss Martha. I hope I can meet Mr. Jesus some day and thank him for healing my Abba."

"Well, he usually stops in every time he comes to Jerusalem, so I'll be sure and invite you to come and meet him next time."

It was about a year later when Mother said, "Gabriela, stay here and watch your brothers. I'm going to Martha and Mary's house.   Their brother Lazarus is sick, and they don't know what to do.   I'll be back in a little bit."

When Mother returned, she told Gabriela that Lazarus was very sick.

I wish Mr. Jesus were here," said Gabriela.

"Yes, they sent a messenger to his house in Capernaum, but no one knows where he might be.   I'm sure he could heal Lazarus."

But Jesus didn't come, and Lazarus died.

Everyone loved Martha and Mary and their brother Lazarus, so there were family and friends everywhere. Gabriela wished she could stop her ears from hearing the wailing and dirges (sad music) coming from the mourners at Miss Martha's home.

Gabriela had been allowed to spend a little time with Miss Martha, but mostly she stayed at home and kept her little brothers entertained and out of the way so her mother could be with the sisters and try to help.

Gabriela decided to take her brothers to the little river that ran behind Miss Martha's house. She knew that they were welcome to play there anytime, and she didn't think about having to walk right past the family tomb.

She assumed everyone would be at the house, and she was right. But she got a creepy feeling walking past the big stone tomb where she knew that Lazarus' dead body had been put. She was glad her little brothers didn't pay any attention to it.

Once they were past the tomb, she relaxed and enjoyed playing with her brothers along the river. It was very shallow there and they could wade in the water along the edge. The smooth stones were slippery, though, so they had to be careful. The boys tried to catch minnows with their hands — but, of course, were not successful.

Gabriela sat down in the grass along the edge and kept a good eye on her brothers as they splashed and played. She was thinking that they should start home soon so she could start dinner, when she realized that they were trapped.

For some reason, the mourners had all moved to the tomb and there seemed to be quite a crowd. From where she sat, she could see Miss Martha and Miss Mary talking with some man. There seemed to be hundreds of mourners gathered around them.

Gabriela called her brothers to come and sit beside her. She didn't want them playing in the water without supervision — and she wanted to watch and see what was happening at the tomb. The three of them watched as some men opened the tomb.

"What are they doing?" asked her brothers.

"I don't know. Let's just watch and see." The boys obediently watched and were rewarded with a very funny sight. A man came out of the tomb all wrapped up in cloth like a mummy. He had strips of cloth all over him so that he could barely walk, and he had cloth all over his face, so he couldn't see where he was going. The boys giggled and even Gabriela thought it looked funny.

Then the men who had opened the tomb began to unwrap the man and take the cloths off. Gabriela couldn't believe her eyes. The man looked like Lazarus. But it couldn't be. He was dead, and this man was alive and moving around and hugging Miss Martha and Miss Mary and the man that was with them.

Gabriela's mind was filled with questions and confusion. *What just happened?*

As she watched, the crowd began to move back toward the house, but the mourning music had stopped, and the crowd was celebrating. Gabriela took her brothers home where she got them all dried off and presentable. She thought she would start dinner, but she couldn't stand not knowing what was going on.

"Promise to be on your best behavior, and we'll go to Miss Martha's and see what has happened."

Both boys promised to be good, and she took them each by hand and walked over to Miss Martha's house.

Everyone was celebrating, and the crowd was getting larger and larger. They were saying that Jesus had raised Lazarus from the dead. It was too crowded to safely hold onto the two boys, so she took them back home to wait for her mother to come.

When Mother arrived, she was very excited about what she had seen. She described it to Gabriela and the boys. Gabriela asked if she could please go to see Mr. Jesus, but her mother said that he was already gone. He had left immediately after he had told the men to unwrap Lazarus.

Gabriela was so disappointed that she had missed meeting Jesus. Her mother hugged her and promised her that next time Mr. Jesus came, she would make sure Gabriela got to meet him.

Then Gabriela and the boys told Mother what they had seen. At least they had seen the miracle happen — even though it was from a distance.

After Lazarus was raised from the dead, the Pharisees were really upset. Many people were believing that Jesus was the Messiah. The Pharisees put out word that anyone who saw Jesus should report it to them immediately.

Early one morning, Miss Martha came over. "Keturah, I have a big favor to ask," said Miss Martha.

"Anything! You know that. How can I help you?" replied Keturah, Gabriela's mother.

"This morning, a disciple of Jesus came and asked if they could meet with us for the Sabbath meal. But they want to meet somewhere besides our house, since the Pharisees are watching us so closely. I was wondering if you would mind hosting Jesus and about 20 of his disciples, and of course us, for the Sabbath? I could help you with all the cooking and preparation."

"Oh, Martha, that would be an honor and privilege. Gabriela has still not been able to meet him personally and thank him for healing Simon. I'll have to ask Simon, but I know the answer is yes. Gabriela, go to Abba's store and ask him if it's okay — but keep it a secret — don't let anyone else know."

"And Gabriela, remind your Abba to keep it a secret, too. Otherwise, he might invite the whole town!" said Miss Martha.

So, Gabriela ran to Abba's store and talked with him privately. He, too, was thrilled to be able to do something for Jesus and promised to keep it secret.

On Friday night, Jesus and his disciples arrived at Gabriela's house, and she was finally able to meet him. She felt all tongue-tied and stayed busy helping Mother and Miss Martha in the kitchen. It surprised her that everyone seemed so serious and quiet — not at all the way Miss Martha had described Mr. Jesus.

Jesus reclined with Abba and Lazarus and four of his disciples. The other disciples and the women and children reclined at the other tables. Miss Martha, Mother and Gabriela were busy serving the tables, but Miss Mary had disappeared.

Just as the meal was ending, Miss Mary returned with a beautiful alabaster (white glass) bottle. She went to Jesus' couch and broke open the bottle. Immediately the room was filled with an amazing fragrance.

Spikenard was only used by royalty for special occasions — like a coronation or a wedding. And it was used to anoint a body for burial. Miss Mary had been given this bottle as a gift and had not even used it at her brother's death. It was very, very expensive perfume, and her most precious possession.

Now, she anointed Jesus's hair with the perfume and then poured it on his feet and wiped it with her own hair. She was worshiping him and singing softly to him.

Gabriela was amazed at the beauty of the moment. How she wished that she had a gift for Mr. Jesus that would please him like Miss Mary's gift.

But then some of the disciples began to fuss about Miss Mary's wasting such a precious gift.

> .... "Why this waste?" they asked. "This perfume could have been sold at a high price and the money given to the poor."[2]

But Jesus quieted them and told them:

> "Leave her alone.... Why are you bothering her? She has done a beautiful thing to me. ....She poured perfume on my body beforehand to prepare for my burial."[3]

And the room grew quiet again.

Gabriela didn't understand what was going on, but she knew that something important was about to happen. The disciples were getting ready to go and Gabriela felt that she had to speak to Mr. Jesus.

She went to his couch and knelt before him. She thought it would be hard to talk with him, but it wasn't at all. She said, "Thank you for healing my Abba. I believe that you are the Messiah. And I love you."

"Little one," Jesus said, "that is the most precious gift you can give me." He placed his hand on her head and then he left with his disciples.

———————

[1] Luke 10:40
[2] Matthew 26:8-9
[3] Mark 14:6,8

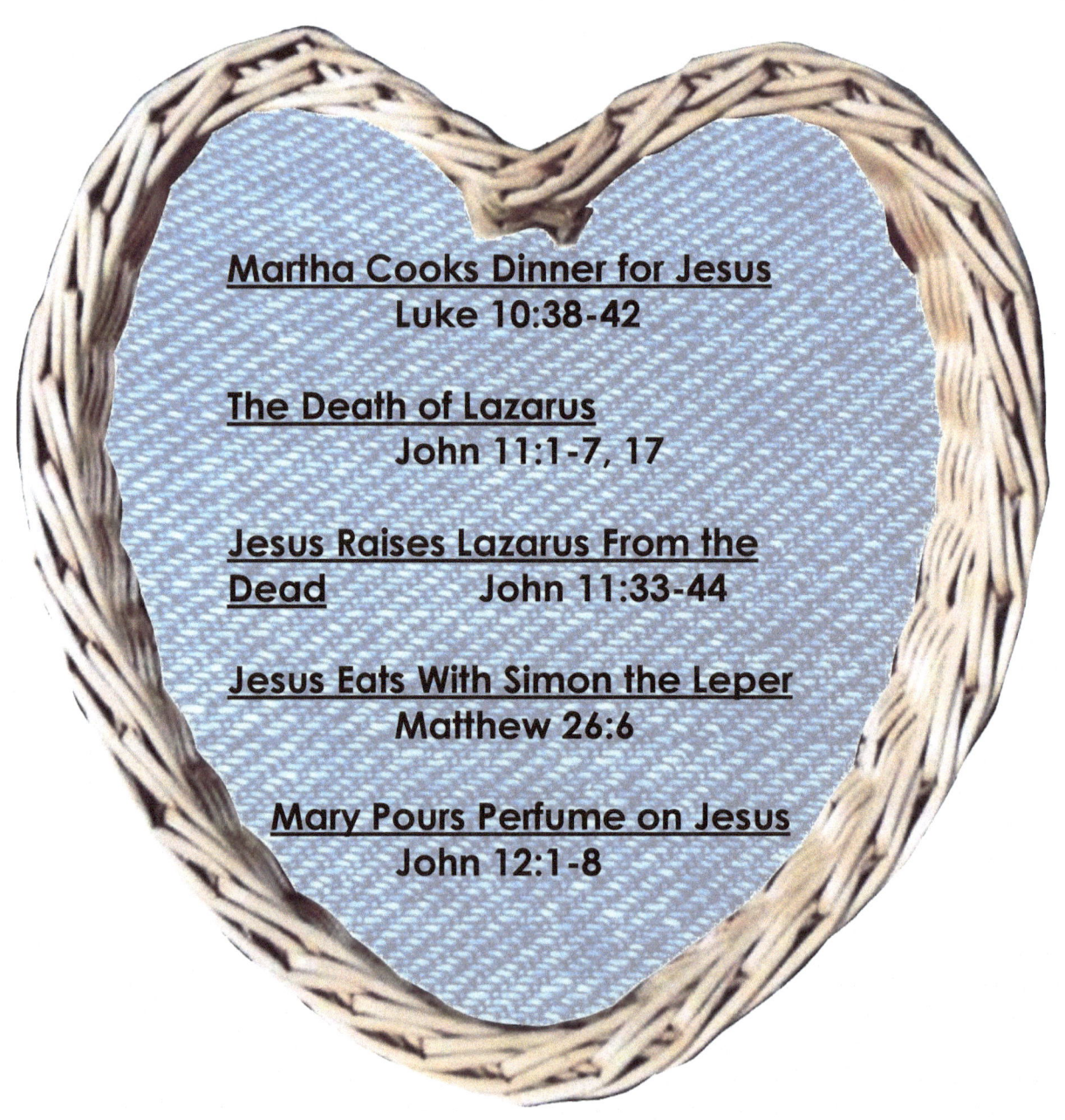

Martha Cooks Dinner for Jesus
Luke 10:38-42

The Death of Lazarus
John 11:1-7, 17

Jesus Raises Lazarus From the Dead   John 11:33-44

Jesus Eats With Simon the Leper
Matthew 26:6

Mary Pours Perfume on Jesus
John 12:1-8

Chapter 21
THE STORY OF MATTISON

Mattison's dad was a Pharisee and a member of the Sanhedrin living in Jerusalem. He was best friends with the High Priest, Caiaphas. The Sanhedrin was the group that governed the Jewish people directly under Rome. They were the most elite and supposedly the most spiritual leaders of the Jews. They made all the rules (under Rome, of course).

"Mattison, come into my study; I need to ask you a question."

"Coming, Dad."

"Mattison, I am going to send your mother and the girls out of the city for a couple of weeks. I thought I would make sure what you wanted to do. I felt you would choose to stay in Jerusalem for Passover, but if you prefer to go to the shore with your mother and sisters, that can be arranged."

"This will be my first official Passover as a man, and yes, I would prefer to stay in the city. But it is rather a hassle. The crowds get worse every year, and I know you'll be busy with responsibilities. But, yes, I guess I would like to stay just because it's my first Passover as a man. It would be a shame to miss the Seder meal."

"I know you are out of school for the month. Do you have any plans or any projects due?" asked Dad.

"No, I'm pretty much free to study what I please, but I do have one report to complete on whatever I choose to study during the break. It won't take long to throw something together. I don't think the rabbis read them anyway. What have you got on your mind?"

"I just wanted you to know that if you want to stay here, I would enjoy your company. We haven't had much time to talk recently."

"I've been focusing on Roman law and it's been keeping me pretty busy," said Mattison.

"I guess that's why we need to catch up — I thought you were studying Jewish Law."

"It's the future, Dad. I figure I know enough of the Jewish Law, and I need to understand the Roman law to be able to keep Rome happy."

"Well, it's going to be the end of Jewish rule if we don't get this chaos under control. Rome is ready to crack down on us if we don't get the people settled down. And everywhere I turn there's a new uprising."

"Is it really any worse than it's always been? I mean, there have always been uprisings."

"In the past, the revolts have been localized — usually in one city or one region. This man, Jesus, travels from the top of Galilee, all through Samaria and to the bottom edge of Judea. He's got followers in the thousands at any location where he chooses to teach.

"If they plan to take over Jerusalem next week during Passover, we would be outnumbered. We would have to call in Roman troops, and once we do, then Rome will use it as an excuse to oust us. If we can't control the people — they will."

"I didn't realize it was that serious, Dad."

"Well, it is, and that's one reason I want your mother and sisters out of here."

"Wow. How can I help?"

"Son, it will be a big help just to have you around. It's nice to have someone to talk with after a hard day. Now, I've got another meeting to go to tonight and I'll probably be out late again. Your mother and sisters will be leaving in the morning. I'll try to be here to see them off. But I'll definitely plan to see you tomorrow night for Sabbath dinner."

Mattison and his dad felt strange eating the Sabbath meal with just the two of them. He was glad he hadn't left his dad alone. Usually they had friends over, or at least had Mother and the girls here. But this Friday night, they ate together and mostly in silence. When the meal was over, Dad lay back on his cushion and began to talk.

"At the meeting of the Sanhedrin last night, we decided to post spies throughout the city so that we could keep an eye on Jesus and know his every move.

"We also decided that it was too dangerous to try to arrest him during the Passover celebration. He has too many supporters. We need to catch him alone."

"Are you sure he's coming to Jerusalem for the Passover on Friday?" asked Mattison.

"Yes, and in fact there was one report that he and his group of disciples were sighted in Bethany yesterday, but it wasn't verified. If he was there, he didn't stay at the usual place."

On Sunday morning, Mattison and his dad shared breakfast and then his dad headed to the temple while Mattison decided to walk toward Bethany and see if he could do some spying on his own.

Just as he got to the edge of Jerusalem, his jaw dropped as he realized that he was being engulfed in some humongous uprising. A man was riding on a donkey colt like the old kings of Jewish history, and hundreds of people were throwing palm branches and coats and making a carpet for him to enter the city of Jerusalem.

This was not what Mattison had expected. This was not a man and his 12 followers — this was the whole nation of Israel. The people were singing "Hosanna to the Highest." They were proclaiming that Jesus was the rightful King of Israel and that he was coming to take over Jerusalem.

The people were shouting:

... "Hosanna!"

**"Blessed is he who comes
in the name of the Lord!"**

**"Blessed is the coming kingdom
of our father David!"**

"Hosanna in the highest heaven!"[1]

Mattison couldn't move. He was frozen by the shock of it, but also by the beautiful sight of all the people gathered around their King. *Is my mind playing tricks? Is this the Messiah?* He probably stood there for only a few seconds, but it seemed like 30 minutes before he realized he had to get word to his dad.

He ran as fast as he could to the temple. He told them what he had seen, and all the Jewish leaders ran toward the crowd to try to break it up.

Mattison heard one of the Pharisees order Jesus to make his followers stop. But Jesus replied:

> "I tell you," ... "if they keep quiet, the stones will cry out."2

Wow! thought Mattison. *This guy really believes that he is the Messiah. He must be crazy!* But he couldn't stop the thought that also came: *What if he is the Messiah?*

Mattison wanted to be home for dinner to talk with his dad, but his dad never showed up and finally Mattison ate alone. The servants would fix his dad a late plate whenever he arrived.

For the first time in a long time, Mattison had a desire to look at the Jewish Scripture. He went into his dad's study but couldn't find any scrolls, and he certainly didn't want to walk back to the temple. Maybe he would do his report on the various predictions about the Messiah. That could prove interesting.

After breakfast on Monday morning, Mattison decided to walk to the temple and check out what the Jewish Scripture says about the Messiah.   As he got closer, he kept meeting people who were running from the temple. Mattison was terrified that something horrible was happening and he began to run toward the gates. But the people kept pushing him back.

He ran around to the gates on the other side of the temple and the crowd seemed to be less. He was finally able to push his way into the temple courtyard. His eyes could not believe what he saw. Instead of the booths where cows and sheep and doves were sold, he just saw chaos.

Tables were overturned and the courtyard looked like a tornado had just blown through. The animals were all gone, and debris was everywhere.

Mattison was trying to figure out what could have caused such a mess, and where were the animals?

As Mattison looked around, he noticed that Jesus was standing on the temple steps calmly teaching a small group of people. But that small group of people was growing larger as more and more people arrived in the courtyard. Mattison couldn't decide whether to listen to Jesus teach, or to go inside and work on his school project. But while he was deciding, he saw Jesus heal a crippled woman, and then a leper.

Even though he was fascinated, he decided to go inside and look at the scrolls. When he got inside, he found that the room was packed full of scribes who were all seeking the same answers he was. There was no way he was going to be able to do any research on the Messiah today.

Mattison went back to the courtyard and stood to listen to Jesus teach. Jesus taught by telling simple stories called parables. He heard Jesus tell a story about women being prepared for a wedding, and he heard a story about a businessman returning and finding some of his servants prepared and one not prepared. Mattison couldn't figure out what these stories had to do with whether Jesus was the Messiah or not. So, he decided to go and see if he could find some friends to hang out with.

That night his dad told him that Jesus had totally wrecked the courtyard of the temple and that he was behaving more and more like a madman.

Mattison asked what happened to the animals and his dad admitted that none of them were harmed. The animals just wandered around the city streets until the priests could round them all up again. Essentially, no harm had been done — it had just disrupted a whole day of business at the temple. They had made very little money that day and Caiaphas, the high priest, was not happy about that.

"Why don't you arrest him?" Mattison asked.

"Because the people love him, and it would start a riot! We've got to find a way to arrest him when there's not so many crowds.

"Did I ever tell you what happened last year when he was teaching in the temple and we sent the temple guard to arrest him?" asked his dad.

"No, I don't think so. What happened?" asked Mattison.

"Well, we sent an entire temple guard to go arrest Jesus because he was teaching at the temple without our permission. We waited and waited and waited for them to return.

> **Finally the temple guards went back to the chief priests and the Pharisees, who asked them, "Why didn't you bring him in?"**
>
> **"No one ever spoke the way this man does," the guards replied.**[3]

"So, he hypnotized even the soldiers!" Dad shook his head as he remembered that day.

"I'm just glad it wasn't worse at the temple today. He's got a lot of power and I don't understand why he doesn't use it. He seems to have some plan that we just can't figure out."

Mattison told his dad, "I stopped and listened to Jesus teach for a little while this morning. He seems to teach in very simple stories, but I didn't understand the point. He was talking about being prepared. But I'm not sure what he wants us to be prepared for. Do you think it's some kind of secret code?"

"I don't know, Son, I just don't know. I'm going to bed early and try to get some rest. These late-night meetings are killing me."

"Sleep well, Dad. Hopefully, things will settle down soon."

"We got him! Mattison, where are you? We got him!" Dad was yelling as he came in the front door.

"Dad, slow down. You got Jesus?" Mattison asked, "How?"

"Well, we don't have him yet. But this afternoon one of his apostles came and made a deal with us. He will lead us to Jesus when there are no crowds around, and we paid him for his services."

"Dad, are you sure this isn't a trap? That sounds pretty suspicious to me!"

"He says he knows where Jesus spends the nights, and we'll catch him totally unaware. He says he will let us know in a few days when the time will be perfect.

"Until then, we can just relax and let Jesus teach all he wants. Judas — that's the man's name — said that Jesus isn't making any plans to overthrow the temple or Rome, so we can relax."

"Sounds like a follower who isn't happy with the plan," said Mattison.

"Exactly. It seems to me he thought Jesus was planning a big revolt, and now he's disappointed with the lack of action."

Mattison hadn't seen his dad this relaxed in months. He had intended to look up those Scriptures about the Messiah tomorrow. But obviously, that wasn't important now. This man couldn't be the Messiah. Maybe he and his dad could take the day off and go fishing tomorrow. It would do them both good to get out of the city and have some fun.

---

[1] **Mark 11:9-10**
[2] **Luke 19:40**
[3] **John 7:45-46**

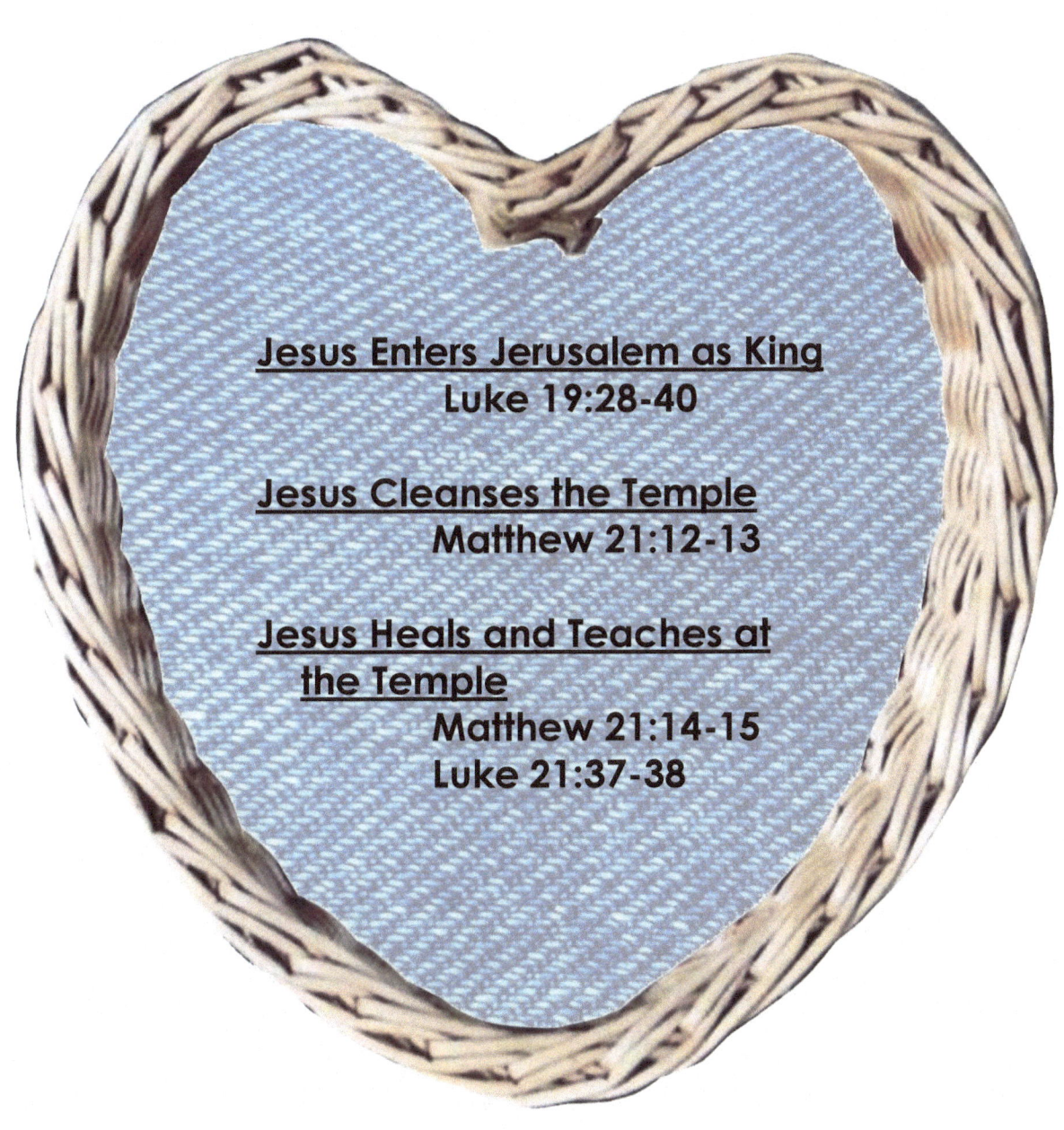

Jesus Enters Jerusalem as King
Luke 19:28-40

Jesus Cleanses the Temple
Matthew 21:12-13

Jesus Heals and Teaches at the Temple
Matthew 21:14-15
Luke 21:37-38

Story of Prepared and Unprepared Ladies
Matthew 25:1-13

Jewish Leaders Plot to Kill Jesus
Matthew 26:3-5

Judas Betrays Jesus
Matthew 26:14-16

Chapter 22

"THE STORY OF JONATHAN & JENAY"

"Jon! Jen! We need to go!"

"Coming, Mother!" they both replied.

"Where are we going?" asked Jenay, who was always up for an adventure.

"There's work to be done. We need to go into Jerusalem to prepare the Passover Seder for Mr. Jesus," said Mother. Jonathan and Jenay knew the Seder was a very special meal celebrated by the Jews each year during the Passover Festival.

"Mr. Jesus has appointed Cousin Peter and Uncle John to go and prepare the lamb, so we will help prepare the rest of the meal. Abba will come later with Mr. Jesus. You two will be the only kids, but there's a lot of things you can do to help."

"We are the only kids left! Everyone else is gone," complained Jonathan, who really missed his group of friends.

"It's okay Jon, you've still got me!" said Jenay cheerfully. Jenay was perfectly satisfied being Jonathan's twin, and didn't really care whether she had anyone else, as long as Jon was there to play with her. But Jonathan was grieving the group of friends who played together as they and their parents followed Mr. Jesus. Many of them had left and were no longer following Mr. Jesus, and others were visiting relatives for the Passover festival.

"Okay, I think I have everything I need. Do you two have your traveling bags? We will camp in Jerusalem tonight."

"Yes, Mother. How far is it to Jerusalem from here?"

"Only six miles. Oh, there's Mrs. Lois and Mrs. Magda. Good morning, you two. May we join you?"

"Certainly. It seems like such an honor to be preparing the Passover Seder for a King. Wasn't last Sunday exciting?" said Mrs. Magda.

The ladies chatted while Jenay and Jonathan ran ahead and then stopped and waited for the ladies to catch up. Soon Cousin Peter and Uncle John joined them and thanked them for their help. That made their ministry team complete. The rest of the group would be celebrating the Passover with friends or family in or near Jerusalem.

"At least we don't have to plan the menu. The Seder meal has been the same for hundreds of years, so I think we can figure this out.   Do you want me to supervise, or do you want to each take a dish and be responsible for it?" asked Mrs. Lois.

Uncle John said that they would take care of preparing the lamb if the ladies would take care of everything else.   Then he very politely apologized to Jonathan.

"Actually, I don't cook — I'm the taster!" said Jonathan, and everyone laughed.

It was agreed that each one would prepare a portion of the meal so that there wouldn't be too much work for anyone. But they also agreed that Mrs. Lois should probably oversee it and be in charge.

They would need to prepare for 22 people since they were planning on serving Jesus, the apostles, themselves and four young men who would arrive later to help set up the rooms.

Each lady figured out which dishes she would prepare. Soon they found themselves at the city walls.

It was really crowded at the city gates because of Passover, and hard to stay together as a group. "So, where are we setting up this Seder meal?" Mrs. Lois asked.

"Well, it's a mystery," said Uncle John. "Jesus said that as we came into the city of Jerusalem, we should watch for a man carrying a water jar. When we see him, we are to ask him if we can use his guest room to prepare the Seder for Jesus."

"Oh, I like mysteries!" said Jenay.

"And Jesus always provides just what we need. So, I suppose there will be an oven to bake the bread, as well as space to prepare everything else that we'll need," said Mrs. Lois, who was in charge of making the unleavened bread that was an essential part of the Seder meal.

In a few minutes, Jonathan spotted the man and ran back to point him out to Uncle John and Cousin Peter so that they could do the talking.

The man took them to an upstairs room that was perfectly suited for their group. There was a large dining room for Jesus and the apostles to eat their Seder, a preparation area for the food, a second dining room off to the side, and an outdoor cooking area in the back courtyard.

Cousin Peter and Uncle John left to go and purchase a couple of lambs. They would need to butcher them according to the Jewish Scripture and roast them over an open fire.

The women and Jenay and Jonathan headed to the market to purchase the supplies they would need for their particular dishes. They had found baskets in the cabinets and asked permission to use them at the market. They had to hurry because some of the dishes would need to cook all day.

Jenay's and Jonathan's mother, Kayla, was in charge of the fish sauce. They needed to find fresh fish and the right herbs and vegetables to season it. Jenay and Jonathan each carried a basket while Mother was able to juggle the rest in her bags.

The menu included the roasted lamb, a bean stew, olives and olive oil, unleavened bread, bitter herbs, the fish sauce, dates, and wine. As the women returned to the kitchen and began cooking, they seemed to find plenty of things for the kids to do to help.

The owner of the building showed them where the nearest well was, and Jonathan and Jenay spent a lot of time carrying water jars to the preparation area and the outside kitchen.

Once Mother got the fish sauce prepared, Jenay could stir it over the fire while Mother and Jonathan made another trip to the market to get more supplies.

Jonathan talked with some boys who were playing in the street outside the courtyard. He was surprised to discover that for them, even though Passover started at sunset, they didn't eat the Seder meal until the following evening.

Jonathan went to where his mother and the other ladies were working and asked why they celebrated the Seder earlier than other people. Mrs. Lois explained that according to the Jewish Scripture, the Seder meal was to be eaten on the first night of Passover. And most of the people who lived in Galilee had always done it that way. But the people in Jerusalem didn't agree. They celebrated their Seder meal on the second night of Passover. Since Jesus and most of his disciples were from Galilee — they were celebrating tonight.

The four young men, Yanis, Mark, Enis, and Joel, arrived in plenty of time to set up the tables and reclining couches for Jesus and the apostles. Jesus had requested that he be allowed to share this meal alone with just his apostles. The rest of the disciples would eat their Seder in the second dining room.

Yanis, the son of a priest, would be leading their Seder meal there. So, they got that room all set up, too. Then the young men hung out in the courtyard with Cousin Peter and Uncle John as they finished roasting the lambs. Jonathan was proud to get to hang out with the "men."

Jenay preferred being in the preparation room with the ladies, helping chop the vegetables and herbs.

All was finally ready, and Jesus and his apostles arrived just as the sun was setting. Jesus came into the preparation area and thanked the helpers before going to the table.

The ladies set all the dishes on the table for Jesus and the apostles so that they could be alone for this special Passover celebration as Jesus had requested. Then the ladies set a similar feast on the table in the other room, and all the helpers gathered there for their special meal.

Since Jonathan was officially the youngest, he got to ask the question, "Why is this night different from all other nights?" Yanis did a good job leading the group through their Seder. It was his first time to lead, and Mrs. Lois had to remind him of a few details, but everyone was relaxed and enjoyed their meal together.

The helpers in this room had been following Jesus for over three years, so they knew each other well. They felt like family and loved each other like brothers and sisters. They were all excited about Jesus announcing that he was the Messiah. They felt that Rome would soon be overthrown and Jesus would be crowned king. They could hear Jesus and the disciples talking in the other room, and they sounded more serious than usual.

When the helpers had finished their meal and enjoyed some leisurely conversation, Mrs. Lois reminded them that they were here to work and needed to clean everything up before leaving. The young men took care of cleaning up the outside kitchen and making sure no debris was left behind.

The women and children cleaned the preparation room and their dining room. They weren't sure how much longer Jesus would be teaching his apostles, and since it was getting late, Joel and Mark walked with Mrs. Lois and Mrs. Magda to the olive garden to find a place to camp for the night.

Mother and Jonathan and Jenay would wait until Jesus was finished teaching, and then clean up their table. Yanis and Enis decided to wait with them so that they could hear more of Jesus' teaching, help with the final cleaning, and then walk with the little family across the ravine to the olive garden.

They all sat quietly against the wall listening to Jesus teach. Jenay remembers him saying:

> "**My command is this: Love each other as I have loved you.**"[1]

The next thing she remembered was Mother shaking her and Jonathan awake and saying it was time to leave.

Jesus and his apostles had already left, the table had been cleared and the dishes put away. Mother was trying to get Jenay and Jonathan awake enough to walk to the olive garden. They would camp there with the rest of the group.

When they finally arrived at the garden and found where the others were sleeping, they were surprised that Jesus and his disciples were not there. But it was so late and had been such a busy day that everyone was asleep within minutes.

"RUN!" "RUN!" "GET OUT OF THE GARDEN!" "HIDE!" "RUN!"

Jenay and Jonathan had only been asleep about an hour when they were awakened by screaming men. They grabbed Mother's hands and ran as fast as they could. But no one knew where they were running or what they were running from.

Some of those in the olive garden ran to friends or family in Jerusalem. Others ran to other camping spots that they had used around Jerusalem. Some ran all the way to Bethany to Martha and Mary and Lazarus' house.

 Jenay and Jonathan ran with their mother into the city and hid by a stream. They forgot their blankets and travel bags, so they just cuddled together trying to figure out what had happened.

It took a long time before Jenay and Jonathan could get calm enough to go back to sleep on Mother's lap. But for Mother, there was no sleep. She wanted to know what happened and where Jesus was and where her husband, James, was. James was one of Jesus' best friends and more than likely, he was wherever Jesus was.

She was also trying to figure out what to do next, and it looked like the best solution would be to go to her sister's house. She lived in Jerusalem and always told them they were welcome. Her sister, Oprah, and her husband, Nehemiah, didn't believe that Jesus was the Messiah. Kayla dreaded hearing the "I told you so!" *But what else can I do? I don't have a penny, or blanket, or travel pack.* She had left everything in the garden, and she had two children to protect. Yes, when the sun came up, she would go to her sister's house. Oprah would take them in.

Jenay and Jonathan were very tired, but when the sun came up, their mother insisted they get up and move around. They washed their faces in the stream and then Mother led them to Aunt Oprah and Uncle Nehemiah's house.

Aunt Oprah welcomed them and fed them a good breakfast. She suggested that Jenay and Jonathan might want to take another nap since they had had such a rough night. They agreed. Mother tucked them in bed and then told them that she was going out to check on their Abba and see if she could find out what happened in the garden.

By mid-morning Jenay and Jonathan were awake. They played with their cousins and tried to relax — but they were always listening and watching for their mother to return and bring them news.

At noon, the sun suddenly quit shining and the children ran into the house. The servants lit lamps and it seemed like the middle of the night. No one could explain what was happening, but Jenay and Jonathan were worried. *Where are Mother and Abba and our friends? Did everyone get out of the garden safely last night? And what is going on?*

Mother arrived back at Aunt Oprah's house after dinner and apologized for being gone so long. She also apologized to Oprah's family for being such a poor guest, but asked if she could speak to Jenay and Jonathan alone for a few minutes. Oprah's family could tell that she was upset and excused them. The three of them went upstairs to the bedroom. There, Mother began to cry, and the three of them just huddled together in a heap until she was able to tell them the terrible news.

"Mr. Jesus is dead. He has been crucified."

Jenay and Jonathan were old enough to know about crucifixion — every Jew knew what a horrible, horrible death it was.

Mother had talked with Uncle John and he had assured her that everyone else had gotten out of the garden safely. He was sure they were in hiding somewhere, and that their Abba was safe. Mother assured them that Abba would find them soon.

Jenay and Jonathan stayed in the bedroom while their mother went downstairs to tell Aunt Oprah's family the news. They just wanted to be alone and didn't feel like playing games with their cousins.

All day on the Sabbath, Jenay and Jonathan and their mother were treated kindly at Aunt Oprah's, but it wasn't the same as being with their friends who loved Mr. Jesus.

They were eager to find their Abba and the other followers. Just as soon as the sun went down, Mother told Aunt Oprah and Uncle Nehemiah that they were going out to explore and see if they could find their Abba, but would return by bedtime.

"Where are we going, Mother?" asked Jenay.

"I know a couple of places where I think the others might be. Right now, let's go to Mrs. Mary's house — Mark's mother. Her house is large enough to host the disciples, and I'm hoping we can find Abba there."

"Do you think they might have gone to Mr. Lazarus' house?" asked Jonathan.

"Hmm, might be. We'll just take it one step at a time. I'm sure we'll find them somewhere," assured Mother.

Several of the followers of Jesus were gathered at Mrs. Mary's house. It was good to be with others who were also grieving Jesus' death, but the sadness was so hard. Each hug reminded them that Jesus was dead and that they were no longer his disciples.

Mrs. Mary told them that the apostles were hiding in the rented room where they had last seen him for the Passover Seder, but they had locked the doors and weren't letting anyone in. So, Mother and Jonathan and Jenay went back to Aunt Oprah's house for the night.

Mother agreed to meet Mrs. Mary and some of the other ladies to properly prepare Jesus' body for burial at sunrise tomorrow. There hadn't been time to properly wash and wrap the body in spices before the Sabbath.

On Sunday morning, Jenay and Jonathan were eating breakfast with their cousins when Mother returned. Her face was flushed, and she was yelling, "HE'S ALIVE! HE'S ALIVE! The stone was rolled away, and the angels say that Jesus is alive!"

Aunt Oprah was concerned that her sister had gone crazy. She encouraged her to sit down and drink a cup of juice. She insisted that all the stress of seeing the crucifixion had made her go insane. Jenay and Jonathan gathered around her and hugged her and asked her to tell them again what had happened.

"I met Mrs. Mary and the other ladies. There were about 10 of us who went to the tomb. But when we got there, the tomb was empty. Jesus wasn't there, but two angels were. They reminded us that Jesus had told us that he would be killed, but on the third day, he would come alive."

"Mother, we've seen Mr. Jesus raise other people from the dead, couldn't he raise himself?" asked Jenay.

"I believe he has!" said Mother.

Aunt Oprah continued to insist that it was just wishful thinking. But Mother was determined that they go to find Abba and see what was happening. They hoped to find Abba at the room where they had eaten the Passover Seder.

It was pure chaos there. The courtyard was packed. The rooms were packed. Cousin Peter and Uncle John had talked with an angel. The women had talked with two angels. Miss Mary Magdelena had actually talked with Jesus, and she was certain that it was really, really him. Everyone wanted to hear the stories over and over and over, and the joy was overflowing — mixed with so many questions.

Jenay and Jonathan were relieved to get to hug their Abba. Then they were sent outside to play in the courtyard. But even there, the crowds were getting bigger and bigger. *Is it true? Is it just wishful thinking?*

In the afternoon, Mother and some of the other women began to bake some bread and prepare a light meal for everyone to eat. Jenay and Jonathan were once again sent to the well to get lots of jars of water. Some of the older boys helped them. Disciples who lived close by brought in some fish and cheese so that no one would have to cook much. Someone brought a bucket of dates. They had to eat in shifts since there wasn't enough room for everyone.

Gradually the crowd began to thin, and Mother said it was time for them to head back to Aunt Oprah's. They were grateful to have a place to stay, but wished they could stay with the group like old times.

Everyone agreed that it was dangerous to stay together after dark. They were too afraid that the Roman soldiers would decide to attack all the followers of Jesus. Everyone felt safer staying hidden and scattered and behind locked doors.

On Monday morning, Jenay and Jonathan and Mother were eating breakfast with Aunt Oprah's family when their Abba, James, arrived. He was glowing with joy. Even Aunt Oprah commented that he looked incredibly happy.

"I <u>am</u> happy. Jesus is alive, and it is true that he is the Messiah, the Lamb of God. I got to see him last night and talk with him and now I understand why he had to die.

"Nathaniel and Oprah, thank you so much for caring for my family during these hard days. We are going to be staying in Jerusalem for another week or so before we return to Galilee. I was wondering if you want me to find other lodging for my family, or should they plan to stay here with you?"

"Oh, that's ridiculous!" said Aunt Oprah. "Of course they are welcome here anytime. I want to hear more about this Jesus that you follow and maybe we'll have more time to talk this week."

"Well, the reason I'm here is that I haven't had any time with my family in several weeks, and so I thought we would go camping for a couple of days and just relax a bit. We'll probably go over toward the Jordan and catch some fish. I promised the guys I would be back in town before the Sabbath. So, I will return them to you — if you are sure it's okay."

"Of course, it's okay!" said Aunt Oprah and Uncle Nehemiah together.

Once they left Aunt Oprah's, Mother reminded Abba that they had left all their traveling bags in the olive garden. They really owned nothing.

"I left mine, too," said Abba. "We'll stop by the market and find what we need before we leave town. Then I know a little camping site that's not too far. Hopefully it won't be crowded."

Jenay and Jonathan were so happy to see Abba and Mother together again, walking hand in hand, and talking about all the events of the week. They had much to catch up on. And soon, they found the perfect place to camp.

The first thing Abba wanted to do was go fishing, so he and Jonathan headed to the Jordan River. Jenay and Mother laid out the new blankets and repacked the new travel bags, then they began to collect firewood to cook the fish.

How good it felt to be doing "normal" things again as a family! During dinner Jenay asked, "Abba, tell us about seeing Mr. Jesus alive."

"Well, we were all in that room on Sunday night," Abba began his story, and the others settled back on their blankets munching on the wonderful fish. "You three had left and most everyone else had gone, too. There were maybe 20 people still around the tables.

"After dark we locked the doors for fear the Romans would come after us. We posted a watchman downstairs to make sure no one surprised us.

"But boy, were we surprised!

"I just blinked and Mr. Jesus was standing right there looking at us.

We asked him how he got in because the doors were locked. He said that doors and tombs could not hold him anymore. We thought he was maybe a ghost, but he insisted he wasn't.

"Then he asked if we had any food left over. The ladies made him a plate and he sat and ate and talked with us just like old times. It was amazing."

"So, did he really die?" asked Jonathan.

"Oh, yes. No one lives over a Roman crucifixion. Lots of people saw him die."

"I saw him die," Mother said softly. "And I saw two men put him in the tomb. I know he was dead."

"And now he's alive. It's a miracle just like the little girl he brought back to life — only this is even better!" Jenay clapped her hands with happiness.

"Yes, this is even better because Mr. Jesus died as the Lamb of God to pay for our sins. Do you kids know what 'Messiah' means?" asked Abba.

"I know that he's the promised one," said Jenay.

"I think it means he'll conquer Rome or something like that," said Jonathan.

"Yes, he is the promised one and someday he will conquer Rome and rule the whole world, but that's not what the Messiah is. A Messiah is someone who rescues us from danger," explained Abba.

"What danger, Abba?" asked Jenay.

"The danger is our sins. If our sins are not paid for — then we can't be near to God. And there's no way we can pay for our sins!" said Abba.

"God has been promising to send us a Messiah to pay for our sins for over 1700 years. All of us have sins. Mr. Jesus was the Lamb who paid for everyone's sin — the Jews and the Gentiles. He paid for your sins and my sins. He paid for your past sins and your future sins. He paid for everybody's sins.

"Now that Mr. Jesus has died and sin has been paid for, there's only one thing that people have to decide."

"What's that, Abba?" asked Jenay.

"They have to decide whether they want to follow Mr. Jesus and let him pay for their sins, or whether they want to live their own way."

"You followed Mr. Jesus, didn't you, Abba?" asked Jonathan.

"Yes, when Mr. Jesus asked me to follow him, I did. I didn't understand a lot about what that meant, but every day he's taught me more and more about what it means to follow him."

"Mother, when did you decide to follow Mr. Jesus?" asked Jenay.

"Well, when your Abba came home and told me that he was going to follow Mr. Jesus, I made the choice to follow your Abba. But I didn't really understand who Mr. Jesus was until I listened and learned some more.

"One day I was listening to him teach and I realized that I wanted Mr. Jesus to be my rabbi. I wanted to follow him and obey him and learn to be like him. Now I know that he's my Messiah."

"I want to follow Mr. Jesus, too," said Jenay.

"Me, too," said Jonathan.

"That makes your mother and me very happy. We know that you don't understand everything about Mr. Jesus — we don't either — but we are happy that you want to be obedient to Mr. Jesus and learn to do things his way — the New Way," said Abba.

"You've heard Mr. Jesus teach a lot. He said that if we loved him, we would obey him. What are some things you think he wants you to do right now to show that you are following him?" asked Mother.

Jenay asked, "Do you remember the night after the Seder when we were waiting for Mr. Jesus to finish teaching so that we could clean up the table?"

"Yes," said Mother.

"Well, the last thing I heard Mr. Jesus say on that night at the Seder was to love one another the way he loves us," said Jenay. "I want to learn to love everyone the way Mr. Jesus does."

"Mr. Jesus was always reminding us kids to obey and honor our parents. I want to do that," said Jonathan.

"Those sound like great ways to get started following Mr. Jesus. I'm glad you've both made your decision to follow him. And remember, if you have any questions, your mother or I, or actually anyone in the group, would be glad to help you."

"What's going to happen now?" asked Jenay.

"Will the group get back together?" questioned Jonathan.

"You said we were going back to Galilee. Will everything get back to normal then?" asked Mother.

"I don't know for sure. But Jesus said he would meet us in Galilee at the end of the month, so I assume he'll teach us more there and resume the ministry." That made everyone feel happy.

The family had a relaxing few days camping together. On Thursday they hiked back to Aunt Oprah's house and said goodbye to Abba again. He would be staying with the apostles at the rented room.

Jenay and Jonathan enjoyed playing with their cousins, and Mother enjoyed answering Aunt Oprah's questions about Jesus. On Wednesday, Abba stopped by to visit and said they should be ready to leave for Galilee on Friday after breakfast. Aunt Oprah invited Abba to come for breakfast on Friday, and she asked Abba some more questions about Jesus.

On Friday morning, just as soon as Abba arrived, Aunt Oprah announced that she believed that Jesus was the Messiah and wanted to be his follower, too. Abba, Mother, Jonathan and Jenay were thrilled with her decision. Abba gave her directions to Mary's house (Mark's mother). He told her to go there to meet with the other followers. Breakfast was a sweet time of celebration even though they were saying "goodbye." They were already looking forward to their next visit in a few weeks and promised to tell her everything that happened in Galilee.

It took them only three days to reach Capernaum after a restful Sabbath. It was mostly downhill and they were experienced travelers. And besides, you can always walk faster when you are headed home. They had rented out their house, so they would be staying with Grandpa Zebedee and Grandmother Salome. They would see lots of cousins and aunts and uncles while they were there, besides neighbors and friends. It would be great to be back.

Jenay and Jonathan loved being in Capernaum. They played at the beach, and sometimes Grandpa Zebedee put them to work picking up rocks or driftwood for his fishing nets.

There was a small row boat that they were allowed to play in, as long as an adult was on the beach to make sure they didn't get too far out to sea. They spent hours rowing — mostly round and round in circles because Jenay's arms weren't as strong as Jonathan's.

It was a nice change from being in Jerusalem for the past month. They soaked up the sunshine and loved being near the sea.

One night when they arrived home for dinner, they found that their dad had gone out with some of the other apostles on a fishing trip. "I wish he'd invited me," whined Jonathan. "I would like to go on a real fishing trip."

"Maybe next time," said his mother. "I think this trip was just for the apostles. They need time together. You ought to ask Grandpa Zebedee if he will take you fishing next time we visit."

"Oh, that would be cool! Can I go ask him now?"

"No, because he's probably already gone tonight and it's time for dinner. But maybe tomorrow afternoon you could ask him if he'll take you the next time we visit. Don't ever wake him up in the mornings!"

"Yes, Mother."

"Your dad will also need to sleep tomorrow morning after a night of fishing, so you two need to plan to play at the beach or at least stay outside."

"Okay, Mother. Grandpa Zebedee wanted us to collect rocks for his fishing nets, and we've been piling them up. We've got some pretty big mountains of rocks. Do you want to come and see them tomorrow?"

"Sure! That sounds like a good way to let your Abba sleep," said Mother.

But the next morning, Abba didn't come home at sunrise as expected. Grandmother Salome let Jenay and Jonathan go ahead and eat breakfast without him, but they could tell that Mother was worried. Usually fishing trips ended at dawn, then the fishermen cleaned their nets and were home in time for breakfast.

When it was almost noon, Mother said, "Let's walk down to Grandpa Zebedee's shop and see if he knows where Abba and the rest of the men are. I just want to make sure their boat is back safely."

When they talked with Grandpa Zebedee, he assured them that all was well. He pointed to a cove that was about three miles down the beach and they could plainly see the boat floating close to the beach. He was sure the men were just enjoying time together and there was nothing to worry about.

Jenay and Jonathan were showing Mother their piles of rocks when the men arrived. The men brought Grandpa Zebedee a huge net filled with fish. He asked if they were still fresh and they assured him that they had taken them out of the water only long enough to count them and then put them back. Abba and Uncle John, Cousin Peter and Cousin Andrew had all fished for Grandpa long enough to know the rules. He wouldn't sell or process fish that had been out of the water too long. "You must have had a great night of fishing. That's quite a haul!"

"You could say that," said Cousin Peter, looking at the other guys and laughing.

"Jon! Jen!"

"Yes, Abba?"

"Your mother and I are going home and I'm going to take a nap. Grandmother is planning a special dinner for us, so don't be late."

"Okay, Abba," they replied together.

Jonathan and Jenay continued to play on the beach, and watched as their cousin Benji and his helpers Samson and Solomon cleaned and checked the nets to prepare them for the fishermen. They knew not to bother the boys while they worked.

Grandpa Zebedee sent the boys home early and closed up the shop since this was going to be a family get-together for Jenay and Jonathan's last night there. Benji and his dad, Uncle Jonas, walked home with them, too. All four of Grandpa Zebedee's sons and their families would be there for the farewell dinner.

After a bountiful feast, everyone settled on cushions around the courtyard, and Uncle John and Abba began to share about their night of fishing.

"Dad, do you remember the day that Jesus called us to follow him?" asked Abba.

"How could I forget?" replied Grandpa Zebedee. "I thought I was ruined — three boats that brought in nothing. I've never seen anything like that. Then Jesus came along, and I had more fish than I've ever caught. Oh, yes, I remember it well."

"Well, it happened again," said Abba.

"What happened again?" everyone wanted to know.

Uncle John told the story:

"There were seven of us fishing in the large boat, so we were using a round net. We fished and we fished and caught nothing. Some of the guys had never been deep-water fishing, so they were disappointed, and it really made us look bad. We are <u>supposed</u> to be fishermen.

"We were coming in a little before sunrise, and I was just steering the boat in the shallows close to the coast, when a man called out from the beach. It was too dark to see his face, but he called out to us:

>..."**Friends, haven't you any fish?....**"[2]

"We told him 'No' and he said:

>... "**Throw your net on the right side of the boat and you will find some....**"[3]

"We were in fairly shallow water, but we obediently dropped our net. Suddenly, it was so full of fish, we couldn't lift it; we had to drag it. It took all of us to push the load onto the shore.

"The minute I saw the net full of fish, I knew it was Jesus. Peter did, too, and he just jumped overboard and started running toward him. I had to steer the boat, or I would have jumped in, too. Jesus said to bring him some fish and we had a big ol' fish fry right there on the beach. It was great."

Long after the women and children had gone home and been tucked into beds, the four brothers and their dad Zebedee talked into the night. Uncle John and Abba shared with them that Jesus was leaving the ministry with the apostles and would be returning to Heaven soon.

They told them that Jesus had said there would continue to be trouble with the Pharisees and Rome, and many of the followers would be killed. The three men encouraged Abba and Uncle John to remain faithful and to know that they would care for their families if necessary.

There was much love shared between these brothers and their dad, and all wanted to be obedient followers of Jesus.

At sunrise the next morning, Jenay and Jonathan were sad to leave their grandparents' home again, but they were headed to Jerusalem and that meant they would get to see Aunt Oprah again. Grandmother had invited all the apostles to breakfast before they got on the road to Jerusalem. Somehow that made it easier to say goodbye to Grandmother Salome and Grandpa Zebedee.

By Monday afternoon the group of disciples was close to Bethany. Cousin Peter and Mr. Thomas ran ahead to ask Lazarus about lodging for the group for the night. They hoped to spend the night before going into Jerusalem tomorrow.

By the time the rest of the group arrived, Martha and Mary had prepared a nice dinner for them and arranged lodging. Jenay and Jonathan were excited that their family was assigned to Simon the Leper's house since they were told that there were kids to play with there.

Soon after dinner, Miss Martha walked with Mother, Jenay, and Jonathan to Mr. Simon and Mrs. Keturah's house so they could get settled. Jenay and Jonathan immediately liked Gabriela and her older brothers. Her little brothers were only four years old and were already in bed. Jenay was excited to sleep in Gabriela's room, but Jonathan slept in the courtyard with Gabriela's two older brothers to make room for their parents. At the first sign of sunlight, Jonathan woke up with two four-year-old boys jumping on top of him to welcome him.

Jabet and Jared were identical twins and there was no way for Jonathan to keep up with which was which. "My sister is my twin — but you can tell us apart!"

"I'm glad God didn't make Jared a girl!" said Jabet.

"I'm glad God made Jenay a girl — because we don't get confused as to who is who!" laughed Jonathan.

"We don't get confused!" said either Jabet or Jared.

"We just have fun confusing everyone else," said the other.

"Who is ready for breakfast?" Mrs. Keturah called.

"Me! Me! Me!" came the replies. The two older boys had already eaten and left for Hebrew school.

After breakfast Tuesday morning, Mother and Jenay and Jonathan thanked their hostess and said goodbye. They went back to Miss Mary, Miss Martha, and Mr. Lazarus' home thinking that they would be traveling into Jerusalem. But when they walked in the door, Mr. Jesus was there.

Mr. Jesus knelt down and hugged first Jonathan and then Jenay. He knelt with one arm around each of them as he talked with them for just a few minutes. He told them that he was proud of them for being his youngest followers and that he would always love them. Jenay threw her arms around Mr. Jesus and hugged him tightly. She told him how glad she was that he was alive.

He smiled and said, "Me, too!" He hugged them both again.

When Jesus stood up, he told the group that he needed to change the plans. He wanted to go camping overnight with just the apostles. Kayla and the children could stay an extra day to visit with Mary and Martha and Keturah. They quickly agreed, and the men said their goodbyes and were out the door. Jesus said they would be back sometime on Wednesday — probably late.

All day Tuesday the women visited and enjoyed being together. They knew that the men were happy because they were with Jesus, and the children were happy to have friends. They were content, and it felt like a holiday. Chores were left undone and they snacked on leftovers.

Early Wednesday morning, Gabriela asked permission to take Jenay and Jonathan, and of course her two little brothers Jared and Jabet, on a hike up the mountain behind Mrs. Martha's house. There was a nice trail that wasn't too steep, and there was a stream where they liked to skip rocks. Since Jenay and Jonathan were so used to camping out, their mother felt it should be perfectly safe. The mothers packed them a bag of snacks and sent them on their way — grateful that they were happily entertained.

The kids took their time and enjoyed playing in the stream along the way.

Gabriela and her brothers told about seeing Mr. Lazarus raised from the dead.

Jenay and Jonathan told about their times of traveling with Mr. Jesus.

Gabriela told about Mr. Jesus healing her Abba, and the children were having a great time and were becoming best friends.

"Shhhhh!   Get down!"

whispered Jared and Jabet. All the kids quickly jumped off the trail and hid in the brush.

"What is it?" whispered Gabriela, who wasn't at all sure whether there was something to hide from, or whether her brothers were just trying to scare them.

"Look!" said Jared.

Up ahead in a clearing stood Mr. Jesus and his apostles.   Mr. Jesus was talking and the 11 men were all listening carefully.

"Let's get closer and see if we can hear what they are talking about!" said Jabet.

"Maybe we shouldn't," said Jenay. "It's probably private."

Gabriela couldn't decide whether to just stay on the trail and walk past them, or to turn around and go home. So, for just a minute or two the children stayed hidden, watching the men, but not being close enough to hear their conversation.

They were still trying to figure out what to do when they saw Mr. Jesus reach out and touch each apostle on the head like he was blessing him. Then, with his hands still stretched toward them, Mr. Jesus began rising up into the sky.

"Wow!" whispered the kids all at once.

They sat hidden in the bushes and watched as Mr. Jesus rose up and up and up into the sky. They watched until they couldn't see him anymore.

When they looked back at the apostles, they saw two angels talking with them. They didn't know what to do. Gabriela and Jenay were crying and Jonathan wiped tears off his cheeks. The younger boys were just watching in awe.

The angels were talking to the men and pointing up at the sky where Mr. Jesus had gone. They couldn't hear what was said, but they could see that the apostles were excited and happy.

Suddenly the angels were gone, and the men just stood and looked at each other. Then somebody began to sing songs of worship. They fell on their knees and praised God for what they had experienced.

The children stayed hidden and quiet in the bushes until one of the men started singing this Psalm of David:

> Praise the LORD.
> Praise God in his sanctuary;
> Praise him in his mighty heavens.
> Praise him for his acts of power;
> Praise him for his surpassing greatness.
> Praise him with the sounding of the trumpet,
> Praise him with the harp and lyre,
> Praise him with timbrel and dancing,
> Praise him with the strings and pipe,
> Praise him with the clash of cymbals,
> Praise him with resounding cymbals.
> Let everything that has breath praise the LORD.
> Praise the LORD.[4]

Then one of the twins yelled, "I KNOW <u>THAT</u> ONE!" and burst out of his hiding place and raced toward the men to join in the singing. Of course, the other twin was right behind him and the three older children chased after them.

The older children felt certain that they would be in trouble for disturbing the men. But instead the apostles welcomed the children, and they began to dance and sing the Psalm over and over together.

As they finally ended the Psalm and sat on the grass together, Uncle John asked Jenay and Jonathan what they were doing up on the mountain. Jenay explained that they had packed a picnic and were letting Gabriela show them her beautiful mountain.

"A picnic sounds like a wonderful idea," said Cousin Peter. "I believe we have a bag of apricots to share." And the children and the men sat together eating snacks and sharing about their favorite times with Mr. Jesus.

One of the twins asked, "Where did Mr. Jesus go?"

And the other asked, "How did he do that?"

The apostles laughed and tried to explain that although Mr. Jesus was a human, he was filled with supernatural power from God. That's why he could do miraculous and supernatural things.

"But where did he go?" insisted Jared.

"He went to Heaven to be with his Father, God," said Cousin Peter.

"But I liked him!" pouted Jabet.

"Yes, we liked him, too," agreed Mr. Thomas, "but he needed to go home. Hey, do you kids want to know a secret?"

They were eager to hear what Mr. Thomas had to tell them.

"Did you see the two angels that talked with us?"

All the kids nodded, "Uh-huh."

"Those angels told us that someday Mr. Jesus will come to earth again. What do you think of that?"

"Cool!"

"Before Mr. Jesus died, he told us that someday he would come back and get us and take us to live in Heaven with him and his Father. He said he would prepare rooms for us so that we would feel welcomed. Mr. Jesus said:

> **'My Father's house has many rooms; if that were not so, would I have told you that I am going there to prepare a place for you? And if I go and prepare a place for you, I will come back and take you to be with me that you also may be where I am.[5]'**

Everyone was dreaming of heavenly homes and wondering when Jesus would come back. It was a special memory for all of them as they enjoyed their picnic in the grass.

Jenay put her arm around her Abba and asked, "What are you thinking, Abba?"

He told her that he was thinking about how much he and the other apostles had changed in their three years with Mr. Jesus. They were learning to love all people, not just Jew or Gentile; or rich or poor; or healthy or sick. He said, "I remember Mr. Jesus teaching us:

> **... 'Let the little children come to me, and do not hinder them, for the kingdom of heaven belongs to such as these.'"[6]**

---

[1] **John 15:12**
[2] **John 21:5**
[3] **John 21:6**
[4] **Psalm 150**
[5] **John 14:2-3**
[6] **Matthew 19:14**

Preparing the Passover for Jesus
Mark 14:12-16

Jesus Gives New Commandment
John 13:34-35

Jesus Teaches About Heaven
John 14:1-3

**Everyone Deserted Jesus
When He was Arrested**
Matthew 26:56

Jesus Was Crucified
John 19:18,30

Darkness Covered the Land
Luke 23:44-45

Many Women Watched Crucifixion
Matthew 27:55-56

Jesus was Placed in a Tomb
John 19:38-42

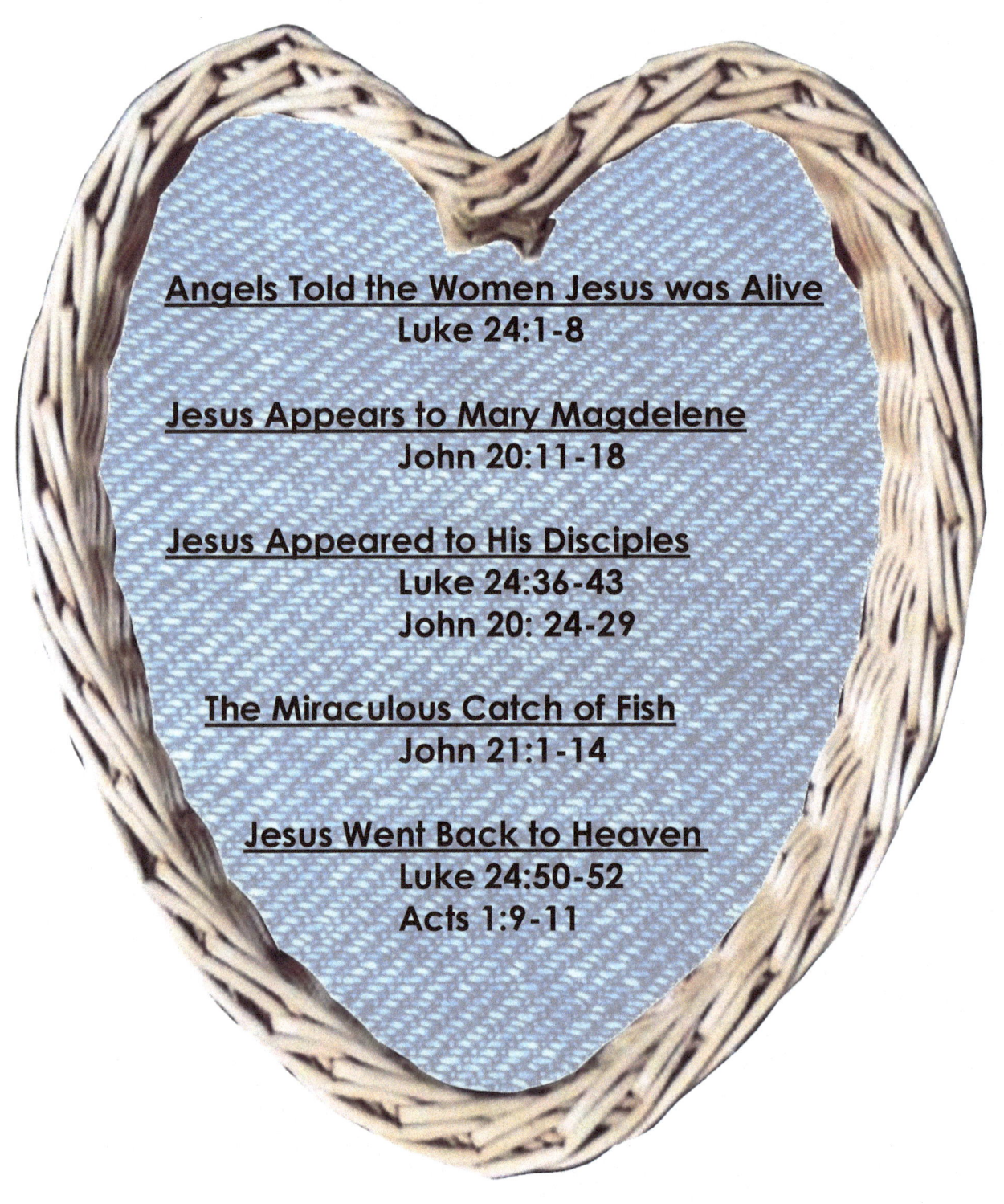

Angels Told the Women Jesus was Alive
Luke 24:1-8

Jesus Appears to Mary Magdelene
John 20:11-18

Jesus Appeared to His Disciples
Luke 24:36-43
John 20: 24-29

The Miraculous Catch of Fish
John 21:1-14

Jesus Went Back to Heaven
Luke 24:50-52
Acts 1:9-11

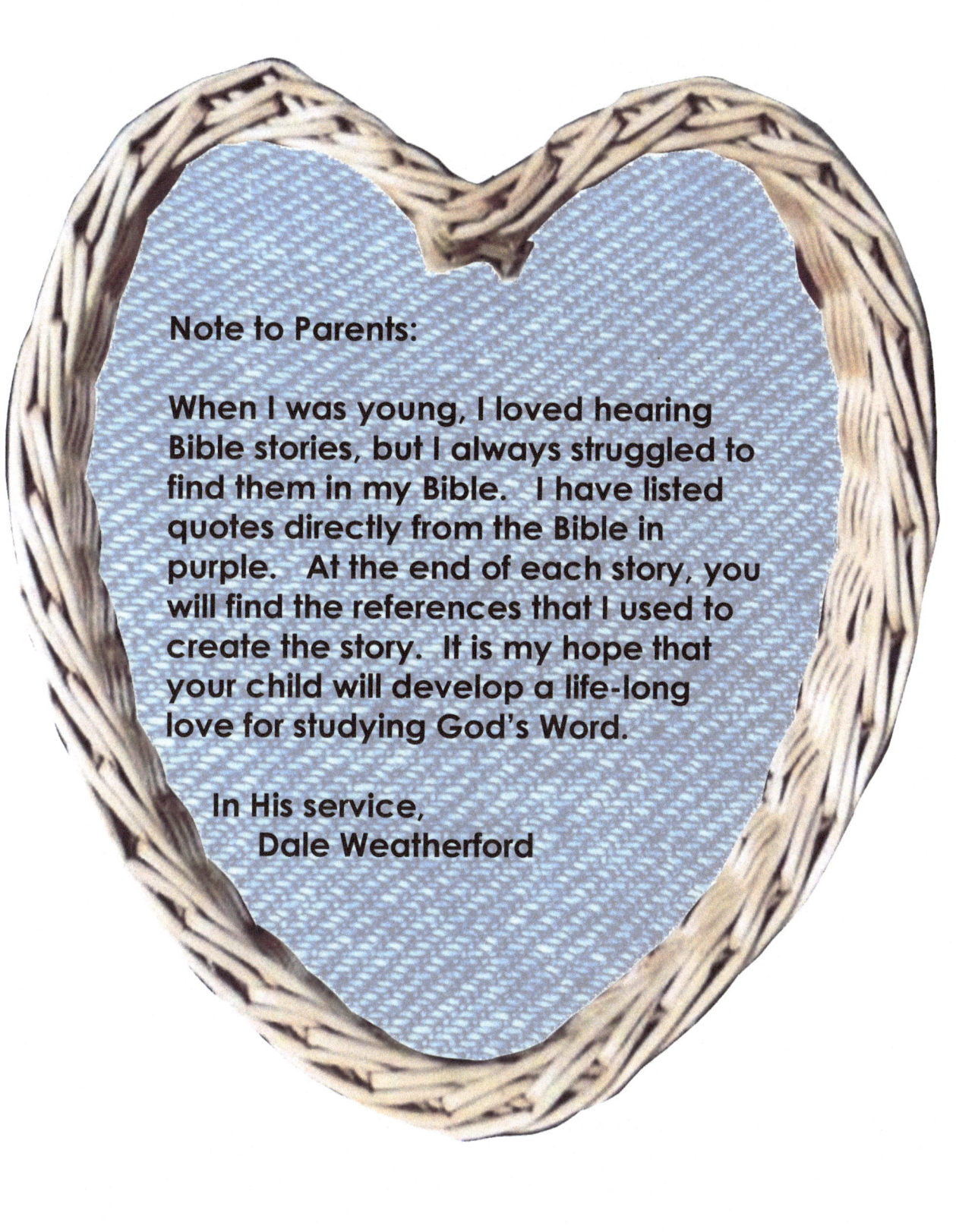

Note to Parents:

When I was young, I loved hearing Bible stories, but I always struggled to find them in my Bible. I have listed quotes directly from the Bible in purple. At the end of each story, you will find the references that I used to create the story. It is my hope that your child will develop a life-long love for studying God's Word.

    In His service,
        Dale Weatherford

The following have provided free illustrations that have helped make this book possible:

Berserkon.com
Cliparts.zone
Clker.com
Freeimages.com
Freesvg.org
Microsoft Word
Pikrepo.com
Pixabay.com
Pxfuel.com
Unsplash.com
Wikimedia.org